Religious Discrimination and Hatred Law

In 2006 two new pieces of legislation came into force: Part 2 of the Equality Act and the Racial and Religious Hatred Act. Both pieces of legislation mimic existing legislation on racial discrimination and racial hatred. However, there are many fundamental differences between race and religion which will make the operations of these new laws far more problematic than racial laws.

This book provides a holistic overview of religion and the law, looking at the new pieces of legislation, together with existing Human Rights provisions of Article 9 of the European Convention on Human Rights, the 2003 Employment Discrimination Regulations and the 2001 Religiously Aggravated Offences. By looking at the entire subject in one book it is possible to draw comparisons which might not appear immediately obvious, and to deal in more depth with the definition of and distinctions between religion and belief. Addison challenges some common but simplistic views on what religious beliefs are and how they are accommodated by the law.

Neil Addison is a practising barrister and former Senior Crown Prosecutor with experience in both criminal and civil court at all levels.

Religious Discrimination and Hatred Law

Neil Addison

Routledge·Cavendish
Taylor & Francis Group
LONDON AND NEW YORK

First published 2007 by Routledge-Cavendish
2 Park Square, Milton Park, Abingdon, Oxon OX14 4RN

Simultaneously published in the USA and Canada
by Routledge-Cavendish
270 Madison Ave, New York, NY 10016

*Routledge-Cavendish is an imprint of the Taylor & Francis Group,
an informa business*

© 2007 Neil Addison

Typeset in Times by RefineCatch Limited, Bungay, Suffolk
Printed and bound in Great Britain by
Antony Rowe Ltd., Chippenham, Wiltshire

British Library Cataloguing in Publication Data
A catalogue record for this book is available from the British Library

Library of Congress Cataloging in Publication Data
A catalog record for this book has been requested

ISBN10: 0–415–42030–X (pbk)
ISBN10: 0–415–42027–X (hbk)

ISBN13: 978–0–415–42030–3 (pbk)
ISBN13: 978–0–415–42027–3 (hbk)

Dedicated to the memory of

My mother
Rose Eileen Addison (Loughran)

my mother-in-law
Norah Mary O'Hare (Gordon)

and our good friend
Kathleen MacAuley

Three very remarkable ladies
to whom Rita and I owe a great deal

Requiescat in pace

Contents

Table of cases

Table of legislation

Useful websites

More links available at the author's	www.religionlaw.co.uk
Religion and Law Web Site	www.religionlaw.co.uk/linkstext.htm
Lawyers Christian Fellowship	www.lawcf.org
Association of Muslim Lawyers	www.aml.org.uk
World Council of Churches	www.wcc-coe.org
Church of England	www.england.anglican.org
Catholic Church in England and Wales	www.catholic-ew.org.uk
The Church of Scotland	www.churchofscotland.org.uk
Evangelical Alliance	www.eauk.org
The Christian Institute	www.christian.org.uk
The Orthodox Church in Britain	www.orthodox.clara.net
MCB – The Muslim Council of Britain	www.mcb.org.uk
The Organization of the Islamic Conference (OIC)	www.oic-oci.org
Ahmadiyya Muslim Community	www.alislam.org
The Chief Rabbi	www.chiefrabbi.org
Network of Sikh Organisations	www.nsouk.co.uk
The Buddhist Society	www.thebuddhistsociety.org
Hindu Forum of Britain	www.hinduforum.org
Bahai Community of the UK	www.bahai.org.uk
National Secular Society	www.secularism.org.uk
British Humanist Association	www.humanism.org.uk
LDS (Mormon) Church	www.lds.org.uk
The Pagan Federation	www.paganfed.org
Delia Venables (THE Legal Reference Site)	www.venables.co.uk
The Religion and Law Research Consortium	www.religlaw.org
Faithworks	www.faithworks.info
ACAS	www.acas.org.uk

Glossary of terms

(Brief explanations of some of the religious terms, expressions and names which are used in this book)

Agnostic   Someone who may believe in the existence of God but who does not accept any religion.

Ahmadiyya Muslims   (Sometimes also called Ahmadi, Qadiani or Lahori Muslims) Are members of a worldwide religious movement which started in 1889 in the Punjab. They are regarded as heretical by both **Sunni** and **Shia** Muslims because they believe that their founder Hadhrat Mirza Ghulam Ahmad was the Messiah. Because of this they are not regarded by other Muslims as actually being Muslims at all and can be the victims of discrimination from them. In consequence they are not allowed to enter **Mecca** and are not affiliated with other Muslim organisations in Britain. However, Ahmadiyya would tend to identify themselves simply as Muslims for the purposes of any census or survey.

Apostate   A person who leaves or renounces their religion. Apostasy is the act of leaving or renouncing a religion.

Atheist   Someone who does not believe in God.

Bible   The holy book of the Christian religion commonly divided into two sections 'The Old Testament' and 'The New Testament'. The first five books of the Old Testament are known to Jews as the **Torah** or law. The New Testament contains the **Gospels** which tell of the life, death and resurrection of **Jesus Christ**. Though the Bible is regarded with reverence by Christians it is not regarded as holy in itself but what it says is holy. For that reason there are no specific rules or customs regulating how it is to be treated or handled other than that it should not be treated deliberately disrespectfully.

Book of Mormon   See **Mormons**.

Catholic (also known as Roman Catholic)   The largest Christian denomination in the world. The most important binding aspect of the Catholic Church is the acceptance of the role of the Bishop of Rome as the Pope and supreme leader of the Church.

Church   Has a double meaning in Christianity. 'The Church' is the title used for a collection of individuals and organisations forming a single denomination, for example the Catholic Church or the Church of England; whilst a church is a building used for Christian worship. Some Christian Churches or groups prefer to use the title chapel for the building rather than church.

Dharma   The teachings of the Buddha.

Ecumenical Council   Councils of bishops which discuss and decide on the essential beliefs of Christianity. There were seven Councils held between 325 and 787 which are particularly important in Christian history and whose declarations are still accepted as binding by Catholic, Orthodox and many Protestant Christians.

Gospels   See **Bible**.

Granthi   A Sikh religious leader and teacher usually attached to a **Gurdwara**.

Gurdwara   A building used by Sikhs for prayer and where the **Guru Granth Sahib** is kept. Every gurdwara has a **langar** attached to it where food is served to anyone without charge. The term **langar** is also used for the communal meal served at the gurdwaras.

Guru Granth Sahib   The holy book of the Sikhs. A collection of the teachings of the first ten Sikh gurus, it is believed by Sikhs that the Guru Granth Sahib now replaces the teaching role of the gurus.

Hajj   Hajj means the pilgrimage to **Mecca** and is one of the five pillars of Islam which every Muslim is supposed to perform at least once during their life. Hajj can only be performed during certain specified dates known as Dhu al-Hijjah.

Halal   A Muslim phrase meaning 'permitted'. It is commonly applied to food which is either halal or **haram**, i.e. either permitted or forbidden. All vegetarian food is halal but for meat to be halal the animal must be killed in a particular way by an authorised halal slaughterman (who must be a Muslim). Some meat, such as pork, can never be halal.

Haram   A Muslim phrase meaning forbidden. It is commonly applied to food which is either **halal** or haram. Pork is always haram as is alcohol.

Hijab   A headscarf covering the hair and ears which is worn by many female Muslims who consider that it is required under **Shariah** law. Wearers of the hijab are sometimes referred to as hijabee. Many other variations of Muslim female dress are often collectively referred to as hijabs.

Icon   A Christian religious picture. Icons are especially associated with the worship of the **Orthodox Church** and are painted, following very strict traditional rules, by persons who are themselves practising Christians.

Imam   A Muslim religious leader and teacher usually attached to a **mosque**.

Jesus Christ   The founder of the Christian religion whose life is detailed in the New Testament in the **Bible**. Christians believe that he was born in the Holy Land (today Israel and Palestine), taught and worked miracles and was crucified at around the age of 33, and three days later he rose from the dead. Jesus is regarded by Muslims as a great prophet but Christians have always regarded Jesus as far more than a mere prophet. He is regarded as the Son of God or God in human form walking the earth.

Jilbab   An all-encompassing female garment covering the hair, ears, arms and legs and also hiding the shape of the body, and which is worn by some female Muslims who consider that the wearing of the **hijab** does not adequately meet the requirements of **Shariah** law.

Joseph Smith   See **Mormons**.

Koran   Often spelt Quran or Q'ran. The Koran is the holy book of Muslims who believe that it was divinely revealed to their prophet **Mohammed** over a period of 23 years. It provides the main basis for Muslim beliefs and **Shariah** law. In Muslim belief copies of the Koran should be treated with immense respect, should not be placed on the ground and should be covered with a cloth when not being read. Copies of the Koran which are used in court for Muslim witnesses to take the oath are usually enclosed within green covers to protect them from being directly touched. Usually it is Arabic versions of the Koran which are treated with this respect. Translations from Arabic are often not regarded with the same reverence.

Kosher   Meaning food that has been prepared in accordance with Jewish law. All vegetarian food is kosher but for meat to be kosher the animal must be killed in a particular way. Some food such as pork or shellfish can never be kosher. The term kosher can also cover how food is prepared and served as well as the food itself. For example meat and dairy products should never be served together and meat should never be cooked or kept in any container which has been used to cook or keep any dairy products.

Langar   See **Gurdwara**.

Lourdes   A town in southern France and a major pilgrimage centre for Catholics who believe that the **Virgin Mary** appeared there to Saint Bernadette in the mid-nineteenth century.

Mass   The main religious service of the Roman Catholic Church. In the Church of England it is often referred to as the service of Holy Communion and in the Orthodox Church as the Holy Liturgy. The common factor across all churches is the use of bread and wine to commemorate the last supper of **Jesus Christ** on the day before his crucifixion.

Mecca   Also called Makkah. A city in Saudia Arabia which was the birthplace of **Muhammad**. It is where the annual **hajj** takes place. Under Saudi law non-Muslims are banned from entering Mecca.

Mormons   Refer to themselves as members of 'the Church of Jesus Christ of Latter Day Saints' or LDS but are popularly known as Mormons because of their belief in '**The Book of Mormon**'. Mormons believe that the Book of Mormon was divinely revealed to their prophet **Joseph Smith** in America in 1830 and that it tells the history of America prior to the arrival of Europeans and visits to America by **Jesus Christ** after his resurrection. Mormons were notorious for their practice of polygamy, though this has been banned by the Church since 1890. Because they believe that the Book of Mormon is equal in authority to the **Bible**, as well as having other distinctive beliefs, Mormons are regarded as quite separate from other Christian Churches and groups. Their headquarters are in **Salt Lake City**, Utah, USA. Mormons do not drink tea, coffee or alcohol.

Mosque   A building used by Muslims for prayer. Each mosque should have a quibla which indicates the direction of Mecca, and prayers should be said in that direction

Muhammad   The founder of **Islam** who lived in Arabia 570 to 632. Believed by Muslims to have been divinely inspired to reveal the **Koran** and to be the final prophet of God (**Allah**). When the name Muhammad is said or written by Muslims they commonly add 'Peace be upon him' or write pbuh.

Niqab   A mask covering the face with the exception of the eyes. Worn by some Muslim females, usually as part of a jilbab, and associated with a particularly strict interpretation of **Shariah** law.

Orthodox Christians (also known as Eastern Orthodox)   The second largest Christian denomination in the world. The main Orthodox Churches in Britain are the Greek, the Russian and the Antiochian. Whilst many Orthodox Churches in Britain continue to use Greek or Russian in their services many, especially the Antiochian Church, are increasingly using English.

Priest   Title for a religious figure in Christian and Hindu and some other religions. The distinctive nature of a priest is that besides being a religious leader and teacher he (or she) also has certain functions or powers which are unique to their priestly role. For example, in Christianity whilst any Christian can lead prayers or teach the faith only a priest can say **Mass**.

Protestant   In the sixteenth century many churches in Europe split from the **Catholic Church** over disagreements concerning the role of the Pope and various aspects of Christian worship. The main protestant Churches in Britain today are the Church of England, Church of Scotland, Methodist Church and Baptist Church, though there are many others with varying degrees of difference between them.

Rabbi   A Jewish religious leader and teacher usually attached to a **synagogue**.

Sangha   The Buddhist community at large.

Salt Lake City   The capital of the state of Utah, USA, Salt Lake City is also the headquarters and spiritual heart of the Mormon Church. It was founded in the mid-nineteenth century by Mormons fleeing from persecution in the rest of the United States.

Shariah law   Is the legal system instituted by the Muslim prophet **Muhammad** and developed subsequently by Muslim leaders and **Imams**. It is based both of the words of the **Koran** and also the accepted records of the hadiths or traditions of the Prophet (Muhammad). Shariah includes both civil and criminal law though in many parts of the Muslim world Shariah is now applied only to family and inheritance law. In Britain Shariah is often referred to in arguments over the correct or acceptable form of dress for females.

Shia Mulims   (also called Shiite) The second largest group in Islam and in Britain. Their division with **Sunni** Muslims dates back to the death of Muhammad when Shia believe that Ali, the son in law of Muhammad, should have been appointed as the Prophet's successor. There are few differences of religious practice between Sunni and Shia though there are specific Shia festivals such as Ashura. In Britain the distinctions between Sunni and Shia Muslims are not greatly emphasised and both strands are represented in the main Muslim organisations.

SSPX (Society of Saint Pius the Tenth) See **Tridentine Mass**.

Sunni Muslims   Form the largest percentage of Muslims internationally and in Britain. Their division with **Shia** Muslims dates back to the death of Muhammad and centres on who was his legitimate successor. In Britain the distinctions between Sunni and Shia Muslims are not greatly emphasised and both strands are represented in the main Muslim organisations.

Synagogue   A building used by Jews for prayer. A synagogue is where the rolls of the **Torah** or law are kept.

Thomist Christian   (Also known as Malabar Christians) The oldest Christian denomination in India they trace their establishment back to the Apostle Thomas (doubting Thomas) who is believed to have travelled to India and established Christianity there.

Torah   Jewish term meaning the law. Technically used only to refer to the first five books of the Bible, 'Torah' can also mean the totality of Jewish law.

Tridentine Mass   The traditional form of the Roman Catholic **Mass** which was said in Latin. It was replaced in the 1960s by a new form of Mass said in the language of the congregation. Many Catholics still regard the Tridentine Mass as the 'true Mass' and the **Society of Saint Pius the Tenth** (SSPX) is a group which split from the Catholic Church in order to maintain the Tridentine Mass.

Ummah   The Muslim community throughout the world.

Vihara   A Buddhist social, study and meditation centre.

Virgin Mary   Also known as 'Our Lady', 'The Blessed Virgin', 'The Mother of God' 'The Madonna' and 'Holy Theotokos'. The mother of **Jesus Christ**. For Catholic and Orthodox Christians the veneration, but not the worship, of Mary is an important part of Christian devotion.

Introduction

In 1995 I wrote a short story, 'The Cold Jihad', which imagined the world in the year 2020 locked in a new Cold War between the West and a united, nuclear-armed, Islamic world stretching from Istanbul to Pakistan and from Kazakhstan to Casablanca. Looked at 11 years later, this minor short story is nightmarishly close to becoming prophetic.

What I did not consider in that, admittedly very short, story was the fate of religious minorities stuck on the wrong side of the 'Koranic Curtain' which I visualised as dividing the world. However, the question of religious minorities in the West, how they will affect our society, and indeed arguments over whether they should be allowed to affect our society, is becoming potentially the most important issue facing the future of Europe. The suicide bombings in London on 7 July 2005 were the first incidents of religious warfare in England since the end of the seventeenth century and are a terrifying development which would have been dismissed as impossible only 30 years ago.

Like it or not, religion is increasingly being regarded as an inherent source of identity and not merely a system of belief. In consequence, discrimination and hatred laws which were designed to deal with racial identity are being adapted to cover religious identity also. This process reached a legal crescendo in early 2006 with the passing of anti-religious discrimination legislation in the Equality Act 2006, anti-religious hatred legislation in the Racial and Religious Hatred Act 2006 and the House of Lords decision in the case of *Shabina Begum v Denbigh High School* [2006] UKHL 15, which involved a claim by a 13-year-old that she had the legal right to insist that she be allowed to wear an Islamic jilbab in defiance of the school rules regarding uniform.

This book is the first attempt to bring all these legal developments together and to look at them as a whole. In theory, they can each be looked at separately, a chapter on religious discrimination in a textbook on discrimination, a mention of religious hatred in textbooks on criminal law. The problem with that approach is that it perpetuates the assumption that religious discrimination is merely a variation on a theme, nothing more than an extension of existing discrimination laws; but I beg to differ. Race is fixed but religion is changeable, in all of human history nobody has ever changed their race (with the possible exception of Michael Jackson) but millions change their religion. Also, there are no degrees of race which an individual can alter or choose for themselves, but with religion choice does exist; a person can choose to believe or not to believe, can be intensely devout or merely occasionally devout. Finally, of course, there may be situations in which religious discrimination might be regarded as understandable in a way that racial discrimination could never be. Disliking someone because of their race or skin colour is impossible to defend rationally but disliking someone because of their religious beliefs may be as understandable as disliking someone because of their political beliefs. It is dangerously simplistic to assume that 'we all believe in the same God', since it ignores the fact that there have been some pretty weird and unpleasant religions in human history.

However, the debate on whether religious discrimination and hatred laws should be passed is now over. The powers that be have clearly decided that the legislation is required in order to ensure justice and community cohesion. I hope they are right but I fear that they are wrong and that the legislation will fall victim to the law of unintended consequences, creating division rather than curing it. Race discrimination law has, in the main, tried to make people colour blind and to minimise differences between citizens. Religious discrimination law, by contrast, has the potential to make people emphasise their differences and to demand that *their* special needs be given special attention. If that happens, then it is likely to lead to more division in society rather than more cohesion; however, only time will tell.

In writing this book I have had to come up with various examples of discrimination, hatred, etc. in order to show how the various pieces of legislation may work and, in doing so, I hope I have spread the examples around all religions in a suitably non-discriminatory way. If any member of any religion feels that I have unfairly picked on them or that I have given an unrealistic example – 'members of *my* religion would never behave that way' – then I hope they will understand the difficulties in trying to cover the infinite variety of possible human actions and will forgive me for any unintended offence which I may have given.

I am grateful to Faithworks for their permission to reproduce sections from their excellent series of guides to the Employment Equality (Religion or Belief) Regulations 2003, my thanks are also given to ACAS for permission to reproduce the whole of their guidance on the regulations as Appendix C-2.

I would like to thank my wife, Rita, who has patiently endured my spending many hours in my office with 'that other woman', as she refers to my computer; my senior clerk John Stewart, his indefatigable team of clerks and my colleagues in New Bailey Chambers who have patiently listened while I have tried to explain what I am writing about this time; also Simon Calvert, Don Horrocks, Alex Lawrence-Mills, Patrick Sookhedeo, Martin Holst, Evan Harris, Keith Porteous Wood, Andrea Minichiello Williams,

Nick Grant, James Dingemans, my daughter Rachel, and many others who have taken the time to assist me with information and guidance or to read and correct my chapters as the book progressed. As for the faults that remain, '*mea maxima culpa*' as we Catholics (used to) say.

The law is correct as of 22 June 2006.

Neil Addison
New Bailey Chambers
Liverpool and Preston

Chapter 1

What is a religion?

The question of what is the true religion, or indeed whether there is such a thing as the true religion, is a question for theologians. Why religion exists and why some succeed and others fade is a question for philosophers and historians. Whether a particular belief constitutes a religion, a philosophy or a political opinion can, however, be a question which has to be decided by lawyers. Now that legislation has been passed, dealing with religious discrimination and religious hatred, courts may find themselves having to draw fine distinctions between religious beliefs, philosophical beliefs, political beliefs and personal opinions. Depending on the particular wording of the legislation in question, where the courts draw the line could determine whether or not a person is guilty of unlawful discrimination or guilty of particular criminal offences.

For example, religiously aggravated criminal offences (Chapter 7) and the criminal offence of religious hatred (Chapter 8) both involve hostility or hatred towards 'a group of persons defined by reference to religious belief or lack of religious belief', i.e. it is clear that these particular pieces of legislation only apply in relation to 'religious belief'. Article 9 of the European Convention of Human Rights (Chapter 2), by contrast, applies to either 'religion or belief'. In employment legislation (Chapter 4), tribunals have to consider discrimination based on 'any religion, religious belief, or similar philosophical belief', whilst s 44 of the Equality Act 2006 (Chapter 3) defines 'religion or belief' as follows:

(a) 'religion' means any religion,
(b) 'belief' means any religious or philosophical belief,
(c) a reference to religion includes a reference to lack of religion, and
(d) a reference to belief includes a reference to lack of belief.

Whilst Art 2 of the First Protocol of the European Convention on Human Rights (Chapters 2 and 5) refer to 'religious and philosophical convictions'.

The *Oxford English Dictionary* offers the following definitions:

Religion A particular system of faith and worship. Action or conduct indicating a belief in, reverence for, and desire to please, a divine ruling power; the exercise or practice of rites or observances implying this. Recognition on the part of man of some higher unseen power as having control of his destiny and as being entitled to obedience, reverence and worship.

Belief Mental acceptance of a proposition, statement or fact as true, on the ground of authority or evidence; assent of the mind to a statement, or the truth of a fact beyond observation on the testimony of another, or to fact or truth on the evidence of consciousness; the mental condition involved in this assent.

Philosophy A particular system of ideas relating to the general scheme of the universe; a philosophical system or theory. Also more generally, a set of opinions, ideas or principles, a basic theory, a view or outlook. Used especially of knowledge obtained by natural reason, in contrast to revealed knowledge.

It is probably fair to say that, in the majority of legal cases, the question of whether a belief is or is not a religion or whether a person is or is not a member of a religion is not in dispute. Courts are entitled to apply their knowledge of life and to take judicial notice of facts which are well known. For example, if a woman wearing a hijab is attacked by someone who shouts 'I hate you f***ing Muslims', then the defendant would be charged with religiously aggravated assault and a court would give short shrift to any argument that Muslims were not a religious group. However, what would be the situation if a Muslim shopkeeper regarded Muslim women who do not wear the hijab as 'bad Muslims'? If he refused to serve a Muslim woman who was not wearing a hijab, would he be guilty of religious discrimination? Are they both members of the same religion, or does the fact that they interpret or apply the same religion differently mean that they, in practice, have different beliefs? And what of people who have deeply held political beliefs which form an essential part of their personality and life? Should their beliefs be regarded as less worthy of protection than the beliefs of someone else who is only a nominal member of a religious group?

There are two main sources of law on the question of what is a religion, namely cases involving charity law and European and UK cases involving Art 9 of the European Convention on Human Rights. Under English charity law, a legitimate charitable purpose is 'the advancement of religion' and, because charity status brings many financial and other benefits, many groups have sought to be defined as religions. However, some of the case law involving charities has to be approached with caution, since quite often the court was looking not at whether a particular group or belief constituted a religion but whether its purposes were for the 'advancement of a religion' and therefore had an element of public benefit. For example, a purely contemplative or secluded religious order does not classify as a charity because there is no element of public benefit associated with their activities, even though those activities are clearly religious in nature. *Cacks v Manners* [1871] LR 12; *Gilmour v Coats* [1849] AC 426.

The most comprehensive statement of what classifies as a religion in English law, the distinction between religion and belief, and the way in which courts should approach these two concepts was given in the case of *Barralet v Attorney General* [1980] 3 All ER 919. In this case an 'ethical society', whose objectives were 'the study and dissemination of ethical principles and the cultivation of a rational religious sentiment', applied for registration as a religious charity. During the case the judge, Dillon J, was referred to an opinion by the United States Supreme Court relating to the beliefs of a (non religious) conscientious objector where the Supreme Court had said that, in its opinion: 'a sincere and meaningful belief which occupies in the life of its possessor a place parallel to that filled by the God of those admittedly qualifying for exemption on the grounds of religion comes within the statutory definition'. However, this approach of making religious and nonreligious beliefs comparable was rejected by Dillon J, who said (at p 924):

In a free country, and I have no reason to believe that this country is less free than the United States, it is natural that the court should desire not to discriminate between beliefs deeply and sincerely held, whether they are beliefs in a God or in the excellence of man or in ethical principles or in Platonism or some other scheme of philosophy. But I do not see that that warrants extending the meaning of 'religion' so as to embrace all other beliefs and philosophies. Religion as I see it is concerned with man's relations with God and ethics are concerned with man's relations with man. The two are not the same and are not made the same by sincere enquiry into the question, what is God. If reason leads people not to accept Christianity or any known religion but they do believe in the excellence of qualities such as truth, beauty and love, or belief in the Platonic concept of the ideal, their beliefs may be to them the equivalent of a religion but viewed objectively they are not a religion . . . It seems to me that two of the essential attributes of religion are faith and worship; faith in a God and worship of that God. This is supported by the definition of religion given in the *Oxford English Dictionary*, although I appreciate that there are other definitions in other dictionaries and books. The *Oxford Dictionary* gives us one of the definitions of religion: 'A particular system of faith and worship. Recognition on the part of man of some higher unseen power as having control of his destiny and as being entitled to obedience, reverence and worship'.

What constitutes 'worship' was considered by the Court of Appeal (Civil Division) in the case of *R v Registrar General ex p Segerdal* [1970] 3 All ER 887, in which the court decided that a 'chapel' used by the Church of Scientology was not a place of worship. In reaching their decision, the court considered the 'creed' of the church and the activities which took place in the 'chapel' and held that these did not constitute religious worship. In that case Buckley LJ said (at p 892):

> Worship I take to be something which must have some at least of the following characteristics, submission to the object worshiped, veneration of that object, praise, thanksgiving, prayer or intersession.

However, in both these judgments it was accepted that the law could not give an absolute and definitive interpretation of religion. In both cases it was accepted that Buddhism should be regarded as a religion even though Buddhists do not worship a supreme being and Buddhism is, in many ways, more of a philosophy than a religion. However, Buddhism does include prayers, ritual and worship and has a viewpoint regarding the ultimate destiny of the human personality, or soul, after death, which means that, for all practical purposes, it is indistinguishable from a religion which includes a god.

The point in *Barralet* that 'religion is concerned with man's relations with God and ethics are concerned with man's relations with man' is still a valuable and relevant distinction to be made. Communism in the 1930s, for example, had many aspects of similarity with religion, perhaps because Stalin was an ex-student from a seminary. Certainly, under Stalin the works of Marx and Lenin were raised almost to the status of divine scripture and many commentators noted that Communist parades and meetings had a ritualistic, quasi-religious atmosphere. However, Communism was concerned only with the relationship of humans to each other and to the state and did not concern itself with the destiny of the individual after death. For that reason, though quasi-religious in many ways, it was never a religion and was never regarded as such.

Another way of distinguishing between a religion and a belief is the extent to which it is possible to be a member of a religion and another organisation. It is, for example, possible for both Mormons and Muslims to be members of the Labour Party but it is not possible for a Mormon to be a Muslim or a Muslim to be a Mormon. A purely personal definition that I suggest is 'religion is what I do, belief is what I think', i.e. religion is communal, belief is personal. I may go to the same church as my co-religionists and say the same prayers but whether I believe the same things as them is another matter.

One attempt to define religion is in s 2(3) of the Charities Act 2006:

> . . . 'religion' includes—

(i)   a religion which involves belief in more than one god, and

(ii) a religion which does not involve belief in a god.

It is doubtful if this definition actually changes anything. Charity law already gives equal treatment to polytheistic religions (religion which involves belief in more than one god) such as Paganism, non-theistic religions (religion which does not involve belief in a god) such as Buddhism and monotheistic religions (religion which involves belief in one god) such as Christianity, Islam and Judaism. It is probable that the *Barralet* decision relating to the distinction between 'religion and ethics' will continue to be applied and anything lying outside the definition of religion will fall within the definition of 'belief'.

In the Australian case of *Islamic Council of Victoria v Catch the Fire Ministries Inc.* [2004] VCAT 2510 there was an attempt to argue that Islam was not a religion. This point was argued on technical legal grounds but the judge took the view that the decision as to whether or not Islam was a religion was a question of fact and not a question of law:

> 376 The question of whether Islam is a religion was raised by the respondent. The Tribunal's view is quite simple, and that is that it is a religion. The expert witnesses who were called by the complainant each conceded that it was a world religion. An obscure argument was put by Mr Perkins based upon a number of essentially legal issues. The respondent seeks to deny that Islam is a religion by reference to a decision that the law of blasphemy only applies to Christianity. The basis of that view is in doubt in this State and, indeed, may not even exist (see the view of Harper J in *Pell v. The Council of the Trustees of the National Gallery of Victoria* (1988) 2 V.R. 39). The fact that there is an absence of strict division between church and State does not detract from the con-clusion that Islam is a religion. The relationship between the two may be an issue, but to suggest that there is no such thing as an Islamic religion does not stand scrutiny. The above is demonstrated by the fact that Islam, which has adherers, in excess of one billion people through-out the world; who regard the Qur'an as equivalent to the Bible; that it agrees substantially with Christian beliefs save for particular events; that it is accepted by millions of people as a religion by which people live their lives based upon the teachings of the Qur'an and Hadiths; that it has a structured organisation which teaches and promotes its views; and finally has places of worship world wide, that is, mosques, has to deny any argument that it is not a religion.

However, though courts have an important and legitimate role in deter-mining what constitutes religion or religious belief, it is no part of the role of secular courts to take sides in religious controversy or to decide which particular religious belief is correct. Two cases illustrate this point clearly. In *Amicus v Secretary of State for Trade and Industry* [2004] EWHC 860 (Admin) the Amicus trade union were objecting to s 7(3) of the Employment Equality (Sexual Orientation) Regulations 2003, which exempted 'employment for purposes of an organised religion' from the regulations (Chapter 4). Amongst other points it was argued that Christian groups which were opposed to homosexuality were theologically wrong in their understanding of the teaching of the Bible. This approach was categorically rejected by Richards J in paras 36–39 of the judgment:

> 36 The NUT disputes the existence of a coherent theological basis for the interveners' views on sexual morality, in particular on homosexuality and homosexual behaviour. The evidence before the court includes witness statements, extracts from the Bible and other material directed to this issue. In my view, however, it is not an appropriate issue for this court to entertain. First, this is a judicial review challenge in the context of which the interveners' beliefs have an illustrative rather than determinative function, helping in particular to cast light on the background to regulation 7(3) and on the competing claims between which a balance has to be struck. Secondly, and in any event, I consider that the resolution of the theological dispute raised by the NUT would take the court beyond its legitimate role.

> 37 In *R (Williamson) v. Secretary of State for Education and Employment* [2003] QB 1300, which raised the question whether the claimants' belief in the use of mild corporal punishment as part of a Christian education was a 'belief' for the purposes of article 9 of the Convention, Arden LJ observed that the court's function at the fact-finding stage was to decide what the claimants' beliefs were and whether they were genuinely held:

>> 'Religious texts often form the basis from which adherents develop specific beliefs. It is not the court's function to judge whether those beliefs are fairly based on the passages said to support them' (1370B-C, para 252).

> Although the other members of the court did not adopt the same approach, it is one that seems to me to have a great deal to commend it.

> 38 A more extreme case, relating as it did to a doctrinal assessment of the fitness of a rabbi, but again one that points to the appropriateness of judicial restraint in this general area is *R v. Chief Rabbi, ex parte Wachmann* [1992] 1 WLR 1036. In that case Simon Brown J stated that 'the court would never be prepared to rule on questions of Jewish law' and that, in relation to the determination of whether someone is morally and religiously fit to carry out the spiritual and pastoral duties of his

office, the court 'must inevitably be wary of entering so self-evidently sensitive an area, straying across the well-recognised divide between church and state' (1042G–1043A).

39 I should also note a case on which Mr Dingemans has placed substantial weight, namely the decision of the US Supreme Court in *Boy Scouts of America v. Dale* (2000) 8 BHRC 535, where it was said (at 541h–542b):

> 'The [New Jersey Supreme Court] concluded that the exclusion of members like Dale 'appears antithetical to the organization's goals and philosophy' . . . But our cases reject this sort of inquiry; it is not the role of the courts to reject a group's expressed values because they disagree with those values or find them internally inconsistent . . . The Boy Scouts asserts that it 'teaches that homosexual conduct is not morally straight' and that it does 'not want to promote homosexual conduct as a legitimate form of behavior' . . . We accept the Boy Scouts' assertion . . .'

Such an approach is certainly in line with that which I consider to be appropriate in the present case in relation to religious beliefs.

Following the *Amicus* case, the fact that it is not for secular courts to take sides on theological questions was restated in unequivocal terms in the House of Lords case of *R (Williamson) v Secretary of State for Education and Employment* [2005] UKHL 15, where several Christian schools were arguing that legislation restricting corporal punishment in Christian schools violated their right to freedom of religion under Art 9 of the European Convention on Human Rights. This case involved arguments as to whether the Bible did in fact *require*, as opposed to *permit*, corporal punishment. Lord Nichols said (at para 22):

> '22 It is necessary first to clarify the court's role in identifying a religious belief calling for protection under article 9. When the genuineness of a claimant's professed belief is an issue in the proceedings the court will inquire into and decide this issue as a question of fact. This is a limited inquiry. The court is concerned to ensure an assertion of religious belief is made in good faith: 'neither fictitious, nor capricious, and that it is not an artifice', to adopt the felicitous phrase of Iacobucci J in the decision of the Supreme Court of Canada in *Syndicat Northcrest v Amselem* (2004) 241 DLR (4th) 1, 27, para 52. But, emphatically, it is not for the court to embark on an inquiry into the asserted belief and judge its 'validity' by some objective standard such as the source material upon which the claimant founds his belief or the orthodox teaching of the religion in question or the extent to which the claimant's belief

conforms to or differs from the views of others professing the same religion. Freedom of religion protects the subjective belief of an individual. As Iacobucci J also noted, at page 28, para 54, religious belief is intensely personal and can easily vary from one individual to another. Each individual is at liberty to hold his own religious beliefs, however irrational or inconsistent they may seem to some, however surprising. The European Court of Human Rights has rightly noted that 'in principle, the right to freedom of religion as understood in the Convention rules out any appreciation by the state of the legitimacy of religious beliefs or of the manner in which these are expressed': *Metropolitan Church of Bessarabia v Moldova* (2002) 35 EHRR 306, 335, para 117. The relevance of objective factors such as source material is, at most, that they may throw light on whether the professed belief is genuinely held.

23   Everyone, therefore, is entitled to hold whatever beliefs he wishes. But when questions of 'manifestation' arise, as they usually do in this type of case, a belief must satisfy some modest, objective minimum requirements. These threshold requirements are implicit in article 9 of the European Convention and comparable guarantees in other human rights instruments. The belief must be consistent with basic standards of human dignity or integrity. Manifestation of a religious belief, for instance, which involved subjecting others to torture or inhuman punishment would not qualify for protection. The belief must relate to matters more than merely trivial. It must possess an adequate degree of seriousness and importance. As has been said, it must be a belief on a fundamental problem. With religious belief this requisite is readily satisfied. The belief must also be coherent in the sense of being intelligible and capable of being understood. But, again, too much should not be demanded in this regard. Typically, religion involves belief in the supernatural. It is not always susceptible to lucid exposition or, still less, rational justification. The language used is often the language of allegory, symbol and metaphor. Depending on the subject matter, individuals cannot always be expected to express themselves with cogency or precision. Nor are an individual's beliefs fixed and static. The beliefs of every individual are prone to change over his lifetime. Overall, these threshold requirements should not be set at a level which would deprive minority beliefs of the protection they are intended to have under the Convention.

Lord Nicholls' view that a religion needs some form of intellectual coherence conforms with the judgment in the case of *X v UK* [1977] 11 DR 55, where the European Commission on Human Rights held that because the Wiccan 'religion' had no clear structure or belief system, it did not qualify as a religion for the purposes of Art 9. It is also important to note the distinction Lord Nicholls made between religious belief and manifestations of religious belief because it is a distinction which is often misunderstood. For example, during the parliamentary debate on Pt 2 of the Equality Bill (Chapter 3), Home Office Minister Paul Goggins MP said (*Hansard* 6 December 2005, col 145):

> We know from case law that religion has to be consistent with human dignity; it must have a cogency, seriousness and sense of cohesion about a particular series and set of beliefs. We would expect a philosophical belief to betray the same hallmarks, although it does not revolve around belief in a particular deity.

The reference to religion having to be 'consistent with human dignity' is a common misreading of the European Court of Human Rights case of *Cosans v UK* 25 February 1982, where the court was considering not the meaning of the word 'religion' but the meaning of the phrase 'philosophical convictions' and said (para 36):

> In its ordinary meaning the word 'convictions' . . . denotes views that attain a certain level of cogency, seriousness, cohesion and importance . . . As regards the adjective 'philosophical', it is not capable of exhaustive definition . . . The expression 'philosophical convictions' in the present context denotes, in the Court's opinion, such convictions as are worthy of respect in a 'democratic society' . . . and are not incompatible with human dignity.

A person therefore can have religious beliefs which are not 'worthy of respect in a democratic society' (an extraordinarily vague and subjective concept) but they still have a religious belief. For example, the Ancient Aztecs worshipped the sun god Huitzilopochtli by means of gruesome human sacrifices, in which hearts were torn from living bodies and offered up to Huitzilopochtli in order to ensure that he (i.e. the sun) would return the next day. By no definition could the beliefs and practices of the Aztecs be regarded as 'worthy of respect in a democratic society' but there can be no argument that their beliefs did constitute a religion.

What the European and UK cases seem to be saying is that if the beliefs and practices of a religion are 'incompatible with human dignity' and are not 'worthy of respect in a democratic society', then those beliefs and practices will not be treated by the law as being 'religious' beliefs. Having said that, the barrier would be set very high. The Muslim insistence on women wearing the hijab and the Jewish practice of circumcision could both be regarded as beliefs which are 'not worthy of respect' and 'incompatible with human dignity' but they are not so unworthy or so incompatible that they are not protected by the law.

Therefore, when a court or tribunal is considering a case involving a question of religious belief, it is not for it to decide whether the religious belief is properly held and conforms with the view of the majority of members of the religion. What it must decide, as a question of fact is 'what is the belief which is claimed to be held?' and, having answered that question, it must then go on to answer the following questions:

(a) Is the belief sincerely held rather than being a mere pretence?
(b) Is the belief more than merely trivial, does it possess a degree of seriousness and importance?
(c) Is the belief capable of some degree of coherence and of being understood so that it can be communicated?
(d) Does the belief constitute a set of opinions, ideas or principles as opposed to an opinion on a particular issue of the day?
(e) Does the belief involve man's relationship with a god (however defined) and worship of that god?
(f) Is the belief compatible, or incompatible, with human dignity?

If the court, or tribunal, can answer 'yes' to questions (a)–(e) (on a fairly low level of proof) then it is dealing with a religion and, if it can only answer 'yes' to (a)–(d) then it is dealing with a belief. In either case, if the answer to (f) is that the belief in question is 'incompatible with human dignity' then the law will not recognise or protect the religion, or belief, in question. It is important, however, with (f), to recognise that it is very much a long stop and it is not up to a believer to convince a court that their beliefs are compatible with human dignity; rather the onus is on anyone who claims that a religious belief is 'incompatible with human dignity' or 'not worthy of respect in a democratic society' to prove their claim to a high standard. Courts and tribunals must remember that they are only required to respect a person's right to have a religion or belief; they are not required to respect, to like or to approve of the religion or belief itself. What is fundamental is that the court or tribunal can only go behind a claim to have a belief in order to decide if the belief is sincerely held or is a pretence, they cannot go behind a belief in order to establish whether it is a correct belief.

It may well be, however, that in the majority of cases courts and tribunals will find it simpler to assume, in the absence of argument to the contrary, that the particular belief in question is a religion and then go on to decide if it is thereby protected by the specific statutory provision being relied on. This was the approach adopted by the European Commission for Human Rights in the case of *Chappell v UK* [1987] 53 DR 241, where it said, in regard to Druidism:

> The Commission has not found it necessary to decide whether or not Druidism can be classified as a religion within the meaning of Article 9

para. 1 (Art. 9–1). It has assumed, for the purpose of this application, that it is a religion or belief as it finds the complaint anyway manifestly ill-founded.

The final word, as always in a legal textbook, goes to the House of Lords and the judgment of Lord Walker in para 54 of *R (Williamson) v Secretary of State for Education and Employment* [2005] UKHL 15:

> In my opinion it is certainly not necessary, and is probably not useful, for your Lordships to try to reach a precise definition [of Religion]. Courts in different jurisdictions have on several occasions had to attempt the task, often in the context of exemptions or reliefs from rates and taxes, and have almost always remarked on its difficulty. Two illuminating cases are the decisions of Dillon J in *In re South Place Ethical Society* [1980] 1 WLR 1565 and that of the High Court of Australia in *Church of the New Faith v Commissioner of Pay-Roll Tax (Victoria)* (1983) 154 CLR 120, both of which contain valuable reviews of earlier authority. The trend of authority (unsurprisingly in an age of increasingly multi-cultural societies and increasing respect for human rights) is towards a 'newer, more expansive, reading' of religion (Wilson and Deane JJ in the *Church of the New Faith* case at p 174, commenting on a similar trend in United States jurisprudence).

In summary, the attitude of courts when faced with the question 'what is the definition of religion' is possibly best summed up in the (probably apocryphal) remark attributed to a US Supreme Court Justice who, when asked to define pornography, said: 'I can't define it; but I know it when I see it.'

Chapter 2

Religion and human rights

Historically, Britain did not recognise a legal right to religious freedom, though there was a pragmatic acceptance of religious diversity where this seemed appropriate. For example, after the capture of Quebec in 1759, Britain legalised, and indeed pampered, Roman Catholicism in French-speaking Canada, even though Catholicism was still banned in Britain itself. In British India, Hindus and Muslims were each allowed to retain their personal religious laws and practices, though Shariah criminal law was replaced by English criminal law and the Hindu customs of suttee (widow burning) and thugee (worship of Kali, goddess of death) were suppressed.

During the late eighteenth and early nineteenth centuries, legal restrictions on Protestant dissenters and Roman Catholics were progressively removed and, since then, for all practical purposes, there has been complete religious freedom in Britain. In 1948 Britain was a supporter of the historic Universal Declaration of Human Rights, passed by the United Nations, Art 18 of which declares the universal right to freedom of thought, conscience and religion. This clause was incorporated almost word for word into Art 9 of the European Convention on Human Rights, which was signed by Britain in 1951 as one of the founder members of the Council of Europe. Following the passing of the Human Rights Act 1998, Art 9 now forms part of English law and provides:

(1) Everyone has the right to freedom of thought, conscience and religion; this right includes freedom to change his religion or belief and freedom, in community with others and in public or private, to manifest his religion of belief, in worship, teaching, practice and observance.

(2) Freedom to manifest one's religion or beliefs shall be subject only to such limitations as are prescribed by law and are necessary in a democratic society in the interests of public safety; for the protection of public order, health or morals or for the protection of the rights and freedoms of others.

Closely allied to Art 9 is Art 10 (Freedom of Expression), which provides:

(1) Everyone has the right to freedom of expression. This right shall include freedom to hold opinions and to receive and impart information and ideas without interference by public authority and regardless of frontiers. This Article shall not prevent States from requiring the licensing of broadcasting, television or cinema enterprises.

(2) The exercise of these freedoms, since it carries with it duties and responsibilities, may be subject to such formalities, conditions, restrictions or penalties as are prescribed by law and are necessary in a democratic society, in the interests of national security, territorial integrity or public safety, for the prevention of disorder or crime, for the protection of health or morals, for the protection of the reputation or rights of others, for preventing the disclosure of information received in confidence, or for maintaining the authority and impartiality of the judiciary.

It is common for human rights claims to allege breaches of both Arts 9 and 10, though the approach of the courts has usually been to choose one of the rights as being the principal right in question and to decide the case by reference to that right. For example, in the cases of *Sahin v Turkey* 10 November 2006 and *Hammond v DPP* [2004] EWHC 69 (Admin) breaches were alleged of both Arts 9 and 10. In the case of *Sahin*, the European Court of Human Rights decided that Art 9 was the important article, whilst in the case of *Hammond* the High Court decided to concentrate on Art 10.

The case law of the European Court of Human Rights indicates that Art 9 rights are not confined to natural persons but extend to organisations; but there is a distinction between the rights to 'freedom of thought and conscience' and rights to 'freedom of religion' because only individuals can have 'thoughts' or a 'conscience': *Company X v Switzerland* [1981] 16 DR 85; *Verein 'Kontakt-Information-Therapie' v Austria* [1988] 57 DR 81. However, it has been accepted that representatives of religious groups and organisations can claim the full protection of Art 9 on behalf of their members: *X and Church of Scientology v Sweden* [1979] 16 DR 68; *Chappell v UK* [1987] 53 DR 241.

Article 9 provides an absolute right to freedom of belief and a qualified right so far as manifestation of belief is concerned. This means that the state cannot restrict or make it illegal to have particular beliefs but it can restrict or make illegal certain activities which could constitute 'manifestation' of that religion. For example, under Art 9 an individual has an absolute right to believe in the omnipotence of the Aztec sun god Huitzilopochtli but they do not have any right to 'manifest' this belief by performing a human sacrifice to Huitzilopochtli such as was done by Aztec priests.

These two separate principles were summarised by Lord Nicholls in paras 15–17 of *R (Williamson) v Secretary of State for Education and Employment* [2005] UKHL 15:

15. Religious and other beliefs and convictions are part of the humanity of every individual. They are an integral part of his personality and individuality. In a civilised society individuals respect each other's beliefs. This enables them to live in harmony. This is one of the hallmarks of a civilised society. Unhappily, all too often this hallmark has been noticeable by its absence. Mutual tolerance has had a chequered history even in recent times. The history of most countries, if not all, has been marred by the evil consequences of religious and other intolerance.

16. It is against this background that article 9 of the European Convention on Human Rights safeguards freedom of religion. This freedom is not confined to freedom to hold a religious belief. It includes the right to express and practise one's beliefs. Without this, freedom of religion would be emasculated. Invariably religious faiths call for more than belief. To a greater or lesser extent adherents are required or encouraged to act in certain ways, most obviously and directly in forms of communal or personal worship, supplication and meditation. But under article 9 there is a difference between freedom to hold a belief and freedom to express or 'manifest' a belief. The former right, freedom of belief, is absolute. The latter right, freedom to manifest belief, is qualified.

17. This is to be expected, because the way a belief is expressed in practice may impact on others. Familiar instances of conduct shaped by particular religious beliefs are the days or times when worship is prescribed or encouraged, the need to abstain from work on certain days, forms of dress, rituals connected with the preparation of food, the need for total abstinence from certain types of food or drink, and the need for abstinence from all or some types of food at certain times. In a more generalised and non-specific form the tenets of a religion may affect the entirety of a believer's way of life: for example, 'thou shalt love thy neighbour as thyself'. The manner in which children should be brought up is another subject on which religious teachings are not silent. So in a pluralist society a balance has to be held between freedom to practise one's own beliefs and the interests of others affected by those practices.

One of the most fundamental cases under Art 9 is *Kokkinakis v Greece* [1993] 17 EHRR 397, which is invariably referred to and re-emphasised by the European Court of Human Rights whenever it is considering Art 9 claims. Kokkinakis was a Jehovah's Witness who was prosecuted under a Greek law which made it a criminal offence to 'proselytise', i.e. to attempt to convert others (invariably members of the Greek Orthodox Church) to another religion. He appealed to the European Court of Human Rights on the basis that the law infringed his rights under Art 9.

In paras 31 and 33 of its judgment, the court laid down the fundamental principles underlying Art 9:

31. As enshrined in Article 9 (art. 9), freedom of thought, conscience and religion is one of the foundations of a 'democratic society' within the meaning of the Convention. It is, in its religious dimension, one of the most vital elements that go to make up the identity of believers and their conception of life, but it is also a precious asset for atheists, agnostics, sceptics and the unconcerned. The pluralism indissoluable from a democratic society, which has been dearly won over the centuries, depends on it.

32. AWhile religious freedom is primarily a matter of individual conscience, it also implies, inter alia, freedom to 'manifest one's religion'. Bearing witness in words and deeds is bound up with the existence of religious convictions. According to Article 9, freedom to manifest one's religion is not only exercisable in community with others, 'in public' and within the circle of those whose faith one shares, but can also be asserted 'alone' and 'in private'; furthermore, it includes in principle the right to try to convince one's neighbour, for example through 'teaching', failing which, 'freedom to change one's religion or belief', enshrined in Article 9, would be likely to remain a dead letter.

33. The fundamental nature of the rights guaranteed in Article 9 para. 1 is also reflected in the wording of the paragraph providing for limitations on them. Unlike the second paragraphs of Articles 8, 10 and 11 which cover all the rights mentioned in the first paragraphs of those Articles, that of Article 9 refers only to 'freedom to manifest one's religion or belief'. In so doing, it recognises that in democratic societies, in which several religions coexist within one and the same population, it may be necessary to place restrictions on this freedom in order to reconcile the interests of the various groups and ensure that everyone's beliefs are respected.

Applying these principles to the *Kokkinakis* case the court held that the restrictions on proselytising in Greece were 'not necessary in a democratic society'. It is, however, worth noting that in the case of *Larissis v Greece* [1998] 27 EHRR 329 the court accepted that the Greek Air Force had been entitled to court-martial three air force officers who were Pentecostalist Christians and who had attempted to convert Greek airmen. The court noted in para 51:

the hierarchical structures which are a feature of life in the armed forces may colour every aspect of the relations between military personnel, making it difficult for a subordinate to rebuff the approaches of an individual of superior rank or to withdraw from a conversation initiated by him.

Therefore, the prosecution was legitimate in order 'to protect the rights and freedoms of others', i.e. lower-ranking airmen.

The court also noted in para 45 of the *Larissis* case:

> Article 9 does not, however, protect every act motivated or inspired by a religion or belief. It does not, for example, protect improper proselytism, such as the offering of material or social advantage or the application of improper pressure with a view to gaining new members for a Church.

The court in the *Kokkinakis* case had laid down the reasoning to be gone through in deciding whether Art 9 had been breached:

(a) Has the right to manifest religious belief been interfered with?
(b) If yes, was the interference 'prescribed by law'?
(c) If yes, did the interference pursue a legitimate aim within the meaning of Art 9.2?
(d) If yes, was the interference 'necessary in democratic society'?

However, it is important to recognise that this merely reflects the train of reasoning that will be undertaken by courts in deciding cases brought under Art 9. There is no requirement that a public body must follow exactly the same line of reasoning itself. In the case of *Begum v Denbigh High School* [2005] EWCA Civ 199 the Court of Appeal decided that Denbigh High School had acted unlawfully because it had not applied the same line of reasoning as the European Court of Human Rights in deciding whether a Muslim pupil could rely on Art 9 in order to demand the right to wear an Islamic jilbab in school. This approach was, however, roundly rejected by the House of Lords when the school appealed against the Court of Appeal decision. In *Begum v Denbigh High School* [2006] UKHL 15 Lord Hoffmann stated (para 68):

> 68. Article 9 is concerned with substance, not procedure. It confers no right to have a decision made in any particular way. What matters is the result: was the right to manifest a religious belief restricted in a way which is not justified under article 9.2? The fact that the decision-maker is allowed an area of judgment in imposing requirements which may have the effect of restricting the right does not entitle a court to say that a justifiable and proportionate restriction should be struck down because

the decision-maker did not approach the question in the structured way in which a judge might have done. Head teachers and governors cannot be expected to make such decisions with textbooks on human rights law at their elbows. The most that can be said is that the way in which the school approached the problem may help to persuade a judge that its answer fell within the area of judgment accorded to it by the law.

Whilst Lord Bingham noted, in para 30, that a court reviewing a decision must not become bogged down in the question of the procedure that was followed:

> 30. Proportionality must be judged objectively, by the court (*Williamson*, above, para 51). As Davies observed in his article cited above, 'The retreat to procedure is of course a way of avoiding difficult questions.'

The concept that any interference with the exercise of rights under Art 9 (and indeed most other articles) must be 'prescribed by law' is fundamental to how the Convention and the Human Rights Act 1998 work. The rule of law is described in the preamble to the Convention as part of the 'common heritage' which the signatories share. No interference with a right protected under the Convention is permissible unless the citizen knows the basis for the interference because it is set out in an ascertainable law which is accessible and certain and, in the absence of such detailed authorisation by the law, any interference, however justified, will violate the Convention.

The phrases 'prescribed by law' or 'in accordance with the law' mean that there must be an ascertainable legal regime governing the interference in question but they mean more than a mere search for some national legal rule which permits the interference; a national rule will not constitute a law for Convention purposes unless it has appropriate qualities to make it compatible with the rule of law. The classic definition of 'prescribed by law' was laid down by the European Court of Human Rights in *Sunday Times v United Kingdom* [1979] 2 EHRR 245 (para 49):

> 49. Firstly, the law must be adequately accessible: the citizens must be able to have an indication that is adequate in the circumstances of the legal rules applicable to a given case. Secondly, a norm cannot be regarded as a 'law' unless it is formulated with sufficient precision to enable the citizen to regulate his conduct: he must be able – if need be with appropriate advice – to foresee, to a degree that is reasonable in the circumstances, the consequences which a given action may entail. Those consequences need not be foreseeable with absolute certainty: experience shows this to be unattainable. Again, whilst certainty is highly desirable, it may bring in its train excessive rigidity and the law must be able to keep pace with changing circumstances. Accordingly, many

laws are inevitably couched in terms which, to a greater or lesser extent, are vague and whose interpretation and application are questions of practice.

What is sufficiently certain will depend on the circumstances. Statute law, secondary legislation, principles of common law and internal rules laid down by organisations are all acceptable. In the European Court of Human Rights case of *Sahin v Turkey* ECtHR Application no 4477/98 10 November 2005 the court accepted that regulations made by the Vice Chancellor of Istanbul University, which prohibited female students from wearing the Islamic headscarf, and prohibited male students from having beards, were rules 'prescribed by law'. Similarly in the case of *Begum v Denbigh High School* [2006] UKHL 15 the House of Lords accepted that rules laid down by the school regulating the acceptable forms of school uniform were 'prescribed by law'. In both cases the logic was the same. The student concerned knew what the rules were, they were able to regulate their conduct in accordance with those rules and the rules were laid down by a person or body with authority to make regulations for the university or school. In para 88 of the *Sahin* case the European Court of Human Rights said:

> 88. Further, as regards the words 'in accordance with the law' and 'prescribed by law' which appear in Articles 8 to 11 of the Convention, the Court observes that it has always understood the term 'law' in its 'substantive' sense, not its 'formal' one; it has included both 'written law', encompassing enactments of lower ranking statutes (*De Wilde, Ooms and Versyp v. Belgium*, judgment of 18 June 1971, Series A no 12, p. 45, § 93) and regulatory measures taken by professional regulatory bodies under independent rule-making powers delegated to them by parliament (*Bartold v. Germany*, judgment of 25 March 1985, Series A no. 90, p. 21, § 46), and unwritten law. 'Law' must be understood to include both statutory law and judge-made 'law' (see, among other authorities, *Sunday Times v. the United Kingdom* (no. 1), judgment of 26 April 1979, Series A no. 30, p. 30, § 47; *Kruslin*, cited above, § 29 in fine; and *Casado Coca v. Spain*, judgment of 24 February 1994, Series A no. 285-A, p. 18, § 43). In sum, the 'law' is the provision in force as the competent courts have interpreted it.

The court also accepts the idea that 'ignorance of the law is no defence' so, for example, if a person was to open a religious building in defiance of publicly available planning laws and regulations, it would be no defence that they did not know about the planning laws and regulations. The court has accepted in *Manoussakis v Greece* [1996] 23 EHRR 387 that planning restrictions on places of worship are acceptable under Art 9.

Whether a restriction on the manifestation of religious belief 'pursues a legitimate aim' or 'is necessary in a democratic society' will depend on a balancing exercise of the interests of the believer and of those affected by the belief. If the restriction or practice is merely applied because 'that is the way it has always been done' then that would not be justifiable. For example, in *Buscarini v San Marino* [1999] 6 BHRC 638 the court held that a law requiring persons elected to the San Marino Parliament to take an oath on the Gospels was not 'necessary in a democratic society'. However, where a restriction on the manifestation of religious belief is imposed for a specific and considered reason, or is imposed as a condition of employment, then the European Court of Human Rights is usually reluctant to interfere. This was noted by Lord Bingham in paras 22–24 of *Begum v Denbigh High School* [2006] UKHL 15:

> 22. What constitutes interference depends on all the circumstances of the case, including the extent to which in the circumstances an individual can reasonably expect to be at liberty to manifest his beliefs in practice'. As the Strasbourg court put it in *Kalaç v Turkey* (1997) 27 EHRR 552, para 27,
>
> > 'Article 9 does not protect every act motivated or inspired by a religion or belief. Moreover, in exercising his freedom to manifest his religion, an individual may need to take his specific situation into account.'
>
> The Grand Chamber endorsed this paragraph in *Sahin v Turkey* (Application No 44774/98, 10 November 2005, unreported), para 105. The Commission ruled to similar effect in *Ahmad v United Kingdom* (1981) 4 EHRR 126, para 11:
>
> > '. . . the freedom of religion, as guaranteed by Article 9, is not absolute, but subject to the limitations set out in Article 9(2). Moreover, it may, as regards the modality of a particular religious manifestation, be influenced by the situation of the person claiming that freedom.'
>
> 23. The Strasbourg institutions have not been at all ready to find an interference with the right to manifest religious belief in practice or observance where a person has voluntarily accepted an employment or role which does not accommodate that practice or observance and there are other means open to the person to practise or observe his or her religion without undue hardship or inconvenience. Thus in *X v Denmark* (1976) 5 DR 157 a clergyman was held to have accepted the discipline of his church when he took employment, and his right to leave the church guaranteed his freedom of religion. His claim under article 9 failed. In *Kjeldsen, Busk Madsen and Pedersen v Denmark* [1976] 1 EHRR 711, paras 54 and 57, parents' philosophical and religious objections to sex

education in state schools was rejected on the ground that they could send their children to state schools or educate them at home. The applicant's article 9 claim in *Ahmad*, above, paras 13, 14 and 15, failed because he had accepted a contract which did not provide for him to absent himself from his teaching duties to attend prayers, he had not brought his religious requirements to the employer's notice when seeking employment and he was at all times free to seek other employment which would accommodate his religious observance. *Karaduman v Turkey* (1993) 74 DR 93 is a strong case. The applicant was denied a certificate of graduation because a photograph of her without a headscarf was required and she was unwilling for religious reasons to be photographed without a headscarf. The Commission found (p 109) no interference with her article 9 right because (p 108) 'by choosing to pursue her higher education in a secular university a student submits to those university rules, which may make the freedom of students to manifest their religion subject to restrictions as to place and manner intended to ensure harmonious coexistence between students of different beliefs'. In rejecting the applicant's claim in *Konttinen v Finland* (1996) 87-A DR 68 the Commission pointed out, in para 1, page 75, that he had not been pressured to change his religious views or prevented from manifesting his religion or belief; having found that his working hours conflicted with his religious convictions, he was free to relinquish his post. An application by a child punished for refusing to attend a National Day parade in contravention of her beliefs as a Jehovah's Witness, to which her parents were also party, was similarly unsuccessful in *Valsamis v Greece* (1996) 24 EHRR 294. It was held (para 38) that article 9 did not confer a right to exemption from disciplinary rules which applied generally and in a neutral manner and that there had been no interference with the child's right to freedom to manifest her religion or belief. In *Stedman v United Kingdom* (1997) 23 EHRR CD 168 it was fatal to the applicant's article 9 claim that she was free to resign rather than work on Sundays. The applicant in *Kalaç*, above, paras 28–29, failed because he had, in choosing a military career, accepted of his own accord a system of military discipline that by its nature implied the possibility of special limitations on certain rights and freedoms, and he had been able to fulfil the ordinary obligations of Muslim belief. In *Jewish Liturgical Association Cha'are Shalom Ve Tsedek v France* (2000) 9 BHRC 27, para 81, the applicants' challenge to the regulation of ritual slaughter in France, which did not satisfy their exacting religious standards, was rejected because they could easily obtain supplies of meat, slaughtered in accordance with those standards, from Belgium.

24. This line of authority has been criticised by the Court of Appeal as overly restrictive (*Copsey v WWB Devon Clays Ltd* [2005] EWCA Civ

932, [2005] 1 CR 1789, paras 31–39, 44–66), and in *Williamson*, above, para 39, the House questioned whether alternative means of accommodating a manifestation of religions belief had, as suggested in the *Jewish Liturgical* case, above, para 80, to be 'impossible' before a claim of interference under article 9 could succeed. But the authorities do in my opinion support the proposition with which I prefaced para 23 of this opinion. Even if it be accepted that the Strasbourg institutions have erred on the side of strictness in rejecting complaints of interference, there remains a coherent and remarkably consistent body of authority which our domestic courts must take into account and which shows that interference is not easily established.

Lord Bingham also warned against any tendency by courts or litigants to try to apply judicial creativity so as to extend Art 9 beyond the parameters established by the European Court of Human Rights (para 29):

> . . . the purpose of the Human Rights Act 1998 was not to enlarge the rights or remedies of those in the United Kingdom whose Convention rights have been violated but to enable those rights and remedies to be asserted and enforced by the domestic courts of this country and not only by recourse to Strasbourg.

There will be no 'interference' with rights under Art 9 if it is the result of a restriction imposed by a law of general application. Thus, in *Stedman v UK* [1997] 23 EHRR CD 168 the European Commission of Human Rights rejected an application from a shop worker dismissed as a result of her refusal to work on Sundays; the Commission said that: 'the applicant was dismissed for falling to agree to work certain hours rather than her religious belief as such and was free to resign and did in effect resign from her employment'. Similar decisions were made in the cases of *X v UK* [1981] 22 DR 27, which involved a Muslim teacher who had difficulty getting to a mosque on Friday, and *X v Finland* Application 24949/94, 3 December 1996, where a Seventh Day Adventist railway worker was dismissed for refusing to work on a Friday. In both cases the court held that there was no violation of Art 9. These cases were followed, somewhat reluctantly, by the Court of Appeal in *Copsey v WWB Devon Clays Ltd* [2005] EWCA Civ 932, where it held that a requirement for a shop worker to work on a Sunday did not infringe Art 9. In *Copsey*, however, the court did emphasise that these decisions only related to claims under Art 9 and different decisions might be made regarding claims of unlawful discrimination under employment legislation (Chapter 4).

The European Court of Human Rights has also held that freedom to 'practice' a belief or religion does not always guarantee the right to behave in public in a way which is dictated by the belief. In *Arrowsmith v United Kingdom* [1980] 19 DR 517, when a pacifist distributed a leaflet intended to discourage soldiers from serving in Northern Ireland, the European Commission on Human Rights held that the distribution of the leaflet did not constitute a 'manifestation' of belief.

A further distinction has been drawn between expression of religious belief and communications which are commercial in nature. Advertisements which use religious content to promote sales of goods are commercial, as opposed to informational, and the assertions in them will not be protected by Art 9. For this reason there was no breach of Art 9 when an injunction was obtained prohibiting advertisements, by the Church of Scientology, for the sale of an 'E-meter', which was an electronic instrument alleged to be able to measure the 'electrical characteristics of the static field' surrounding a body and thereby to indicate whether a person had been relieved of their sins. Although the Church of Scientology claimed that the meter was a 'religious artefact', the court held that the advertisement did not constitute a manifestation of belief: *X and Church of Scientology v Sweden* [1979] 16 DR 68. The relevance of this case is that businesses selling religious items or religiously associated services, such as pilgrimage holidays, will not be able to rely on Art 9 in any arguments over legislation prohibiting religious discrimination in goods and services (Chapter 3).

In addition to cases brought under Art 9, the European Court of Human Rights has also had to consider the phrase 'religious and philosophical convictions' in Art 2 of the First Protocol to the Convention (Chapter 5). In the case of *Cosans v UK* 25 February 1982 the court was considering a claim by parents that their children should not be subject to corporal punishment because the parents disagreed with corporal punishment. The parents, however, did not disagree on religious grounds but because the infliction of corporal punishment was contrary to their 'philosophical convictions' and the court defined this phrase in para 36:

> In its ordinary meaning the word 'convictions' . . . denotes views that attain a certain level of cogency, seriousness, cohesion and importance . . . As regards the adjective 'philosophical', it is not capable of exhaustive definition . . . the expression 'philosophical convictions' in the present context denotes, in the Court's opinion, such convictions as are worthy of respect in a 'democratic society' . . . and are not incompatible with human dignity.

The points made by the European Court about 'beliefs worthy of respect in a democratic society' and 'not incompatible with human dignity' are quite often assumed to cover religious beliefs protected by Art 9 but it is clear from the judgment in *Cosens* that this is not the case. A religious belief does not have to be 'worthy of respect' in order to be protected by Art 9. However, the 'manifestation' of religious belief will not be protected under Art 9 if the 'manifestation' is not compatible with human dignity.

One of the most contentious areas of 'manifestation' of religious belief which has come before the courts is the wearing of Islamic dress by women and the question of whether wearing such dress is, or should be, protected by Art 9. There are various categories of Islamic female dress, starting with the 'hijab' (headscarf) and its Turkish equivalent the 'batortusu', moving on to the 'jilbab' (a long dress and headscarf) or its Iranian equivalent the 'chador', then the 'niqab' (a face mask with only the eyes showing, usually worn with the jilbab) and finally the 'burqa' (an all-encompassing garment with the eyes looking through a grille or mesh of material). The issue of restrictions on Islamic dress has been considered by the European Commission on Human Rights and the European Court of Human Rights in the cases of *Dahlab v Switzerland* ECmHR Application no 42393/98 15 February 2001; *Karaduman v Turkey* [1993] 74 DR 93; *Sahin v Turkey* ECtHR 29 June 2004 and 10 November 2005, and the subject has also been exhaustively considered by the High Court, Court of Appeal and House of Lords in the case of *Begum v Denbigh High School* [2004] EWHC 1389 (Admin); [2005] EWCA Civ 199; [2006] UKHL 15.

The starting point is the principle, established in the *Dahlab* case, that the hijab (and therefore all the other forms of Islamic dress) constitutes 'a powerful external symbol' of religious belief and also that the hijab was 'hard to square with the principle of gender equality'. All the cases have accepted that restrictions may be imposed on the wearing of Islamic dress in public institutions. Though the justifications vary in detail, all generally revolve around the concept of 'protection of the rights and freedoms of others'. Because the wearing of Islamic dress can be associated with sympathy for extremist groups, and because women can be pressurised into wearing Islamic dress, public bodies can impose restrictions on the wearing of Islamic dress in order to protect vulnerable women from pressure. On the same basis, in the *Begum* case, it was accepted that allowing variations in Islamic dress in schools could be divisive because those pupils who chose to wear the jilbab could claim to be 'better' Muslims than those who chose only to wear the hijab. The House of Lords also noted that other schools were available where Shabina Begum could wear the jilbab and Lord Hoffmann commented (para 50): 'Article 9 does not require that one should be allowed to manifest one's religion at any time and place of one's own choosing ... people sometimes have to suffer some inconvenience for their beliefs.' However, the House of Lords did not accept that restrictions could be imposed on Islamic dress merely because many people, including many Muslims, did not like it, as Lady Hale said (para 96):

> If a woman freely chooses to adopt a way of life for herself, it is not for others, including other women who have chosen differently, to criticise or prevent her ... the sight of a woman in full purdah may offend some people, and especially those western feminists who believe that it is

a symbol of her oppression, but that could not be a good reason for prohibiting her from wearing it.

Art 9 only protects manifestation of religion but very often it is not the practice of religion which creates controversy but rather the expression of religious views, for example the expression of religious views condemning homosexuality can arouse opposition. In those circumstances it will often be the case that it is Art 10 (Freedom of Expression) which the courts need to consider rather than Art 9. In the case of *Handyside v UK* [1976] 1 EHRR 737, para 49 the European Court of Human Rights gave a ringing, and much quoted, endorsement of the importance of freedom of speech:

> Freedom of expression constitutes one of the essential foundations of such a society, one of the basic conditions for its progress and for the development of every man. Subject to paragraph 2 of Article 10, it is applicable not only to 'information' or 'ideas' that are favourably received or regarded as inoffensive or as a matter of indifference, but also to those that offend, shock or disturb the State or any sector of the population. Such are the demands of that pluralism, tolerance and broadmindedness without which there is no 'democratic society'.

A similar point was made by Sedley J in the High Court case of *Redmond-Bate v DPP* EWHC no CO/188/99 23 July 1999, where he said:

> . . . ours is a society of many faiths and none, and of many opinions. If the public promotion of one faith or opinion is conducted in such a way as to insult or provoke others in breach of statute or common law, then the fact that it is done in the name of religious manifestation or freedom of speech will not necessarily save it. It may forfeit the protection of Articles 9 and 10 by reason of the limitations permitted in both Articles (provided they are necessary and proportionate) in the interests of public order and the protection of the rights of others . . .
>
> Free speech includes not only the inoffensive but the irritating, the contentious, the eccentric, the heretical, the unwelcome and the provocative provided it does not tend to provoke violence. Freedom only to speak inoffensively is not worth having. What Speakers' Corner (where the law applies as fully as anywhere else) demonstrates is the tolerance which is both extended by the law to opinion of every kind and expected by the law in the conduct of those who disagree, even strongly, with what they hear. From the condemnation of Socrates to the persecution of modern writers and journalists, our world has seen too many examples of state control of unofficial ideas. A central purpose of the European Convention on Human Rights has been to set close limits to any such assumed power. We in this country continue to owe a debt to the jury which in

1670 refused to convict the Quakers William Penn and William Mead for preaching ideas which offended against state orthodoxy.

Similarly, in *R (Williamson) Secretary of State for Education and Employment* [2005] UKHL 15 (para 60), Lord Walker noted: 'in matters of human rights the court should not show liberal tolerance only to tolerant liberals'. These principles seemed to have been overlooked by the High Court in the case of *Norwood v DPP* [2003] EWHC 1564 (Admin), which involved an elderly preacher who held up a sign condemning homosexuality and who was subsequently convicted under s 5 of the Public Order Act 1986 (discussed in Chapter 7). Unfortunately, Mr Norwood died before the High Court case and for that reason the European Court of Human Rights refused to hear an appeal which alleged that the conviction breached Art 10. It is, however, worth noting that in the case of *Åke Green* Supreme Court of Sweden 29 November 2005 the Supreme Court quashed the conviction of Lutheran Pastor, Åke Green, who had been convicted of hate speech following a sermon he had preached on the evils of homosexuality. Because the case had aroused international attention, the court released a press release in English which explained its reasons:

> Although it considers Åke Green's statements to be extremely far-reaching, the Supreme Court emphasizes that he made his statements as part of a sermon preached before his own congregation on a theme discussed in the Bible. Under these circumstances, the Supreme Court is of the opinion that it is likely that the European Court of Human Rights, on consideration of the case, would find it to be an infringement of the European convention to sentence Åke Green for the statements he made in his sermon.

The interrelationship between Arts 9 and 10 has been particularly examined with respect to laws on blasphemy. In the cases of *Gay News v UK* [1982] 5 EHRR 123, *Wingrove v UK* [1996] 24 EHRR 1 and *Otto-Preminger-Institute v Austria* [1994] 19 EHRR 34 the European Court of Human Rights accepted that laws prohibiting blasphemy did not breach the Convention, whilst in *Choudhury v UK* [1991] 12 HRLJ 172 the court held that the fact that English blasphemy law (Chapter 7) protected only Christianity did not breach the Convention.

Since many countries have Constitutions and Bills of Rights which protect religious freedom (Appendix A), lawyers often refer to cases from these countries in order to bolster their arguments. Though invariably received politely unless the case deals with a specific point which has not been considered by the European Court of Human Rights, such cases have been of little value to British courts in resolving cases involving Art 9. Cases from the United States in particular need to be approached with caution since the First Amendment to the United States Constitution is primarily concerned with ensuring the separation of religion from the state. Cases under Art 2(a) of the Canadian Charter of Rights and Freedoms are more relevant but, once again, only if they cover a point not dealt with in European case law. For example, in *Begum v Denbigh High School* [2006] UKHL 15, para 34 the House of Lords considered the Canadian Supreme Court case of *Multani v Commission scolaire Marguerite-Bourgeoys* [2006] SCC 6 but based their decision entirely on European case law. Where 'foreign' cases can be useful is where the question of what is 'necessary in a democratic society' is being argued, since they can show what type of behaviour and restrictions of behaviour are considered acceptable, or not acceptable, in other 'democratic' societies.

Chapter 3

Religious discrimination

Background

Part 2 of the Equality Act 2006 introduces a new concept into British law of 'discrimination on grounds of religion or belief'. Part 2 broadly follows the pattern and wording of established legislation dealing with sex, race and disability discrimination and completes a process which began with the Employment Equality (Religion or Belief) Regulations 2003 (see Chapter 4). Part 2 of the Act applies to Great Britain, i.e. England, Wales and Scotland but does not apply to Northern Ireland where, because of Northern Ireland's unique political problems, separate legislation on religious discrimination has existed for some years. Sections 49–51, 59, 61 and 66(2) and (3) of the Act, which deal with religious discrimination in education, are dealt with in Chapter 5.

The main reason why anti-religious discrimination legislation was passed was because there was a perception, particularly amongst the Muslim community, that existing discrimination law was unfair because Jews and Sikhs were already protected under the Race Relations Act 1976. This arose from the decision in the case of *Mandla v Dowell* Lee [1983] ICR 385, where the House of Lords considered the question of whether a Sikh boy (who was refused entry to an independent school because he wore a turban) was discriminated against on grounds of race as defined in the Race Relations Act 1976. The House of Lords considered the ethnic origins of Sikhs and Lord Fraser gave the following definition of race:

> For a group to constitute an ethnic group, in the sense of the 1976 Act, it must, in my opinion, regard itself, and be regarded by others, as a distinct community by virtue of certain characteristics. Some of these characteristics are essential; others are not essential but one or more of them will commonly be found and will help to distinguish the group from the surrounding community. The conditions which appear to me to be essential are these:
>
> (1) a long shared history, of which the group is conscious as distinguishing it from other groups, and the memory of which it keeps alive;

(2) a cultural tradition of its own, including family and social customs and manners, often but not necessarily associated with religious observance.

In addition to those two essential characteristics the following characteristics are, in my opinion, relevant:

(3) either a common geographical origin, or descent from a small number of common ancestors;
(4) a common language, not necessarily peculiar to the group;
(5) a common literature peculiar to the group;
(6) a common religion different from that of neighbouring groups or from the general community surrounding it;
(7) being a minority or being an oppressed or a dominant group within a larger community, for example a conquered people (say the inhabitants of England shortly after the Norman conquest) and their conquerors might both be ethnic groups.

A group defined by reference to enough of these characteristics would be capable of including converts, for example persons who marry into the group, and of course excluding apostates. Provided a person who joins the group feels himself or herself to be a member of it, and is accepted by other members then he is, for the purposes of the Act, a member . . . In my opinion it is possible for a person to fall into a particular racial group either by birth or by adherence, and it makes no difference, so far as the 1976 Act is concerned, by which route he finds his way into the group.

On the basis of this definition, the House of Lords decided that Sikhs constituted a racial group and subsequently, in *Seid v Gillette Industries Ltd* [1980] IRLR 427, it was decided that Jews also constituted a distinctive racial group. In the case of *Tariq v Young* EOR Discrimination Case Law Digest No 2, however, it was decided that Muslims were not a racial group; similarly in *Crown Suppliers v Dawkins* [1993] ICR 517 Rastafarians were held not to be a racial group, nor were Jehovah's Witnesses: *Lovell-Badge v Norwich City College* (Case No 12506/95/LS December 1999).

Whether this interpretation of the Race Relations Act 1976 was unfair or not is perhaps a matter of debate. Merely because a group has a religion does not stop it also being a race and, whilst someone may stop being a member of a religion, they cannot stop being a member of a race. This was proved during the Nazi period when Christian and atheist Jews were sent to the gas chambers; a notable example being Saint Theresa Benedicta (Edith Stein), who was killed in 1943 in Auschwitz, despite the fact that she had converted to Catholicism in the 1920s and become a Carmelite nun.

In any event, the view that the existing discrimination laws were unfair was accepted by the government and, prior to the 2005 general election, an Equality Bill was passed by the House of Commons but fell when the general election was called. After the election, a new Equality Bill, with much the same provisions, was introduced into the House of Lords and eventually became the Equality Act 2006. For that reason the majority of the parliamentary discussion took place in the House of Lords. As the Equality Bill went through Parliament, it was amended and in consequence a number of clauses in the Bill had different numbers from the equivalent sections in the Act. At the end of this chapter the dates of the parliamentary debates are provided and also details of the numbering of the clauses in the Bill, cross-referenced to the equivalent sections in the Act.

Courts and tribunals dealing with cases brought under the Equality Act 2006 will undoubtedly look at established concepts in discrimination law, particularly where the same form of wording is used in the Equality Act 2006 as is used in other anti-discrimination legislation; precedents under the Race Relations Act 1976 are likely to be regarded as particularly relevant. Where words or concepts are ambiguous and open to interpretation, courts and tribunals may be able to refer to the record of parliamentary speeches set out in Hansard using the principles laid down in the case of *Pepper v Hart* [1993] AC 593, where the House of Lords decided that in certain circumstances courts could refer to Hansard to find out the purpose and meaning of a Bill by reference to the speeches of the minister who introduced the Bill. It is important to note, however, that the principles in *Pepper v Hart* will not permit reference being made to the debates in the House of Commons on the Equality Bill that was introduced prior to the 2005 election since, legally speaking, that Bill was not the Bill that was passed

During several of the parliamentary debates the subject of 'harassment' is mentioned. The Bill originally had a clause, cl 47, dealing with harassment and had references to harassment in several clauses, however, during the debate in the House of Lords cl 47 was removed, as were all the references to harassment. Despite this clause being removed, religious harassment is still illegal and can be dealt with using the Protection from Harassment Act 1997 (Chapter 6).

Section 44 definition of religion and belief

The key sections within the Equality Act 2006 are ss 44 and 45. Section 44 defines 'religion and belief' as follows:

(a) 'religion' means any religion,
(b) 'belief' means any religious or philosophical belief,
(c) a reference to religion includes a reference to lack of religion, and
(d) a reference to belief includes a reference to lack of belief.

The meaning of 'religion' is examined in Chapter 1, but the definitions of 'religious belief' and 'philosophical belief' were discussed in some detail in Parliament. Home Office Minister Paul Goggins MP said (Hansard, 6 December 2005, col 145):

> We know from case law that religion has to be consistent with human dignity; it must have a cogency, seriousness and sense of cohesion about a particular series and set of beliefs. We would expect a philosophical belief to betray the same hallmarks, although it does not revolve around belief in a particular deity.

The reference to religion having to be 'consistent with human dignity' is a common misreading of the European Court of Human Rights case of *Cosans v UK* ECtHR 25 February 1982, where the court was not considering the meaning of the words 'religion' or 'religious belief' but was considering the meaning of the phrase 'philosophical convictions' and said (para 36):

> In its ordinary meaning the word 'convictions' . . . denotes views that attain a certain level of cogency, seriousness, cohesion and importance . . . As regards the adjective 'philosophical', it is not capable of exhaustive definition . . . the expression 'philosophical convictions' in the present context denotes, in the Court's opinion, such convictions as are worthy of respect in a 'democratic society' . . . and are not incompatible with human dignity.

Therefore, for the purposes of the Equality Act 2006, a person can have religious beliefs which are not 'worthy of respect in a democratic society' (an extraordinarily vague and subjective concept) but they still cannot be discriminated against. If they have 'philosophical beliefs' which are worthy of respect then, once again, they cannot be discriminated against but if they have 'philosophical beliefs' which are not worthy of respect then they can be discriminated against. The following examples relating to halal meat may help to clarify these concepts in s 44 which perhaps are not as clear as they might be:

(a) Eating only meat which is halal because that is what the Koran says is a religious belief.
(b) Refusing to eat halal meat because the animal is killed 'in the name of Allah' could be a religious belief if you consider 'Allah' to be a false God.
(c) Refusing to eat any form of meat because animals should not be killed is a philosophical belief 'worthy of respect'.
(d) Refusing to eat halal meat because the halal method of slaughter is cruel compared to other methods could be regarded as a philosophical belief 'worthy of respect' or could simply be regarded as a personal opinion.

(e) Refusing to eat halal meat because you want nothing to do with Muslims is neither a philosophical belief nor a belief 'worthy of respect'.

In reality, the distinctions between religious beliefs, philosophical beliefs 'worthy of respect', philosophical beliefs 'not worthy of respect' and mere personal opinions are rarely that clear cut. The interrelationship of these concepts will doubtless keep the courts busy for some time.

One thing that was made clear in both the Lords and the Commons was that Parliament did not want to see political beliefs or the membership of a political party being treated by the courts as a 'belief' for the purposes of s 44. Questions were raised on this point in both Houses because the definition of 'religion or belief' in s 44 differed from the definition that was already in place in s 2(1) of the Employment Equality (Religion or Belief) Regulations 2003, namely: ' "religion or belief" means any religion, religious belief, or similar philosophical belief'. Concerns were raised that removing the word 'similar' could mean that it would become illegal to discriminate against people because of their political beliefs. Home Office Minister Baroness Scotland said (Hansard, 13 July 2005, col 1109):

> The intention behind the wording in Part 2 is identical to that in the employment regulations. However, in drafting Part 2, it was felt that the word 'similar' added nothing and was, therefore, redundant. This is because the term 'philosophical belief' will take its meaning from the context in which it appears; that is, as part of the legislation relating to discrimination on the grounds of religion or belief. Given that context, philosophical beliefs must therefore always be of a similar nature to religious beliefs. It will be for the courts to decide what constitutes a belief for the purposes of Part 2 of the Bill, but case law suggests that any philosophical belief must attain a certain level of cogency, seriousness, cohesion and importance, must be worthy of respect in a democratic society and must not be incompatible with human dignity. Therefore an example of a belief that might meet this description is humanism, and examples of something that might not – I hope I do not give any offence to anyone present in the Chamber – would be support of a political party or a belief in the supreme nature of the Jedi Knights.

Whilst Home Office Minister Paul Goggins MP said (Hansard, 6 December 2005, col 146):

> ... philosophical belief is not limitless; for example, it would not be possible to claim that belief in the supremacy of a certain football team qualified as a religion or philosophical belief. Nor, indeed, could that claim be made about belief in the principles of a political party, the point raised by the hon. Gentleman. We know that because of the case in April

this year of *Baggs v. Fudge*, in which a member of the British National Party sought to challenge the refusal of an organisation to interview him for a job under the Employment Equality (Religion or Belief) Regulations 2003, which incorporate wording about 'philosophical belief' similar to that in the Bill. That individual's argument, that his support for the BNP constituted a philosophical belief, was thoroughly rejected by the tribunal, so there is no case to suggest that any such political belief would qualify as a religion or belief under the Bill. We are not making up the provisions on the spur of the moment; as I said, there is a precedent for them in the 2003 regulations.

Mr. Grieve: I can understand the rationale in *Baggs v. Fudge*, which concerned an adherence to a political party, as I understand it. That seems to me to be capable of being distinguished from an adherence to a particular philosophical belief. There may be no such difference, but the Minister may understand why I remain slightly troubled by this point. It is one thing to say, 'We refused to interview him because he was a member of the BNP' and another to say, 'We refused to interview him because we knew that he had a belief in white supremacy.' Maybe there is no distinction between those two statements, but I see a capacity for one. I wonder whether we are in danger of opening a door to people to make such arguments.

Paul Goggins: Often those two things, a particular belief and association with an organisation, are inextricably linked. In the end it will always be for the court, the employment tribunal or other judicial setting to determine whether the provisions of a particular employment law are relevant to a particular case. Our job here is to set out in legislation the overall provisions, and that we do, in a way that does not give limitless extent to the concept of philosophical belief, but ensures that it is consistent with the hallmarks of religious belief, such as cogency, which I quoted earlier.

Even though both ministers referred in Parliament to the employment tribunal case of *Baggs v Fudge* ET case No 1400114/05, where a member of the British National Party (BNP) claimed to have been discriminated against contrary to the Employment Equality (Religion or Belief) Regulations 2003, they do not seem to have read the judgment in that case, which makes it clear that the decision was very largely based around the word 'similar'. In para 8 of the judgment the tribunal chairman said: 'The BNP is not a religion, or a set of religious beliefs, or a set of similar (which I take to be similar to religious) beliefs.' It is at the very least arguable that because the definition in s 44 refers to 'philosophical belief', rather than 'similar philosophical belief', this means that people holding political beliefs, especially extreme political beliefs, could be protected by the Equality Act 2006 from being discriminated against. Indeed, the more extreme a political viewpoint is, the more it can be said to constitute a 'philosophy'. For example, it will be illegal under the

Equality Act 2006 for a shop to refuse to serve a customer because the customer is a Muslim. But what if the shop refuses to serve the customer because he is wearing a badge saying 'I love Al Qaeda' and, whilst waiting in the queue, loudly proclaims the opinion that 'actions like 9/11 and 7 July were necessary and justified'? Is a belief that terrorism is necessary and justified a philosophical belief? It is perhaps worth noting that s 3 of the Fair Employment and Treatment (Northern Ireland) Order 1998 provides explicit protection for political as well as religious views:

> 3.—(1) In this Order 'discrimination' means—
>
> (a) discrimination on the ground of religious belief or political opinion; subject to the following caveat . . .
>
> 2(4) In this Order any reference to a person's political opinion does not include an opinion which consists of or includes approval or acceptance of the use of violence for political ends connected with the affairs of Northern Ireland, including the use of violence for the purpose of putting the public or any section of the public in fear

and it can therefore be argued that, since the Equality Act 2006 does not include a similar specific reference to political opinion, it is clear that political beliefs are not covered by the legislation. However, Paul Goggins' comment: 'In the end it will always be for the court, the employment tribunal or other judicial setting to determine whether the provisions . . . are relevant to a particular case' does seem to leave the issue wide open for argument.

One other point that should also be noted in the wording of s 44(c) and (d) is the reference to 'lack' of religion or belief. This was obviously introduced so as to make it clear that the anti-discrimination legislation covered atheists and humanists, i.e. those who lack any religious belief. However, it has a wider meaning, since it includes all those who do not have a particular religious (or philosophical) belief. For example, if a Muslim bookseller refused to sell copies of the Koran to non-Muslim customers, he would be guilty of unlawful discrimination. He would not be guilty of discriminating against any particular non-Muslim because of their individual religion, but he would be discriminating against each of them because of their 'lack of belief' in Islam.

Definition of discrimination

The definition of discrimination is set out in s 45(1):

> (1) A person ('A') discriminates against another ('B') for the purposes of this Part if on grounds of the religion or belief of B or of any other person except A (whether or not it is also A's religion or belief) A

treats B less favourably than he treats or would treat others (in cases
where there is no material difference in the relevant circumstances).

(2) In subsection (1) a reference to a person's religion or belief includes
a reference to a religion or belief to which he is thought to belong or
subscribe.

Section 45(1) covers the relatively straightforward situation of 'direct
discrimination'. For example, if a Sunni Muslim halal butcher (A) refuses to
sell halal meat to an Ahmadyya Muslim (B) whom he regards as a heretic,
that would be direct discrimination. Similarly, if A contaminates the meat,
for example by rubbing it against pork, so it is no longer halal or deliberately
gives B older or poorer quality meat, that is direct discrimination. It is
important to note that even though the discrimination against B has to be 'on
the grounds of religion or belief', it does not necessarily have to be on the
grounds of the religion or belief of B. To return to the halal butcher A; if
A were to refuse to serve a Muslim woman (B) because B had married a
Christian, then that would still constitute religious discrimination against B
even though A was not discriminating against B because of her own religion.

What is more unclear is what the situation is where discrimination occurs
where both A and B are members of the same religion. In the House of Lords
the following hypothetical example was raised by Lord Lester (Hansard,
13 July 2005, col 116) regarding his concerns over the original wording of
cl 46 (the predecessor to s 45):

> . . . a member of the liberal wing of the Jewish faith eats pork and a
> member of the orthodox wing of the Jewish faith strongly objects to any
> Jew or religious Jew eating pork. They are both members of the same
> religion – this is entirely hypothetical, which I am trying to explain with
> an example – but perhaps the orthodox Jew is a bigot who decides to
> discriminate against or to harass the less orthodox or unorthodox Jew for
> eating pork. The problem is whether the exception in Clause 46(2)(a) [i.e.
> the original wording in the Bill] prevents the liberal Jew being protected
> against discrimination or harassment because the discriminator has the
> same religion as the alleged victim . . . normally in discrimination law
> the position of the discriminator vis-à-vis the victim does not matter. In
> other words, if I, or a woman, discriminate against a woman, the gender
> of the discriminator is irrelevant. If a victim is the victim of sex dis-
> crimination, the fact that the discriminator is of the same sex does not
> matter. The same is true of racial discrimination.

Baroness Scotland replied (Hansard, 13 July 2005, col 1118):

> I should say to the noble Lord immediately that there may be a few
> areas where we can look again at the wording. This is not because I am

convinced that we will find any better wording but because there is something here that we need to consider . . . The reason for the amendments
[proposed by Lord Lester] therefore, seems to be to ensure that the person's own religious or other beliefs cannot be used as a justification for
discrimination or harassment on the grounds of religion and belief. If
that is partly what the noble Lord seeks, I understand and sympathise
with the intention behind the amendments. I should like to take the
opportunity to place on record that it is neither the intention nor the
effect of the clauses as currently drafted to allow discrimination or
harassment in such cases . . . So an Orthodox Jew providing a good
facility or service could not lawfully discriminate against or harass
another more secular Jew on the grounds that he was not religious
enough . . . I take the view that he wants to do exactly what we want to
do, save that he is not sure that the wording will achieve what we both
aspire to achieve. We believe it does, but I am very happy to take it away,
look at it further and ensure that we are as confident as we can be that the
matters that should be covered are covered.

Following this exchange, the government came back with amendments
which subsequently became s 45(1). Therefore, it is clear that the intention of
Parliament was that even if A and B are members of the same religion,
A should not be able to discriminate against B simply because B is not
sufficiently religious. However, it may not be necessary to resort to Hansard
to resolve this argument. If we return to Lord Lester's example of the
Orthodox Jew A and the less Orthodox Jew B: if A discriminates against B
because B is not sufficiently religious and eats pork, then A is discriminating
against B because of B's 'lack of belief' in the importance of Jews obeying all
of the rules in the Torah. Both A and B may have the same 'religion' but
because they interpret it and apply it differently they 'lack' the same 'belief'.
Therefore, if s 44(d) is considered and applied, the solution to the problem
of discrimination between members of the same religion arises from the
wording of the legislation itself.
    The main point about s 45(1) is that there is no defence of reasonableness
in it and therefore direct discrimination is always unlawful; or is it? There is
an element of a circular argument in s 45(1) which may on occasions be
important. A only discriminates against B if A refuses to do something
because of the religion, or lack of religion, of B but not if he refuses to do it
because of his own religion. For example, if a Roman Catholic shopkeeper
(A) refused to sell a copy of the Bible to a Mormon (B) because he considered
that B was not a 'proper' Christian, that would be unlawful discrimination. If,
however, A refused to sell a crucifix to a B, a Satanist, because he knew, or
believed, that B intended to use the crucifix in a Satanic ritual then arguably
A would not be guilty of unlawful discrimination. That is because A's refusal
is based on A's own religion and on his belief that an object, such as a

crucifix, is sacred and should not be sold to someone who will not treat it with reverence or respect.

Section 45(2) is designed to cover the situation where discrimination occurs due to incorrect assumptions regarding the religion of the victim. For example, if Catholic shop owner A refuses to sell a statue of the Virgin Mary to Indian gentleman B because A believes that B is an 'idolatrous' Hindu, when actually B is a Thomist Christian, A is still guilty of unlawful discrimination.

Indirect discrimination

Section 45(3) is likely to be a more significant provision than s 45(1) because it deals with the far more subtle concept of 'indirect discrimination'. It reads:

> (3) A person ('A') discriminates against another ('B') for the purposes of this Part if A applies to B a provision, criterion or practice—
>
> > (a) which he applies or would apply equally to persons not of B's religion or belief
> >
> > (b) which puts persons of B's religion or belief at a disadvantage compared to some or all others (where there is no material difference in the relevant circumstances),
> >
> > (c) which puts B at a disadvantage compared to some or all persons who are not of his religion or belief (where there is no material difference in the relevant circumstances), and
> >
> > (d) which A cannot reasonably justify by reference to matters other than B's religion or belief.

The phrase 'provision, criterion or practice' has recently been adopted in sex and race discrimination legislation (2001 and 2003 respectively) in addition to the old wording 'requirement or condition'. Therefore, cases involving the new wording in sex and race discrimination cases will be particularly relevant in assisting courts in interpreting s 45(3). However, courts will have to be cautious if they are referred to discrimination cases decided under the old wording, in particular those cases where particular acts were held not to constitute indirect discrimination; the new wording is clearly intended to have a wider impact than the old wording and will apply in a wider range of situations.

Most cases of discrimination involve allegations of indirect, rather than direct, discrimination and can provide the most difficult areas for people to know where to draw the line and whether a practice which seems innocuous to them could be argued to be indirectly discriminatory. Where an allegation of discrimination is made the initial response should be to look at s 45(3)(d) and decide whether the practice can be justified by reference to factors other than religion. For example, most banks and building societies have a rule that people cannot enter the premises with their face covered. That would be a 'provision, criterion or practice' which was applied equally to everyone entering the bank. For most people such a rule is not a problem and motorcyclists, for example, are used to removing their helmets before they enter a bank and a person who has a scarf across their face in winter will also remove it when entering a bank. However, a Muslim woman who wears a niqab (a veil which covers the face below the eyes) could object to a requirement that she remove her veil in order to be allowed to enter the bank; she could argue that the rule puts Muslim women in general, and her in particular, 'at a disadvantage', since her religious beliefs mean that she has to remain veiled when in the presence of anyone other than her husband and family and therefore the banks rule prevents her using the bank and obtaining its services.

In this situation the bank should be able to 'reasonably justify' its rule by reference to security and the prevention and detection of crime. All banks have CCTV and if someone robs the bank or, less dramatically, cashes a fake cheque, etc., then the CCTV can be viewed by the police to establish identity and can be used in evidence in court. It can reasonably be argued that if the bank were to allow Muslim women to enter its premises wearing a niqab, how are they going to prevent a female, or male, fraudster entering whilst wearing a niqab in order to avoid recognition on CCTV; how is the bank expected to know who is sincerely a practising Muslim and who is merely trying to hide their identity?

However, the situation might be more difficult if the bank also prohibited the wearing of all hats and head coverings. The purpose would still be security and to stop criminals wearing 'hoodies' or baseball caps, which prevented their faces being seen on CCTV. However, such a ban on all head coverings would put Sikhs (who wear turbans) at a disadvantage and also Muslim women who wear the hijab (headscarf) but who do not cover their face. In that situation a bank might have difficulty in 'reasonably' justifying a complete blanket ban and might have to modify its rule so that it prohibited people entering with hats or head coverings which prevented their faces being seen on CCTV. If that was done it would be important for staff to be aware that they should apply such a rule in a non-discriminatory way. For example, if a non-Muslim woman entered wearing an 'ordinary' headscarf because it was a windy day and she was told to remove it whilst a Muslim woman entering at the same time was not told to remove her hijab, then the non-Muslim woman could argue that she was being discriminated against because she was not a Muslim.

Section 45(4) is, in the main, fairly self-explanatory and says:

(4) A person ('A') discriminates against another ('B') if A treats B less favourably than he treats or would treat another and does so by reason of the fact that, or by reason of A's knowledge or suspicion that, B—

(a) has brought or intended to bring, or intends to bring, proceedings under this Part,

(b) has given or intended to give, or intends to give, evidence in proceedings under this Part,

(c) has provided or intended to provide, or intends to provide, information in connection with proceedings under this Part,

(d) has done or intended to do, or intends to do, any other thing under or in connection with this Part, or

(e) has alleged or intended to allege, or intends to allege, that a person contravened this Part.

(5) Subsection (4) does not apply where A's treatment of B relates to B's making or intending to make, not in good faith, a false allegation.

The hypothetical A does not have to be the intended target of the proceedings or allegations in which B is involved. So it would be unlawful discrimination if Hindu shopkeeper A was to refuse to serve, Hindu, customer B because A disapproved of the fact that B was giving evidence in a case of discrimination against Muslim shopkeeper C.

As it is worded, however, s 45(5) does not make a great deal of sense, since how can someone make a 'false allegation' 'in good faith'. It does seem that the draftsman has confused the concepts of a wrong or incorrect allegation with the concept of a false allegation, since it is perfectly possible to make an incorrect allegation in good faith. What s 45(5) appears to mean is: 'Subsection (4) does not apply where A's treatment of B relates to B's making or intending to make a false allegation. An allegation which is made in good faith but which turns out to be incorrect is not a false allegation.'

Goods and services

The main area of discrimination covered by the Equality Act 2006 is in s 46, which makes it unlawful to discriminate in the provision of goods and services, 'discriminate' having the same meaning as in s 45 above.

46 Goods, facilities and services

(1) It is unlawful for a person ('A') concerned with the provision to the public or a section of the public of goods, facilities or services to discriminate against a person ('B') who seeks to obtain or use those goods, facilities or services—

(a) by refusing to provide B with goods, facilities or services,

(b) by refusing to provide B with goods, facilities or services of a quality which is the same as or similar to the quality of goods, facilities or services that A normally provides to—

  (i) the public, or

  (ii) a section of the public to which B belongs, or

 (c) by refusing to provide B with goods, facilities or services in a manner which is the same as or similar to that in which A normally provides goods, facilities or services to—

  (i) the public, or

  (ii) a section of the public to which B belongs, or

 (d) by refusing to provide B with goods, facilities or services on terms which are the same as or similar to the terms on which A normally provides goods, facilities or services to—

  (i) the public, or

  (ii) a section of the public to which B belongs.

The phrase 'a section of the public to which B belongs' was discussed in Parliament and explained by Home Office Minister Paul Goggins as follows (Hansard 6, December 2005, col 155):

> . . . it is also the case that some suppliers of goods, facilities and services choose to provide them in different ways to some sections of the public, for example, by offering preferential terms or discounts to students, the unemployed or old age pensioners. The Bill would prevent a service provider from offering such discounts to a section of the public – for example, the unemployed – but then, on the grounds of religion or belief, refusing to provide that same service to a prospective customer who fell into that category. For example, if a theatre charged £6 per ticket in general but had a concessionary price for the unemployed of £5, it would be unlawful to charge an unemployed atheist the full price while arguing that that was the price that was generally available to the public. If that atheist were unemployed, they would fall within the category to which the theatre had decided to give a discount, and should be able to enjoy that as much as any other unemployed person.

 Section 46(2) lists examples of the types of facilities and services in relation to which discrimination under sub-s (1) would be unlawful:

 (2) Subsection (1) applies, in particular, to—

  (a) access to and use of a place which the public are permitted to enter,

  (b) accommodation in a hotel, boarding house or similar establishment,

  (c) facilities by way of banking or insurance or for grants, loans, credit or finance,

> (d) facilities for entertainment, recreation or refreshment,
>
> (e) facilities for transport or travel, and
>
> (f) the services of a profession or trade.

Some of these are more problematic than they appear. For example, will a bank be 'discriminating' against Muslims if it does not offer Shariah compliant financial services? Certainly such a bank would not be directly discriminating for the purposes of s 45(1) but it might be indirectly discriminating unless it can reasonably justify its refusal, either by reference to government rules making it difficult to offer Shariah compliant financial services, or because it is a small bank and it is not economically viable for it to set up entirely separate financial services. However, a bank that does offer Shariah compliant financial services must remember that it cannot discriminate in whom it offers these services to. Shariah compliant services must be made available to all customers, not just Muslims.

Other problems will arise for travel companies which organise 'pilgrimage'-type tours. They will not be able to restrict these only to members of what would appear to be the interested religion. For example, many companies organise pilgrimages to the annual 'Hajj' in Mecca but if they attempted to restrict sales of such a pilgrimage only to Sunni or Shia Muslims then that would constitute direct discrimination and asking people where they prayed or what type of Muslim they were could constitute indirect discrimination. However, in Saudi Arabia it is a crime for a non-Muslims, or for Ahmaddyya Muslims, to enter the cities of Mecca or Medina and this crime can be punished with the death penalty. Organisers of pilgrimages to Mecca therefore face the unenviable choice of either restricting the pilgrimage to Sunni and Shia Muslims and thereby risk being sued for religious discrimination or alternatively being accused by the Saudi authorities of complicity in a capital crime.

However, the fact that a travel company aims a holiday at a particular group of believers is not a problem. Many Christian travel companies, for example, provide holidays aimed at Christians and include talks from Christian speakers, attendance at church services, etc. Unless the company specifically refused to accept a booking from him, an atheist could not bring a claim for discrimination or complain at the fact that the main speakers on the holiday were religious speakers and that visits to churches included prayers. This aspect of the holiday would be its unique selling point, not religious discrimination.

The importance of the words 'reasonably justify' in s 45(3)(d) and its particular relevance in protecting small businesses was emphasised by Home Office Minister Paul Goggins (Hansard, 6 December 2005, col 150):

> For example, financial considerations might mean that a small business, perhaps a child-minding service, is not in a position to provide kosher

food. That would be a function of the fact that it was a small business with limited financial opportunities, not to do with the religious belief of its potential customers. It would be indirect discrimination, but it would be justifiable because it had occurred as a consequence of financial and practical considerations, and there was no intention to discriminate against an individual or a potential customer.

This remark of the minister may be of especial relevance to small restaurants, hotels and bed-and-breakfast establishments (B&Bs). Concern has been expressed that any business that provides food will be required to provide halal food. If a restaurant or hotel chooses to serve both halal and non-halal meals then that is, of course, its choice but for many that would be unduly complicated because, in order for a meal to be 'halal', the meat not merely has to be stored in a particular way but also has to be stored separately and cooked separately from non-halal meat. Kosher cookery is even more complicated and involves all meat being kept separate from dairy products as well as from contact with non-kosher meat. Deciding to serve only halal or kosher meat would therefore mean a B&B stopping serving the 'full English' breakfast (bacon and eggs being both non-halal and non-kosher!).

In addition, halal meat raises peculiarly sensitive issues of double discrimination. For meat to be halal the animal does not simply have to be killed in a particular way, it also has to be killed by a practising Muslim who first says a prayer to Allah. Therefore, deciding to serve only halal meat means putting non-Muslim slaughtermen out of work and also means serving meat which a Christian might regard as having been 'sacrificed' to a false God and therefore unchristian. In addition, many non-religious people regard halal slaughter as cruel and Sikhs are specifically forbidden to eat halal meat. For these reasons hotels and restaurants can quite properly decide that they do not want to serve halal, or kosher, meat. However, they would be wise to provide an acceptable alternative, such as a vegetarian option, since vegetarian food is both halal and kosher. Provided that such a religiously acceptable option is provided, there should be no basis for a complaint under s 46. If a Muslim or Jew were to argue that such a policy is still discriminatory because they prefer eating meat to eating vegetables, they could be referred to the remarks of Lord Hoffmann in the case of *Begum v Denbigh High School* [2006] UKHL 15, para 50, where he said 'people sometimes have to suffer some inconvenience for their beliefs'. Even though it was dealing with the question of freedom of religion under art 9 of the European Convention on Human Rights (Chapter 2), rather than with religious discrimination, the case of *Begum* does provide useful guidance to courts in how to approach claims of religious discrimination. The essence of the case is 'reasonableness' and 'proportionality' in accommodating personal religious beliefs.

Section 46(3) states that where a person exercises a skill in a particular way for the purposes of a particular religion he will not be compelled, by s 46, to exercise it in a different manner for the purposes of another religion. This was referred to in Parliament as the 'halal and kosher butchers let-out clause', since both these trades operate in accordance with specific religious rules. In principle, there is no reason why a halal slaughterman should not also kill animals in a non-halal way for sale to non-Muslims but he may feel that to do so would prejudice his 'professional' status and so he can decline without being accused of discrimination. However, if a halal butcher did agree to do non-halal slaughtering for a Christian, he could not then refuse to do the same for a Jew. Another example for s 46 would be a painter who specialises in painting religious icons according to the specific rules and traditions of the Orthodox Church who could, quite lawfully, refuse to paint a portrait of the Mormon Prophet Joseph Smith.

Premises

In general terms, ss 47 and 48 make it unlawful to discriminate in the disposal, letting, etc. of premises. For example, if an estate agent were to refuse to sell a property to a buyer because the buyer was a Muslim then that would be unlawful in the same way as it is already unlawful to refuse to sell a house to someone because they are black. Similarly, a Muslim landlord could not refuse to let out a room to someone just because they were a Hindu nor could he charge a lower rent to a Muslim tenant than he would charge to a non-Muslim tenant. Section 47(3) also makes it unlawful for someone to refuse permission for the disposal, i.e. sale, of premises. This is most likely to occur in a situation where a person is the executor of a will and therefore has to give consent to a sale. He could not refuse to sell to a particular buyer simply because of their religion.

However, s 47(4) states that s 47 only applies to properties in Great Britain and so someone can discriminate in relation to the letting, sale, etc. of a property they own abroad. For example, if a Mormon was renting out a property that they owned in Salt Lake City then they could refuse to rent it out to a non-Mormon. This provision would seem to have been inserted in order to allow people to take account of local conditions abroad.

Section 48 details a number of situations where s 47 will not apply. The most important exemption is where the landlord or a near relative resides in the premises ('near relative' being defined in s 48(2)), where there are shared parts in the building and where there is only sufficient room for three households or seven individuals. This exemption was clearly designed to cover situations where a person is letting out part of their own home and would therefore, in effect, be living with their tenant. In that situation it might be asking too much of human nature to ask someone to share their home with someone with whose religious views they disagreed.

However, it should be noted that s 48 does not apply to premises such as hotels and B&Bs, even though in most B&Bs the owner and his family live in the premises. Hotels and B&Bs come under the definition of a service in s 46(2)(b) and there are no exemptions which would allow them to discriminate, however small their business. There was an attempt in the House of Commons to give B&Bs a similar exemption to that in s 48 but it was defeated. Home Office Minister Paul Goggins defined the difference between B&Bs and the type of premises covered by s 48 as follows (Hansard, 6 December 2005, col 158):

> One is short-term accommodation, usually provided on a nightly basis and similar to a hotel, in that someone is there in a highly transitory way. In the case of premises, however, individuals may be resident for considerable periods and be using premises as their home. Indeed, they may be tenants and have solid legal rights to remain in that residence. In that instance, the relationship between the landlord and the resident is clearly much more important to both parties than it would be in the provision of bed and breakfast. One, in essence, provides an overnight service; the other provides a long-term home. There is a fundamental difference between the two, and however large or small the boarding house is, it could never fall into the second category, which is more permanent.

Section 62, 'Care within family', does, however, permit discrimination in situations where the use of the premises is on a very personal or 'family' basis:

> Nothing in this Part shall make it unlawful for a person to take into his home, and treat in the same manner as a member of his family, a person who requires a special degree of care and attention (whether by reason of being a child or an elderly person or otherwise).

Therefore, for example, if a Shia Muslim family offered to foster, or look after, an Iraqi orphan they would be allowed to insist that the child was also a Shia.

Sections 47 and 48 have particular problems for religious organisations and the use of their property. Many churches, for example, rent out church halls to a variety of religious and community organisations and whether the Equality Act 2006 applies to the use of these premises depends on whether or not this letting out is regarded as 'commercial'. If it is 'commercial' then the letting, sale, etc. of the property will fall within the provisions of ss 47 and 48 but if it is not commercial then the letting, sale, etc. of them will be covered by s 57(3)(d) and ss 47 and 48 will not apply. Section 57 is discussed below, but whether a letting of a premises is commercial or not is a question of fact. Many church halls, for example, are used as community centres and let out to organisations such as the Scouts, Women's Institute, etc. and in those circumstances the church should be able to show, without too much trouble, that this use of the premises is not 'commercial'. Similarly, every Sikh gurdwara will have a langar, or kitchen, attached to it where a communal meal is provided after the religious service. If a gurdwara allowed their langar to be used at other times and a fee was paid for that use that would not mean that either the langar or the gurdwara were commercial organisations.

Public authorities

Section 52 makes it unlawful for any public authority to discriminate, save for specific exemptions set out in s 52(3) and (4). The most important of these exemptions are in s 52(4)(f) and (g) and relate to immigration. In simple terms, immigration officials can discriminate on religious grounds if they consider that the presence of a particular individual in the UK would not be for 'the public good'. For example, for many years the leader of the Unification Church, Sun Myung Moon, was refused entry to Britain on public policy grounds and Louis Farrakhan, the leader of the Nation of Islam organisation, continues to be banned, and these, or similar, decisions will not be able to be challenged under the Equality Act 2006. Besides ensuring that bans such as these continue, s 52 will allow immigration officials to expedite immigration procedures for ministers of religion where this is appropriate; for example, a Russian Orthodox priest could be granted immigration rights faster than other Russians if it was accepted that he was needed by a Russian Orthodox parish in Britain.

Save for the specific exemptions set out in s 52, public authorities are not allowed to discriminate in their operations. The question 'what is a public authority' is usually not too difficult to answer but in the religious field it can be controversial. For a number of years both local and central government have been allocating funds to charities so that they can carry out social work functions on behalf of government and many of these charities have a religious base. In *Heather v Leonard Cheshire Foundation* [2001] EWHC Admin 429 it was held that just because a charity carried out paid functions on behalf of government, that did not make it a public body. That decision was criticised in the House of Lords debate on the Equality Bill, especially by Lord Lester, but it remains the law. Therefore, there is no legal requirement for a religious charity to change its ethos or hide its religious symbols merely because it is carrying on activities on behalf of local or central government. If local or central government were to ask, or insist, that a religious charity remove religious symbols etc. as a condition for receiving a grant then that would be a political decision and not something they are required to do because of the Equality Act 2006. In addition, any attempt by local or central government to require a charity to remove religious symbols as a condition of receiving funding could constitute interference with the 'manifestation' of religious belief and would therefore be in breach of Art 9 of the European Convention on Human Rights (Chapter 2).

The issue of 'political correctness' by local authorities in the area of religion and the removal of public religious symbols, usually Christian in nature, is a recurrent one in the media and newspapers and often this is done in the name of avoiding 'offence' to other religions. The issue was raised in Parliament during the debate on the Equality Bill with particular reference to a recent incident where a local authority had removed a cross from its crematorium. It could be considered as either unfortunate or farcical that nobody in the debate seemed aware that Muslims do not cremate their dead and so would have no reason to visit a crematorium (Hansard, 13 July 2005, col 1130):

> **Baroness Scotland of Asthal**: . . . I accept, however, that there is an issue about religious objects. I can see situations where public functions are carried out in church halls or other places associated with worship where objects on display in those premises, such as crucifixes, might conceivably lead to accusations of harassment. Similarly, there may be cases where a display on Divalli in the local library or the use of religious objects as part of religious education might be considered harassment. That is absolutely not what we intend.
>
> **Baroness Carnegy of Lour**: . . . I would just say to her that if one goes as a Christian to a funeral at a crematorium and finds that there is no cross to look at as one puts one's loved one to the flames, it is very distressing. It may well be that it is distressing to a person of some other religion – perhaps a Muslim – to find a cross there. Is there is solution to that? The Government, having got into the issue, must confront it.
>
> **Baroness Scotland of Asthal**: . . . On the point raised by the noble Baroness, Lady Carnegy, I have said that we will take the matter away to consider, but some local authorities have behaved very practically to meet the needs of their disparate communities. For example, if there is a cross at the crematorium and a Muslim family has come to cremate a loved one, the cross is sometimes taken down or covered for that ceremony and put back up when the family has gone. So there are practical, sensitive things that one can do to encourage and enable people to take advantage of public services in a way that offends no one.

What s 52 requires is that public authorities do not discriminate. It does not require them to stop supporting any religious group or festival; it merely requires them to be prepared to support other religious groups and festivals. For example, if a local authority has traditionally displayed a crib in its town centre for Christmas and then removes the crib on the basis that it does not want to 'give offence' to other religions, then it must also cease to support any other religious festival. A local authority that refused to display a crib but then put up lights and decorations for Eid would be guilty of religious discrimination against Christians unless it could show that there were no Christians or no significant number of Christians in its area. The proper approach under the law would be for the local authority to support both festivals equally as Home Office Minister Paul Goggins made clear (Hansard, 6 December, col 195):

> **Paul Goggins**: It is important to recognise the need to ensure that public authorities can support the religious needs and wants of the people whom they serve, in a way that balances protection for people of other beliefs as well. We do not seek to prevent local authorities or any other public authorities from being involved in carol services, celebrations of Divali or other religious activities in which they feel it is right for them to be involved. The hon. Member for Beaconsfield pointed out that these things evolve over time and that there is now a broader range of religious faiths and activities than perhaps was the case in the past. We do not think that this part of the Bill stands in any way against that trend. We feel it is right – this is in some measure a response to the hon. Member for Oxford, West and Abingdon – that public authorities should treat people of all faiths and none fairly. That is the limit that I would place on this . . . public authorities have a duty to respond to the various needs of the religious beliefs of the communities that they serve. Just because a public authority provides a chapel or a service for one community, does not mean that it has to provide that service for all religious beliefs and all religious communities. It may not be necessary in a particular locality for that service to be provided. But it is perfectly in order for such provision as is deemed suitable and appropriate to be made. There is a balance to be struck and that is what we seek to uphold.
>
> **Mr. Grieve**: I am grateful to hear the Minister say that. That is exactly what I thought he would say, and exactly what I want to hear him say. I have to contrast that comment about what a public authority can do with the plain terms of the clause. By saying that it cannot discriminate, subsection (1) seems to me to lay itself open to the possibility of a challenge, because somebody can say, 'You are a public authority and you support an annual Christian civic service. I am a Muslim and I object to that.' What happens then? Perhaps the Minister will take the Committee through what happens next when that challenge is raised. I think that he is saying that the public authority could argue, 'Our decision is reasonable and proportionate in all the circumstances,' but that involves a public authority in potential litigation from which I believe that it is entitled to be protected.
>
> **Paul Goggins**: Careful judgments must be made. Public authorities should have proper processes for deliberating on such matters: they

must gather information and then make decisions. It is perfectly reasonable for a public authority to have differential provision for different faith communities, if that provision can be justified by reference to matters other than the religion or the belief. If the individual Muslim to whom the hon. Gentleman referred is the only person of that religious persuasion in a particular community, it might be disproportionate to expect the public authority to make the same provision for him as for vast numbers of people elsewhere. Public authorities cannot be expected to provide the same level of support and service to everybody, irrespective of financial and other considerations. The differentiation there is not on grounds of religion or belief, but on other rational decisions about resources and what is proportionate in the circumstances.

Public authorities also have to be careful that they realise the full implications of what they are doing if they attempt to remove religious symbols from their buildings or from their staff. Religious symbolism is often more subtle than is realised. For example, if a public authority banned all crosses from its buildings and gave an order that its staff were not to wear any form of cross, even as jewellery, because the cross is a religious symbol, then it would be guilty of unlawful discrimination if it does not also ban its Muslim staff from wearing a hijab and its Sikh staff from wearing a turban. In *Dahlab v Switzerland* ECmHR application no 42393/98 15 February 2001 and *Sahin v Turkey* ECtHR application no 4477/98 29 June 2004 and 10 November 2005 the European Court of Human Rights stated that the hijab was a 'a powerful external symbol' of religious belief and therefore it would be unlawful discrimination for a public authority to ban the wearing of a cross whilst permitting the wearing of the hijab, since both are religious symbols. It could, and undoubtedly would, be argued by such a public authority that there was a difference because the wearing of a hijab is compulsory in Islam but the wearing of a cross is not compulsory in Christianity. There are, however, two problems with that approach. First, it is theologically questionable because the Seventh Ecumenical Council of 787 AD declared that the veneration and display of religious objects such as icons, statues, crosses, etc. is part of the religious duty of Christians; second, it is not for a secular authority to decide what is or is not a religious requirement.

Organisations relating to religion and belief

Sections 57 and 58 are crucially important sections in the Equality Act 2006, since they exempt from its requirements most forms of religious organisation.

57 Organisations relating to religion or belief
(1) This section applies to an organisation the purpose of which is—

(a) to practice a religion or belief,

(b) to advance a religion or belief,

(c) to teach the practice or principles of a religion or belief,

(d) to enable persons of a religion or belief to receive any benefit, or to engage in any activity, within the framework of that religion or belief, or

(e) to improve relations, or maintain good relations, between persons of different religions or beliefs.

(2) But this section does not apply to an organisation whose sole or main purpose is commercial.

(3) Nothing in this Part shall make it unlawful for an organisation to which this section applies or anyone acting on behalf of or under the auspices of an organisation to which this section applies—

(a) to restrict membership of the organisation,

(b) to restrict participation in activities undertaken by the organisation or on its behalf or under its auspices,

(c) to restrict the provision of goods, facilities or services in the course of activities undertaken by the organisation or on its behalf or under its auspices, or

(d) to restrict the use or disposal of premises owned or controlled by the organisation.

The justification for these exemptions arises from the fact that a religion is, by definition, restricted to those who subscribe to its beliefs and therefore religious organisations, churches, mosques, etc. need to be able to restrict membership and use of their facilities. Section 57(3)(d) is likely to be particularly important and makes it clear that churches etc. can legally refuse to allow their premises to be used by religions of which they disapprove. It is important to note, however, that s 57 merely exempts religious organisations from claims of 'religious' discrimination; it does not protect them from other types of discrimination claim. For example, if a Catholic church owned a hall and permitted white Protestant groups to use the hall but refused to allow a black Pentecostal church to use it then it could be open to a claim of racial discrimination and s 57 would not protect it against such a claim.

Section 57(3)(b) permits religions to restrict participation in activities undertaken by the organisation. For example, entrance to a Mormon temple is restricted to Mormons who have been given a 'temple recommend' by their local Mormon bishop. Mormons who are not regarded as particularly pious or religiously active will not be given a temple recommend and this has religious implications for them because certain religious ceremonies of Mormonism, such as having a marriage sealed for eternity or baptism for the dead, can only be carried out in a temple. However, restricting participation in religious activities in this way will be legal under s 57(3)(b). The same will apply even if the activity is not necessarily religious provided it is organised under the 'auspices' of a religious organisation. For example, if a church were to organise a camping holiday for teenagers, it could restrict the holiday to those teenagers who had been confirmed.

Section 57(4), (5) and (6) permit ministers of religion to restrict participation in certain activities of that religion. For example, though a person of any religion, or none, is welcome to attend celebrations of the Divine Liturgy (Mass) in Orthodox Churches, only members of the Orthodox Church are allowed to receive communion. This type of discrimination will continue to be lawful. However, it is important to note that religious organisations do not have an unrestricted right to discriminate. There must be a reason which is relevant to the organisation. Section 57(5) says:

(5) But subsections (3) and (4) permit a restriction only if imposed—

    (a) by reason of or on the grounds of the purpose of the organisation, or

    (b) in order to avoid causing offence, on grounds of the religion or belief to which the organisation relates, to persons of that religion or belief.

The wording of s 57(5) does leave a dangerous scope for troublemaking claims and attempts to drag the courts into religious disputes. This could mean that the Equality Act 2006, far from assisting and encouraging inter-religious co-operation, make it less likely because religious groups may become more cautious about allowing their premises to be used by other faiths. For example, if a church allows a Hindu group to use its church hall for a Hindu service then it might find itself in difficulty if it refused to allow a pagan Wicca group to use the premises also. Hinduism is, arguably, an eastern form of paganism and therefore it could be argued that Western pagans should be treated in the same way as Eastern pagans. There is also the danger of an additional claim of racial discrimination if brown-skinned Hindu pagans are permitted to use a church hall but white-skinned Odinist pagans are refused. Similarly, if a Roman Catholic church allowed its church building to be used for an Anglican service, it may have legal difficulties in refusing a request for the church to be used for a Tridentine (traditional Latin) Mass by the traditionalist but schismatic Catholic group the Society of St Pius X. They would undoubtedly, and understandably, argue that they were less schismatic than the 'Protestant' Church of England.

However, the exact interpretation of s 57(5)(b) is arguable. Unlike reg 7(3)(b)(ii) of the Employment Equality (Sexual Orientation) Regulations 2003 (Chapter 4), there is no requirement that any objection has to come from a 'significant number' of the religion's followers. All that is required is that offence would be caused to 'persons' of the particular religion or belief. Arguably, therefore, if a parish priest and his bishop would be offended by a particular use of church premises, that might be sufficient to justify a restriction because priests and bishops are still 'persons of that religion or belief'. Though the examples given relate to churches etc., s 57 also covers organisations which, though not religious in themselves, relate to religion. For example, both the Christian Institute and the Muslim Council of Britain would classify as religious organisations for the purposes of s 57(b) and (c), whilst inter-faith bodies such as 'Churches Together in Great Crosby' or 'The Merseyside Council of Faiths' would classify under s 57(e).

There may, however, be ambiguous dividing lines between one type of organisation and another. For example, an Association of Muslim Lawyers would be entitled to restrict its membership to practising Muslims because it could claim to be an organisation under s 57(1)(d) 'the purpose of which is ... to enable persons of a religion or belief to receive any benefit, or to engage in any activity, within the framework of that religion or belief', but an organisation set up to study and publicise Shariah law would probably not be able to restrict its membership to practising Muslims because the study of Shariah law is a subject of legitimate interest to non-Muslims.

A booklet, 'Guidelines on Religious Discrimination and Islamic ethos', issued by the organisation Faithworks in collaboration with the Muslim Council of Britain, gives a helpful summary of the Muslim view of the phrase 'religious organisation' which, with the kind permission of Faithworks, is reproduced below:

'Organised Religion' and 'Religious Organisations' in the Muslim Community

- Islam does not comfortably use the term 'organised religion'. It has its own view of the relationship between God, the community of Muslims and the individual Muslim. It usually avoids a hierarchical structure for religious authority. There is a strong focus on an unmediated relationship between the individual Muslim and God whilst at the same time Islam has a strong communal aspect. Therefore, although Islam encourages a personal relationship with God and individual responsibility for intention, thought and action there is also a strong emphasis on creating and sustaining a strong community of believers.

- For Muslims, religious organisations are diffuse and diverse. They can range from mosques, seminaries and schools through to more practical organisations that deliver services such as welfare, food and housing. Certain organisations can be said to have the delivery of the religious practices and rites (e.g. funeral and marriage ceremonies) as their main functions. These types of rules are part of the ibadat of Islam which are rules relating to the religious life of Muslims. Rules of ibadat contrast with rules of muamalat that have a more social, economic or practical aim. The types of organisations that deal with religious practices and rites (ibadate) will include mosques, seminaries (madrasas), organisations and bodies that represent and organise the religion.

- The general structure of Muslim organisations is that they are established (often as a waqf or trust) by a person with charitable funds to further a specific purpose such as education or relief of poverty. The intention of those who set up the trust will be religious. The money is often donated as an act of charity (zakat or sadaqa) which is a key religious practice of Islam. The purpose of the trust may be to further a specific religious purpose as in the case of a mosque. In addition, in some cases the function of the organisation will include a more practical purpose such as education or housing or welfare (muamalat).

Organised Religion within Islam – Islamic Organisations
- Organisations that have as their predominant purpose the provision of facilities and services for worship and religious rites (ibadat) can be 'organised religion'. The full range of functions that are provided by these types of organisations (e.g. welfare, counselling, teaching, advice, use of facilities for general purposes) fall within 'organised religion' – the exercise of religious practices and rites. Within this document these organisations will be understood as the organised religion of Islam and they will be called Islamic Organisations.
- In many cases the key religious practices and rites of Islam can be performed and delivered by persons other than official 'Imams' or those who carry an official title. For example, a communal prayer or a marriage ceremony can be conducted by a Muslim in any building/ organisation (i.e. not necessarily in a mosque). It is important that these contexts are also included within the definition of the organised religion of Islam.

Organisations with a religious ethos – Muslim Organisations
- This is NOT to say that other organisations are not also delivering essential religious functions. Religious practices and rites will also be part of the ethos of these organisations. In this document this range of organisations will be called Muslim Organisations. They are often established as a result of charity (zakat and sadaqa) which is a central practice as required by the doctrine of Islam, by people who come together to fulfil their obligations to God through under-taking good works according to the ethical requirements of Islam. This makes them an essential part of the religious life of a Muslim community.

- The intention (niya) of those who set up the trust and those who are responsible for delivering the results of the work of the trust will be religious. Moreover, the atmosphere in which these results are achieved will also be guided by religious values. However, it is not essential that all the people who are involved in ensuring the functions or results in religious organisations be Muslims.
- What is distinctive about these organisations is that:

  (a) they have been established to further a particular charitable object, by a person often motivated by their obligations to God (through their zakat or sadaqa);

  (b) they are a collection of individuals who come together around the key universal ethical values advocated by Islam to deliver this purpose/object and function.

How s 57 is ultimately going to be interpreted by the courts is difficult to predict because there are two legal principles in conflict. In the Equality Act 2006 Parliament has clearly decided that discrimination on the grounds of religion is wrong and should be stopped and therefore courts will be encouraged to apply a 'purposive' interpretation to the Equality Act 2006 and to interpret s 57 as narrowly as possible; however, under s 3(1) of the Human Rights Act 1998: 'So far as it is possible to do so, primary legislation and subordinate legislation must be read and given effect in a way which is compatible with the Convention rights' and the Convention rights include Art 9 which protects freedom of religion (see Chapter 2). Therefore, courts interpreting s 57 must be careful not to interpret it in a way that would require a religious organisation to act contrary to its beliefs regardless of whether the court regards those beliefs as reasonable or even desirable. This point was made clear by Lord Nichols in para 22 of the House of Lords case *R (Williamson) v Secretary of State for Education and Employment* [2005] UKHL15:

> . . . When the genuineness of a claimant's professed belief is an issue in the proceedings the court will inquire into and decide this issue as a question of fact. This is a limited inquiry. The court is concerned to ensure an assertion of religious belief is made in good faith: 'neither fictitious, nor capricious, and that it is not an artifice', to adopt the felicitous phrase of Iacobucci J in the decision of the Supreme Court of Canada in Syndicat *Northcrest v Amselem* (2004) 241 DLR (4th) 1, 27, para 52. But, emphatically, it is not for the court to embark on an inquiry into the asserted belief and judge its 'validity' by some objective standard such as the source material upon which the claimant founds his belief or the orthodox teaching of the religion in question or the extent to which the claimant's belief conforms to or differs from the views of others professing the same religion.

This judgment must be particularly borne in mind by a court when considering the propriety of arguments that a decision by a religious body is not made because of the 'purpose of the organisation'. The legitimate purposes of a church, for example, can include assisting or encouraging organisations which, though not part of the church, conform to Christian ideals or which the church considers should be encouraged or assisted as an act of Christian love. Therefore, the decision as to which organisations should be allowed to use a church hall is a highly subjective and inherently religious judgment which secular courts should be reluctant to interfere with.

'Commercial' organisations

A particularly important provision which may lead to a great deal of litigation is s 57(2): 'But this section does not apply to an organisation whose sole or main purpose is commercial.' One of the major problem areas is likely to be in respect of religious booksellers most of which are established by committed believers and exist in order to sell books, CDs and other merchandise relevant to one specific religion. Some such booksellers are registered charities, such as the Catholic Truth Society and the Protestant Truth Society, but many are not and, even though making money may not be the prime motivation behind such a shop, it is likely that it would be regarded by a court as a commercial organisation. However, it is important to remember that the Equality Act 2006 does not require a business to become a different type of business. In the same way that a military bookshop can refuse to order a Bible because that is not the nature of its business, a shop selling Catholic books, statues, etc. is not going to be obliged to stock the books of other religions such as the Book of Mormon or the Guru Granth Sahib. Similarly, even though a shop sells, and will take orders for, CDs of hymn singing it could refuse to order a CD of Buddhist chanting; however, if the shop agreed to obtain a CD of Buddhist chanting, for example for a priest wanting it for research, it could not refuse to obtain the same type of CD for a Buddhist. The same problem would arise if the bookshop agreed to obtain a copy of the Book of Mormon for a Catholic priest; thereafter it could not refuse to order one if asked to do so by a Mormon. Similarly, if such a shop gave discounts to Catholic priests it could not refuse to give a similar discount to an imam or a rabbi.

There are also many religious holiday organisations, pilgrimage organisers, etc. which are commercial but which are nevertheless in business as much from a sense of religious conviction as from a purely commercial viewpoint. For all of them, however, the fact that they are a 'commercial' organisation will mean that they will not be allowed to discriminate. For example, a travel company set up by a Sikh which regularly organised trips to the Punjab including tours of the Golden Temple in Armritsar and other Sikh holy sites might find it a bit off-putting if a large group of

Hindus or Muslims made a booking. However, unless the company was a specifically Sikh religious organisation or charity, as opposed to a commercial company with a Sikh ethos, it would not be able to refuse a booking from a non-Sikh.

However, the fact that a religious organisation runs part of its operation on a fee-paying basis will not mean that the entire organisation will therefore automatically become a commercial organisation; for example, most Catholic churches have a small repository or shop at the back of the church where statues, rosaries, etc. are sold, but having such a repository does not make the church a commercial organisation. Similarly, even though many religious communities, such as monasteries, take in paying guests for retreats etc., that will not make the monastery a commercial organisation. The essential difference is that a commercial organisation exists in order to be a business whilst non-commercial organisations exist for other reasons even though they may engage in business. Baroness Scotland said (Hansard, 13 July, col 1164):

> Clause 59 [now s57] provides exceptions for religion or belief organisations to enable them to limit their membership, participation in activities, the provision of goods, facilities and services and the use of their premises. That is the whole purpose. The exemptions do not apply to organisations whose sole or main purpose is commercial. Indeed, it is difficult to see how some of these exemptions, for example on restricting membership, might be relevant to commercial organisations because of course they will want to sell as many things to as many people as possible ... Our current provisions would not prevent Christian groups, for example, from restricting access requiring payment, such as concerts or church lunches, if they decided to do that. Nor would we wish to interfere with activities in that way. But where an organisation is offering a commercial service open to the general public, that should be done without discrimination, whether that service is offered by a religious or secular service. Under our current proposals, if the main purpose of the organisation is to support a particular religious community and the commercial purpose is ancillary to that, it will be covered by our exception. Furthermore, where a commercial organisation occasionally undertakes charitable work – for example, where a Christian firm of solicitors provides pro bono work to the local church – we do not believe that its activities would fall within Part 2, because it would not be its main purpose. However, we do not accept that a commercial organisation that, as a by-product, supports a particular community, should benefit from the exemption in Clause 59 ... In the generality of cases, it is relatively easy to say which is the main purpose and which is the subsidiary purpose.

Religious charities

Religious charities are dealt with under s 58 but it is important to note that a religious charity can be covered by both s 57 and s 58; most churches, mosques, etc. are registered charities but they are also organisations:

> the purpose of which is—
>
> (a) to practise a religion or belief,
> (b) to advance a religion or belief,
> (c) to teach the practice or principles of a religion or belief,

and so they are covered by s 57 as well as s 58. The main purpose of s 58 is to protect charities which have a particular religious purpose behind them. For example, if a charity exists in order to help Catholic children go to Lourdes, it will be allowed to continue to restrict itself to Catholics and would not be obliged to send members of other churches or religions to Lourdes provided that any such restriction is 'imposed by reason of or on the grounds of the provisions of the charitable instrument'. Section 58(1)(b) therefore requires that any religious restriction imposed by a charity must be in accordance with provisions laid out in the specific charitable deed or articles of association under which the charity is established. Trustees of a charity cannot simply adopt a policy of restricting benefits to members of one religion even if, as in the case of trips to Lourdes, it might seem a logical and obvious restriction to impose.

Under s 58(2) the Charity Commission are allowed to discriminate in carrying out their functions. Baroness Scotland explained the reason for this (Hansard, 19 October 2005, col 861):

> The amendment ensures that the Charity Commissioners and the Office of the Scottish Charity Regulator will be able to perform their functions in the best interests of the charity concerned, even if that should involve discrimination. For example, if the regulator needs to appoint a new trustee for a religious charity, they may feel it better to appoint someone who shares the religious belief of the charity concerned over someone with equal qualifications in other areas but who is of another religion or belief. It is right that they should be able to do so without arousing an allegation of discrimination under this part.

Membership requirement

Section 60 provides:

> (1) Nothing in this Part shall make it unlawful for a charity to require members, or persons wishing to become members, to make a

statement which asserts or implies membership or acceptance of a religion or belief.

As was made clear in Parliament, this section was introduced specifically in order to cover concerns which had been expressed by the Scouts and Guides Association. Scouts and Guides are not a religious organisation as such and indeed have a proud history of inter-faith co-operation with Catholic, Muslim, Jewish, etc. Scout and Guide troops throughout the world. However, there are no atheist Scout groups and the Scout promise, which is said by Scouts throughout the world, includes the promise to 'do my duty to God' (however defined or named). Baroness Scotland explained the purpose behind s 60 when she introduced it as an amendment to the Equality Bill in the House of Lords (Hansard, 19 October 2005, Col 862):

> The specific effect of this amendment is to allow the Scouts and Guides to continue requiring their members to say the Promise. This requirement is a necessity if the associations are to remain members of the international movements they represent. In most circumstances, a charity that wished to restrict its membership would do so by ensuring that a charitable instrument adequately reflected its intentions, and it would then be covered by Clause 60. In this case, however, because the establishment of the Scouts and Guides was made by Royal Charter, we felt an additional exemption was justified. This will equally protect any other charities that may exist that are in similar circumstances. This is a narrow exception with a particular purpose.

Section 60 is time limited and no new charities can require such a declaration of belief if they were set up since 18 May 2005. This does not, however, apply to religious charities or organisations. Section 57 permits an organisation, whose purpose is to practise a religion or belief etc., to restrict membership and that must logically include restricting membership to those who subscribe to a specific creed or declaration of belief. In practice, with the exception of the Scouts and Guides, there are unlikely to be many, if any, charities which are non-religious and which would want to impose a declaration of belief.

Other unlawful acts

Under ss 53, 54 and 55 the Commission for Equality and Human Rights, which is created by Pt 1 of the Equality Act 2006, is given the power to bring legal proceedings in respect to 'discriminatory practices', 'discriminatory advertisements' and 'instructing or causing discrimination'. Only the Commission can bring these proceedings and they are likely to be regarded as a last resort if an organisation does not respond to requests from the Commission to alter its practices; for example, if a major supermarket chain adopted a policy that it would never sell halal meat in any of its premises then that would probably constitute the sort of 'discriminatory practice' to which the Commission would be likely to object.

Enforcement

In common with other forms of discrimination, claims of religious discrimination under the Equality Act 2006 must be brought in the county court and cannot be brought in the High Court or in an employment tribunal (s 67). However, a county court dealing with such a claim has the power to make any order which the High Court could make (s 68). Amongst other things this means that the court could make an injunction either ordering the defendant to do whatever he is refusing to do, or ordering him to stop doing whatever it is that the court considers amounts to discrimination; a refusal to obey such an injunction would be a contempt of court for which the defendant could be sent to prison.

Under s 68(4) a court can also award damages, including compensation for injury to feelings; however, under s 68(3) a court shall not award damages in respect of an act contrary to s 45(3) if the respondent proves that there was no intention to discriminate. The purpose of this section is clearly to try to discourage people from rushing off to court over trivial matters which they have not discussed with the other side. For example, if a shop organised a sweepstake competition for customers and all the prizes consisted of wine then that could constitute indirect discrimination of Muslim and Mormon customers who do not drink wine; however, if a claim of discrimination was brought, the shop might well argue that there was no intention to discriminate, they simply had not thought of the point and if any customer had mentioned the problem to them then they would have changed the rules to give a choice of prizes. In any such situation a court would not be entitled to award damages.

Under s 66(5) there is a reverse burden of proof so that:

> In proceedings under this section, if the claimant (or pursuer) proves facts from which the court could conclude, in the absence of a reasonable alternative explanation, that an act which is unlawful by virtue of this Part has been committed, the court shall assume that the act was unlawful unless the respondent (or defender) proves that it was not.

This is a change in the normal rules of evidence and burden of proof which has been adopted in all varieties of discrimination law over the past few years, but a claimant would be foolish to rely on it too much; whatever the statute says, judges will still want solid evidence before they decide that someone is guilty of discrimination.

Section 70 allows for rules of court to specify questionnaires which can be used in religious discrimination cases. If such a questionnaire is sent by a claimant or potential claimant then the response, or lack of response, to the questionnaires can be used as evidence in court and a judge will be able to draw inferences if a defendant has refused to answer a question or has given an evasive or equivocal answer. Once again, this procedure is standard in all discrimination cases.

Any claim must be brought within six months of the act of discrimination which is complained of or, if there are a series of discriminatory acts, the case must be brought within six months of the last act of discrimination. Once again, these time limits are standard in all discrimination claims.

Parliamentary chronology – Equality Act 2006

House of Lords

18/05/2005 HL Bill 2 2005–06 Equality Bill (HL). Lords presentation and first reading Explanatory Notes HL Bill 2-EN also published.

15/06/2005 Equality Bill (HL). Lords second reading debate. Agreed to on question and committed to a Committee of the Whole House.

06/07/2005 Equality Bill (HL). Lords committee stage first day. Clauses 3, 4, 5, 6, 7 agreed to. Clause 6 agreed to as amended. Clauses 1 and 2 agreed to. Schedule 1 agreed to. Clause 3 under consideration.

11/07/2005 Equality Bill (HL). Lords committee stage second day. Clause 8 agreed to. New clauses considered. Clauses 9–29 agreed to. Clause 30 under consideration. Clauses 30–43 agreed to. (Clauses 31, 34 and 43, as amended.) Schedules 2 and 3 as amended agreed to.

13/07/2005 Equality Bill (HL). Lords committee stage third day. Clauses 44 to 93 agreed to. Clauses 50, 52, 53, 54, 55, 75 and 78 as amended agreed to. Schedule 4 agreed to. New clauses considered. Bill reported with amendments. (HL Bill 17 2005–06.)

17/10/2005 Equality Bill (HL). Lords motion on order in which amendments for report stage be marshalled and considered. Agreed to on question (formal).

19/10/2005 Equality Bill (HL). Lords report stage. As amended on report.

26/10/2005 HL 56 2005–06 Government responses to the Equality Bill (HL).

09/11/2005 Equality Bill (HL). Lords third reading debate. Privilege amendment made. Motion that Bill do now pass agreed to on question. Bill passed and sent to Commons.

House of Commons

11/11/2005 Bill 85 2005–06 Equality Bill (HL). Brought from the Lords. First reading (formal). Explanatory Notes Bill 85-EN also published.

17/11/2005 HC Research Paper 05/77. Equality Bill (HL) (Bill 85 of 2005–06). House of Commons Library Research Paper 05/77.

21/11/2005 Equality Bill (HL). Second reading debate. Agreed to on question. Programme motion for proceedings in Committee, on report and third reading agreed to on division (292 to 42). Money resolution agreed to on question (formal). Bill read a second time.

29/11/2005 Equality Bill (HL). Committee stage. First sitting (morning). Programme motion agreed to. Clauses 1 and 2 agreed to. Schedule 1 agreed to, with amendments. Clauses 3 to 6 agreed to. Committee stage. Second sitting (afternoon). Clauses 7 to 10 agreed to, one with amendments.

01/12/2005 Equality Bill (HL). Committee stage. Third sitting (morning). Clauses 11 to 26 agreed to, some with amendments. Committee stage. Fourth sitting (afternoon). Clauses 27 to 31 agreed to, some with amendments. Schedule 2 agreed to, with an amendment. Clauses 32 to 40 agreed to. Schedule 3 agreed to, with amendments. Clauses 41 and 42 agreed to.

06/12/2005 Equality Bill (HL). Committee stage. Fifth sitting (morning). Clauses 43 to 50 agreed to, one with amendments. Committee stage. Sixth sitting (afternoon). Clauses 51 to 79 agreed to, one with amendments.

07/12/2005 HC 766 2005–06; HL 89 2005–06. Legislative scrutiny: Equality Bill. Human Rights Joint Select Committee fourth report with proceedings and appendices.

08/12/2005 Bill 99 2005–06. Equality Bill (HL). As amended in Standing Committee A (Vote) Equality Bill (HL) Committee stage. Eighth sitting (afternoon). Clauses 82 to 89 agreed to. Schedule 4, as amended, agreed to. Clauses 90 to 93 agreed to, some with amendments. New clauses considered. Bill, as amended, to be reported.

16/01/2006 Equality Bill (HL). Report stage and third reading debate. Agreed to on question. Passed. Returned to Lords.

House of Lords

17/01/2006 Equality Bill (HL). Returned from Commons with amendments and a privilege amendment. (HL Bill 63 2005–06.)

01/02/2006 Equality Bill (HL). Commons amendments.

13/02/2006 Equality Bill (HL). Consideration of Commons amendments. Commons amendments considered and agreed to.

16/02/2006 CHAP 3 2006 Equality Act 2006. Royal Assent Explanatory Notes also published.

The clauses of the Bill and the sections of the Act

House of Lords Bill

Clauses 45–46 = Sections 44–45
Clauses 48–61 = Sections 46–59
Clauses 62–72 = Sections 61–71
Clauses 73–80 = Sections 73–80
Clause 47 of the Bill was removed during debate.
Sections 60 and 72 of the Act were added to the Bill as it went through the House.

House of Commons Bill

Clauses 43–79 = Sections 44–80

Chapter 4

Religious discrimination in employment

This chapter deals with the Employment Equality (Religion or Belief) Regulations 2003, except for reg 5 (Harassment), which is dealt with in Chapter 6 and regs 20 and 39, which involve educational establishments and are dealt with in Chapter 5.

Legislation prohibiting racial and sexual discrimination in employment has existed since 1976 but until the passage of the Employment Equality (Religion or Belief) Regulations 2003 there was no specific British legislation prohibiting discrimination on the grounds of religion or belief. There has, however, been such legislation in Northern Ireland for many years because of the unique political situation there.

Prior to the 2003 regulations, only members of the Sikh and Jewish religions were protected from discrimination in employment, since Sikhs and Jews are classified as races as well as being members of a religion: *Mandla v Dowell Lee* [1983] ICR 385 and *Seid v Gillette Industries Ltd* [1980] IRLR 427. In addition, it was possible, in some cases, to use the Race Relations Act 1976 to protect aspects of religion if it could be shown that a particular employment practice, albeit principally hitting at religion, would nevertheless have a disproportionate influence on people of particular racial background. For example, in *Hussain v Midland Cosmetic Sales* EAT/915/00 the Employment Appeal Tribunal decided that refusing to allow a Pakistani woman to wear an Islamic hijab constituted indirect racial discrimination. However, in the cases of *Ahmad v United Kingdom* [1981] 4 EHRR and *Copsey v Devon Clays* [2005] EWCA Civ 932, attempts to use Art 9 of the European Convention on Human Rights (Chapter 2) so as to force employers to give time off on Friday for Muslim prayers (Ahmad) or to protect a Christian employee (Copsey) who refused to work on a Sunday were unsuccessful.

On 27 November 2000 in Directive 2000/78/EC, the European Union adopted a directive on equal treatment in employment and occupation which, amongst other things, prohibited discrimination 'on grounds of religion or belief'. Following this, the government introduced the 2003 regulations to outlaw religious discrimination in the workplace. The outline of the regulations is broadly similar to existing legislation outlawing discrimination on the grounds of race and sex; however, the regulations apply solely to the workplace. Further provisions outlawing religious discrimination in goods and services were introduced in Pt 2 of the Equality Act 2006 and those provisions are considered separately in Chapter 3.

General principles

In principle, the regulations are simple and follow existing well-accepted legislation banning discrimination on the basis of race or sex. Therefore, if someone applies for, or has, a job they should not be discriminated against just because they are a Muslim, a Christian or a member of any other religion. There are, however, exemptions for specifically religious posts, such as priests, or for employers who can claim that for a particular post there is a 'genuine occupational requirement' (GOR) which justifies restricting employment to members of a particular religion.

The basis of the regulations is protection of persons who hold a particular 'religion or belief' which is defined in reg 2 as meaning 'any religion, religious belief, or similar philosophical belief'. This definition will be altered by s 77 of the Equality Act 2006, which will introduce the following definition of religion and belief into reg 2:

(a) 'religion' means any religion,
(b) 'belief' means any religious or philosophical belief,
(c) a reference to religion includes a reference to lack of religion, and
(d) a reference to belief includes a reference to lack of belief.

Whether this new definition introduces any significant change is considered in Chapter 3. The old definition was considered by an employment tribunal in the case of *Baggs v Fudge* ET case No 1400114/05, where a member of the British National Party (BNP), who had been sacked because of his involvement with the BNP, claimed that this constituted discrimination on grounds of belief and was therefore contrary to the 2003 regulations. His claim was rejected by the tribunal chairman, who stated in para 8 of his judgment: 'The BNP is not a religion, or a set of religious beliefs, or a set of similar (which I take to be similar to religious) beliefs.' It is perhaps worth noting that s 3 of the Fair Employment and Treatment (Northern Ireland) Order 1998 provides explicit protection for political as well as religious views:

3.—(1) In this Order 'discrimination' means—

(a) discrimination on the ground of religious belief or political opinion;

subject to the following caveat:

2(4) In this Order any reference to a person's political opinion does not include an opinion which consists of or includes approval or acceptance of the use of violence for political ends connected with the affairs of Northern Ireland, including the use of violence for the purpose of putting the public or any section of the public in fear.

It can therefore be argued that the fact that the 2003 regulations do not include a similar specific reference to political opinion indicates that Parliament did not intend political beliefs to be protected.

Regulation 3 of the regulations defines discrimination as follows:

3(1) For the purposes of these Regulations, a person ('A') discriminates against another person ('B') if—

(a) on grounds of religion or belief, A treats B less favourably than he treats or would treat other persons; or

(b) A applies to B a provision, criterion or practice which he applies or would apply equally to persons not of the same religion or belief as B, but—

   (i) which puts or would put persons of the same religion or belief as B at a particular disadvantage when compared with other persons,

   (ii) which puts B at that disadvantage, and

   (iii) which A cannot show to be a proportionate means of achieving a legitimate aim.

This covers less favourable treatment on the grounds of a person's actual religion or belief and also treatment based on the discriminator's perception of a person's religion (which may be mistaken). For example, let us say an employer A receives an application form from B in the name Joseph Smith and A jumps to the assumption that B is a Mormon and rejects the application because he does not want to employ a Mormon; as it happens, B is a Roman Catholic and not a Mormon, but he has still been discriminated against on the basis of religion even though the discrimination is based on a mistaken assumption.

The anti-discrimination provisions also apply to a person's associations with people of a particular religion or belief, since that will involve discrimination based on 'grounds of religion or belief'. This is made explicit by s 77(2) of the Equality Act 2006, which will change the wording of reg 3(1)(a) to state the following:

3(1) For the purposes of these Regulations, a person ('A') discriminates against another person ('B') if—

(a) on the grounds of the religion or belief of B or of any other person except A (whether or not it is also A's religion or belief) A treats B less favourably than he treats or would treat other persons . . .

Therefore, if a Muslim employer was to sack a Muslim employee because her son had converted to Christianity, that would constitute unlawful discrimination contrary to the 2003 regulations even though the motivation is the religion of the employee's son and not the religion of the employee herself. This follows existing principles which are already established in race discrimination law.

It is also possible to be guilty of discrimination against members of the same religion as oneself. For example, if a Hindu employer (A) refused to employ a fellow Hindu (B) of a lower caste and instead offered the job to C, who was a Hindu of a higher caste, then that would be unlawful discrimination against B even though A, B and C were all members of the same religion.

It is fair to say direct discrimination is relatively easy to recognise and deal with and for that reason is the least common form of discrimination. There are no examples of advertisements which say 'no blacks or Irish need apply' these days, and quite rightly too, but there are still many claims of racial discrimination. The vast majority of such claims are brought on the grounds of indirect discrimination and it is likely that the majority of claims of religious discrimination will also be brought on the grounds of indirect discrimination as set out in reg 3(1)(b). An example of such a possible indirect discrimination is given in the ACAS guidance on the regulations, para 1.3:

> *Example:* An organisation has a dress code which states that men may not wear ponytails. This may indirectly disadvantage Hindu men, some of whom wear a shika (a small knotted tuft of hair worn at the back of the head, as a symbol of their belief). Such a policy could be discriminatory if it cannot be justified.

Another example is given in the guidance on the regulations issued by the Muslim Council of Britain in 2005, para 3.4:

> A company introduces a uniform which does not permit head coverings of any type and requires all female employees to wear knee-length skirts. This applies to all employees equally but disadvantages female Muslim employees who choose to wear the hijab or long skirts.

However, whilst direct discrimination in employment is illegal, unless a general occupational requirement applies, indirect discrimination is legal provided that the employer can show that it is a 'proportionate means of achieving a legitimate end', i.e. the employer has a real business requirement and the action is within the limits of what is necessary to achieve that business need. For example, if a mosque was to employ a cleaner or caretaker, it might want to insist that the person appointed did not own a dog; this would be because Islam regards dogs as unclean and the mosque authorities would want to ensure that no dog hairs were brought into the mosque. Such a requirement could be regarded as indirectly discriminatory but can be defended as necessary to 'achieve a legitimate end', namely to ensure that the purity of the mosque was not contaminated.

The ACAS guidance, para 1.4, gives a good example of a requirement which could constitute indirect discrimination but which could be justified:

> A small finance company needs its staff to work late on a Friday afternoon to analyse stock prices in the American finance market. The figures arrive late on Friday because of the global time differences. During the winter months some staff would like to be released early on Friday afternoon in order to be home before nightfall – a requirement of their religion. They propose to make the time up later during the remainder of the week. The company is not able to agree to this request because the American figures are necessary to the business, they need to be worked on immediately and the company is too small to have anyone else able to do the work. The requirement to work on Friday afternoon is not unlawful discrimination as it meets a legitimate business aim and there is no alternative means available.

And the MCB guidance, para 3.5, gives another example:

> A small toy shop employs four staff. Two Muslim employees request time off for Eid-ul-Fitr in the busy pre-Christmas period. However, the toy shop requires all four staff to work during that period. It would be justifiable to refuse such a request if the shop could not cope without them.

The MCB example pinpoints the issue of 'proportionate means', what may be an acceptable requirement in a small business may be unacceptable in a large business. To take the toy shop example again, if this was the toy department in a large department store and there was only one Muslim employee asking for time off to celebrate Eid then a refusal to allow him any time off in the pre-Christmas period might be difficult to justify.

Another likely ground of claims of unfair discrimination is how a vacancy is advertised. Where a vacancy is filled by word of mouth or by advertising on a church noticeboard there is always the risk of discrimination being alleged. If an employer advertised only by noticeboard in a pub, he would be indirectly discriminating against Muslims and Mormons, who do not drink alcohol. Similarly, an Indian restaurant that advertised for staff only in the *Muslim Weekly* could be alleged to be discriminating against Indian chefs who are Hindu or Sikh; however, it would be acceptable to advertise in both the *Muslim Weekly* and a more general Asian community newspaper. Interview questions on mosque, or church attendance, or whether an applicant's children attend a particular faith school could similarly be regarded as evidence of discrimination.

Rules that a person cannot have a beard or cannot cover his head could be said to be indirectly discriminatory against those who are required to have a beard or cover their head as part of their religious beliefs; however, cases decided under the Race Relations Act 1976 in relation to beards already demonstrate the type of approach tribunals should take. In *Panesar v Nestlé Co Ltd* [1980] IRLR 64, a Sikh was refused a job in a chocolate factory because he would not shave off his beard. In that case the employer's justification for its policy was based on expert evidence about hygiene and succeeded and a similar claim and defence under the religion or belief regulations would be likely to have the same result. However, an employer would have to demonstrate that there is no proportionate means of dealing with the hygiene issue other than to ban beards; for example, had the employer considered if a beard could be covered during working hours.

Time off work in order to attend religious requirements is a contentious and complex area. When the Court of Appeal case of *Copsey v Devon Clays* [2005] EWCA Civ 932 was decided, it was widely interpreted as having decided that Christian employees had absolutely no right to have Sunday as a day of rest. However, the case was not brought under the 2003 regulations but under Art 9 of the European Convention on Human Rights (Chapter 2) and the court merely decided that Art 9 did not apply to private contracts of employment. In para 8(3) of the judgment Lord Justice Mummery pointed this out and made it clear that the question could have been decided differently had it been possible to bring it under the 2003 regulations:

> Although discrimination points occasionally surfaced in the course of argument, this is not a case of direct or indirect discrimination on religious grounds. The Originating Application does not mention discrimination of any kind. The claims set out are for unfair dismissal, breach of Convention rights Articles 8 and 9 and failure to make 'reasonable accommodation' for his religious beliefs regarding Sunday as 'a day of rest in remembrance of the Lord Jesus'. No claim for discrimination on the ground of religion or belief could have been brought by Mr Copsey under the Employment Equality (Religion or Belief) Regulations 2003, which only came into force on 2 December 2003 after the relevant events in this case had occurred.

In the case Mr Copsey had refused to accept changes to his working arrangements which would have required him to work on a Sunday and he had also refused to accept alternative work arrangements which would have given him Sunday off but which would have reduced his wages. Though the case did not involve a claim of discrimination, the following extracts from the judgment are worth noting and may provide guidance to tribunals considering claims of religious discrimination relating to holy days. Lord Justice Rix said (paras 68, 69, 71):

> 68. Nevertheless, the concept of reasonable accommodation is not foreign to either Convention jurisprudence or English law: see *Ahmad v. ILEA* and *Ahmad v. United Kingdom*. And, irrespective of article 9, the concept of unfairness in the law of unfair dismissal is inherent in English employment law, now covered by the Employment Rights Act 1996.

> 69. I would therefore prefer to say, limiting myself to the facts of this case, that, where an employer seeks to change the working hours and terms of his contract of employment with his employee in such a way as to interfere materially with the employee's right to manifest his religion, then article 9(1) of the Convention is potentially engaged. One solution is to find a reasonable accommodation with the employee. If this is found, then there will in the event be no material interference. If a reasonable solution is offered to the employee, but not accepted by him, then I think it remains possible to say that there is no material interference

> 71. It seems to me that it is possible and necessary to contemplate that an employer who seeks to change an employee's working hours so as to prevent that employee from practising his sincere adherence to the requirements of his religion in the way of Sabbath observance may be acting unfairly if he makes no attempt to accommodate his employee's needs. I cannot conceive that a decent employer would not attempt to do so.

Whilst Lord Justice Neuberger said (paras 87, 88, 95, 96):

> 87. At one extreme, might be a case where an employee is engaged specifically on the basis that he will work on a Sunday, and he subsequently comes to believe in a religion that prevents him working on a Sunday, and where the employer has always reasonably required an employee with his particular skills to work on a Sunday, and where there are no other appropriately skilled employees who could work in his place on a Sunday. It might be unfair for the employer to dismiss the employee, even in such a case, without taking any steps to see if the employee's newly acquired religious beliefs could be accommodated. However, I would have thought that it would require pretty exceptional additional facts before the employer could be held to have unfairly dismissed the employee in such a case.

> 88. At the other extreme, might be a case where an employee starts his employment on the specific basis that he will not have to work on a Sunday because of his religious beliefs, where the employer subsequently

requires him to work on a Sunday, and where the employee is able to identify another worker, with his particular skills, who would be prepared to work in his place on a Sunday. In such a case, it would be hard, at least in my view, to see, at least in the absence of further facts, how the employer could challenge his dismissal of the employee as unfair if it was on the basis that he would not work on a Sunday, even if the terms of his contract permitted a variation on the part of the employer so that there was no breach of contract in his requiring the employee to work on a Sunday.

95. In summary, the essential findings of the Employment Tribunal were as follows. Devon Clays were reasonable in initially requiring Mr Copsey to work on some (but by no means all) Sundays, owing to changes in demands for their products. They then did their best to accommodate his requirement not to work on any Sundays. This was initially successful, but it then led to difficulties, not least because of dissatisfaction among other employees. Devon Clays then offered Mr Copsey an arrangement which would have minimised his Sunday working, and, subsequently, a new (admittedly less well-paid) post which would have avoided any Sunday working.

96. The view of the Tribunal was that Devon Clays had done everything they reasonably could have done or could have been expected to do, in the particular circumstances of the case, to accommodate Mr Copsey's desire not to work on Sundays. I do not think that it is inaccurate to say that, if the Employment Tribunal thought anyone had acted unreasonably in this case, it was Mr Copsey. These were, as I have said, clear findings which were open to the Tribunal to make, and which justified their conclusion.

Therefore, under the regulations an employer must consider properly any application to take time off for religious festivals or not to work on specific days. Requests can be refused but any refusal must be on reasonable grounds and based on the needs of the business. If the employee's request can be accommodated within the reasonable requirements of the business then the request should be granted. However, an employee must also be prepared to compromise to meet the legitimate needs of the business and should bear in mind the comments of Lord Hoffmann in *Begum v Denbigh High School* [2006] UKHL 15, para 50:

Article 9 does not require that one should be allowed to manifest one's religion at any time and place of one's own choosing . . . people some-times have to suffer some inconvenience for their beliefs.

Even though that comment related to a claim under Art 9 and not to a claim under the 2003 regulations, it nevertheless sets out a principle which should be borne in mind by a tribunal considering a claim under the regulations.

As was pointed out by Lord Justice Neuberger in *Copsey v Devon Clays* [2005] EWCA Civ 932, decisions on discrimination may vary depending on the nature of the job and whether the religious problem arises because of a change in religion by the employee or because of a job change introduced by the employer. For example, if a Muslim or a Mormon applicant (A) goes for a job interview in a small shop which sells alcohol then A cannot claim religious discrimination if he is turned down for the job because he refuses to have anything to do with alcohol. However, if A is an employee in a shop which has not formerly sold alcohol but which obtains a licence to do so, then the employer must have regard to any religious objections A may have and see whether these objections can be accommodated. If, however, the shop has always sold alcohol and A is a long-term employee who refuses to serve alcohol following a religious conversion, then A is in a much weaker position; as Lord Justice Neuberger said in para 87 of *Copsey v Devon Clays* [2005] EWCA Civ 932:

> It might be unfair for the employer to dismiss the employee, even in such a case, without taking any steps to see if the employee's newly acquired religious beliefs could be accommodated. However, I would have thought that it would require pretty exceptional additional facts before the employer could be held to have unfairly dismissed the employee in such a case.

A particular problem with the wording of the regulations is that they do not appear to require the employer to have any knowledge of the particular requirements of a religion before a practice can be held to be discriminatory. This problem is demonstrated by an example given in para 4.2 of the MCB guidance:

> Be aware that certain routine conduct at interviews may conflict with acceptable practice according to the applicant's religion or belief, such as shaking hands with the opposite sex.
> *Example:* An employer at an interview puts his hand out to shake the interviewee's hand who is a Muslim lady. She refuses to do so. The employer does not understand why and considers her to be extremely rude, which affects her application. Employers could instead wait for the employee to initiate the handshake if they are unsure.

The difficulty with this example is that it assumes that an employer should be expected to be a mind reader and fails to accept that actually the woman in question is in fact being rude, because she is refusing to acknowledge a greeting without giving any explanation for her behaviour. If an employer (A) knows that the religious beliefs of a potential employee (B) prohibit her from shaking hands with males, then it would indeed constitute discrimination for A to insist that B shake hands; similarly, it would be discrimination for A to hold it against B because she does not shake hands or for him to describe her in a reference as 'unfriendly'. However, if A does not know, and B does not tell him that her religious beliefs prohibit her from shaking hands, then A would not be discriminating against B by considering that she was rude in refusing, without explanation, to shake hands. In that case the problem would not arise because of prejudice against the religion or beliefs of B but because of her failure to explain that her actions arise from her religious beliefs.

It is important for employers, employees and tribunals to recognise that allegations of discrimination cannot be looked at solely from the point of view of the person who alleges that they have been discriminated against. It is virtually impossible to organise any workplace or any workplace event in a way that is completely satisfactory to every conceivable religious belief. To take one example, it could be said that to have an office event in which alcohol is served would be discriminatory against Muslims who do not drink alcohol, and the MCB do indeed give such an example, in para 4.2 of their guidance. However, serving alcohol is not specifically discriminatory only to Muslims, many Evangelical Protestants abstain from alcohol, as do Mormons, Roman Catholic 'Pioneers' and teetotal atheists. To have an event in which alcohol is not served but tea or coffee are served instead would be acceptable to Muslims but would still discriminate against Mormons, who refrain from drinking tea and coffee as well as alcohol. Similarly, to suggest that works canteens must serve halal meat in order to avoid discrimination against Muslims ignores the fact that serving only halal meat would itself be discriminatory to Sikhs (who are forbidden to eat halal meat), to Evangelical Christians (because halal slaughter involves a prayer to Allah) and also to persons of any religion, or none, who consider that halal slaughter is unnecessarily cruel; to serve halal beef is discriminatory to Hindus, and to serve meat of any sort is discriminatory to Jains, Khalsa Sikhs and Buddhists.

Therefore, though an employer does have to provide religiously acceptable options in food either at a works event or in a works canteen, it is not necessary for an employer to provide for every conceivable variation of belief and taste because it would not be realistic to do so. Provided that non-alcoholic beverages are available as well as alcohol, and that a vegetarian alternative is being served when meat is non-halal, there should be no basis for a claim of religious discrimination. However, it would be important for an employer to ensure that employees are not mocked because they are not drinking alcohol or choose the vegetarian option because such behaviour could constitute discrimination and harassment.

The type of practice which would probably be regarded as indirectly discriminatory and not accepted as being proportionate could be where an employer insisted that all job interviews take place on a Friday afternoon. Such a requirement would discriminate against Muslims who attend mosque on Friday afternoon and who would therefore be unable to attend the interview and, unless there was an extremely good reason why the interviews had to be on Friday afternoon, it would be reasonable and proportionate for an employer to offer a choice of dates.

In essence, proportionality means a balance between what is the alleged discriminatory effect and the importance of the aim pursued. The more important the reason is for any alleged discriminatory practice, the more likely it is to be proportionate. Let us say, for example, that an employer requires all female staff to wear a particular uniform and an employee alleges that the uniform is indirectly discriminatory to Muslim women who wish to wear a hijab. For many types of employment a uniform is simply created in order to establish a core identity and to ensure common standards of dress and in those circumstances it would be reasonable to require that any hijab worn by a Muslim employee was in the uniform colours but it would not be proportionate to prevent Muslim employees wearing a hijab altogether. However, if the employment is in a uniformed public sector organisation such as the police then different factors may have to be considered.

Police officers exercise power in society and may often be required to intervene between individuals and groups so as to maintain the peace. In those circumstances a police uniform in effect hides the individual and should be a neutral symbol of authority for all citizens. However, a hijab is not neutral but is instead 'a powerful external symbol' of religious belief, according to the European Court of Human Rights in the cases of *Dahlab v Switzerland* ECmHR Application no 42393/98 15 February 2001 and *Sahin v Turkey* ECtHR Application no 4477/98 29 June 2004 and 10 November 2005. Therefore, a police officer wearing a hijab becomes a Muslim police officer rather than merely being a police officer who may, or may not, have a religious belief. In those circumstances the police officer ceases to be a neutral and impartial figure and that may affect her ability to be accepted as carrying out her duties impartially. Also if female Muslim police officers are allowed to wear a hijab then that would mean that police officers of other religions must also be allowed to wear religious symbols, for example a cross on their lapel, otherwise they could claim that they were being discriminated against and such an outcome would be divisive and against the interests of good policing. Therefore, the police can ban uniformed female staff from wearing a hijab on the basis that the police must be seen to be impartial towards all religious groups.

Similar principles could apply to any other public employment. It would therefore be acceptable for a public authority to ban its staff from wearing a hijab or a Sikh turban for the proportionate reason of ensuring that the public authority was seen to be religiously neutral. However, if Muslim staff are permitted to wear a hijab, and Sikh staff permitted to wear a turban, then it would be unlawful discrimination for other staff to be prohibited, or discouraged, from wearing other religious symbols such as a cross. In the media there have been reports of this type of discrimination being engaged in by some employers who have justified their discrimination by stating that the wearing of a hijab is compulsory in Islam but the wearing of a cross is not compulsory in Christianity. However, this argument is theologically questionable, because the Seventh Ecumenical Council of 787 AD declared that the veneration and display of religious objects such as icons, statues, crosses, etc. is a religious duty for Christians, and in any event it is not for a secular employer or tribunal to decide what is, or is not, a religious require-ment: *Amicus v Secretary of State for Trade and Industry* [2004] EWHC 860 (Admin), para 37.

Though it might seem an obvious point, employers are under an obligation to be non-discriminatory and consistent in the application of their rules regarding religious dress, food, holidays, etc. Merely permitting some employees to act or dress in a particular way because that is their religion is not enough; the rules, or a relaxation of the rules, must be applied in an across-the-board way. Therefore, if an employee is allowed to have a beard for religious reasons then all male employees should be permitted to have beards on the same terms. If they are not offered the right to have beards on the same terms then they will be being discriminated against because of their 'lack of belief'. Similary, if an employer decides to allow female Muslim staff to wear long skirts or dresses for reasons of modesty it must allow non-Muslim female staff to do the same. However, the regulations do not require that workplace rules or practices are automatically dropped or changed merely because a member of staff objects to them on religious grounds; but an employer does need to have a reason and a justification for any rules or practices which are objected to and the justification needs to be proportionate to the objective. Finally, any rules must be applied in a way which is fair to all staff and exceptions to any rule should not be made merely to placate one religion without equal consideration being given to the beliefs of employees, or potential employees, of other religions or no religion.

Genuine occupational requirement

Under reg 7 discrimination in employment is permitted in certain circumstances:

> (2) This paragraph applies where, having regard to the nature of the employment or the context in which it is carried out—
>
> (a) being of a particular religion or belief is a genuine and determining occupational requirement;
> (b) it is proportionate to apply that requirement in the particular case; and
> (c) either—

    (i) the person to whom that requirement is applied does not meet it, or

   (ii) the employer is not satisfied, and in all the circumstances it is reasonable for him not to be satisfied, that that person meets it,

and this paragraph applies whether or not the employer has an ethos based on religion or belief.

(3) This paragraph applies where an employer has an ethos based on religion or belief and, having regard to that ethos and to the nature of the employment or the context in which it is carried out—

(a) being of a particular religion or belief is a genuine occupational requirement for the job;

(b) it is proportionate to apply that requirement in the particular case; and

(c) either—

    (i) the person to whom that requirement is applied does not meet it, or

   (ii) the employer is not satisfied, and in all the circumstances it is reasonable for him not to be satisfied, that that person meets it.

Regulation 7(2) clearly applies in situations such as employment of a priest in a church where there it is an obvious and legitimate requirement that the priest is a practising member of the religion in question. However, an employer does not have to be a religious organisation in order to rely on reg 7(2); it merely has to be able to justify having a genuine occupational requirement (GOR) for a particular post. For example, if a hospital wishes to appoint a chaplain, it can lawfully restrict that employment to ordained clergy. Another example might be where a charity wanted to establish a unit to help Christian asylum seekers who had fled persecution in Iraq or Darfur; in that situation the charity might decide that all the employees in the unit should be practising Christians or, alternatively, that they could be members of any religion, or none, provided that they were not Muslims. Such a policy would clearly amount to discrimination but could be justified as being a 'genuine and determining occupational requirement' because of the particular history and background of the asylum seekers the charity was trying to assist and the need to provide staff who would not be regarded suspiciously by them. Similarly, if a local authority or police set up a unit dealing with domestic violence and forced marriage in a predominantly Muslim area it could decide to restrict employment to Muslim women in order to ensure that the unit was trusted by those it was set up assist. In both cases there would be a reasoned justification for what would otherwise constitute unlawful discrimination.

A commercial business might also have an aspect of its work which justifies restricting employment to members of a particular religion. For example, a travel company which, amongst other things, organised pilgrimages to Lourdes, could legitimately decide that its travel reps who go on these trips should be practising Catholics. Whilst the professional part of the job could be carried by a non-Catholic, the nature of the type of customer, and the fact that the job will involve attendance at religious events and explaining religious ceremonies, would mean that in practical terms the job could not be carried out by a non-Catholic; however, there would be no similar reason or justification for stating that the pilot of the airplane or the baggage handler needed to be a Catholic. Similarly, a shop which specialised in Islamic women's clothing, hijabs, jilbabs, etc., could justify a practice of only employing Muslim women in its shop but could not justify only employing Muslim tailors or van drivers.

Though they are separate provisions, reg 7(2) and 7(3) overlap to some extent and it may quite often be the case that decisions to restrict employment may be justified under both provisions. Regulation 7(3) is the more complex and was the most controversial element of the regulations because it is an attempt to try to square a philosophical and legal circle, namely, the fact that under the regulations discrimination of any sort is wrong in principle whilst at the same time respect for religious beliefs means accepting the legitimacy of religious differences and religious rules. However, any restriction under reg 7(3) must relate to a genuine requirement of the post and the mere fact that the employer 'has an ethos based on religion or belief' will not, of itself, be sufficient justification for restricting employment only to members of that religion or belief. For example, a firm of solicitors which was established by partners who are all Muslims and operating in a predominantly Muslim area may well have a Muslim ethos but that would not, of itself, justify it advertising for a Muslim solicitor unless the firm could show that a particular role in the firm could only be carried out by a Muslim. For example, it might be possible to justify an advertisement for a Muslim lawyer to deal with the drafting of wills and probate for Muslim clients because of the need to reassure the clients that their wills would be drafted and applied in accordance with the inheritance rules of Shariah law.

Deciding on whether a post should be restricted to members of a particular religion or belief will also depend on the nature of the post and, in particular, on how public the job is. For example, if the National Secular Society was advertising for a bookkeeper then it would probably not be able to justify excluding religious adherents from the post; however if it was looking for a personal assistant to the Executive Director, with a role which involved answering the telephone and attending public meetings with him, then the Society could justify excluding religious adherents from the post because the role would involve participation in the 'mission' of the organisation and therefore a commitment to its purpose. Conversely, if the National Secular

Society was looking for a cleaner and caretaker for its headquarters building then it could probably not justify restricting the position to non-believers, but if a Mormon temple was appointing a cleaner and caretaker then it could restrict the post to devout Mormons because, under Mormon theology, non-Mormons are not allowed to enter a temple and even then, only Mormons who hold a 'temple recommend'.

The issue of what is a genuine occupational requirement is complex and will change from organisation to organisation and from religion to religion. For that reason the organisation Faithworks, in collaboration with the DTI and various religious organisations, published a series of 'Guidelines on Religious Discrimination and [various religions] Ethos'. With the kind permission of Faithworks, the following examples of GOR are reproduced below. They are not examples which have been tested before a tribunal but they do demonstrate the various factors which any organisation will have to consider when deciding on whether a post qualifies for a GOR under reg 7(3).

Possible Buddhist GORs

Buddhist Centre/Vihara Administrator
The Buddhist Centre/Vihara has a number of activities, which run from its premises, involving paid and unpaid team members – e.g. meditation and Buddhism courses, Dharma Study Groups, a Buddhist writer's group, a mother/toddler meditation group, a depression self-help group. The centre/Vihara Manager is paid and has a support package, but also has other obligations. It has been decided that further support is required to offload some admin work and that this role shall be remunerated. The support role involves general administration – room bookings, clerical duties and some diary management for the centre/Vihara, telephone/ email enquiries, etc. It could easily be argued at a functional level that anyone, of any or no faith, could do this work and therefore this job could be carried out by a Buddhist or non-Buddhist.

However, the Buddhist Centre/Vihara believes it is important that the paid member of staff models the spiritual practice and ethos of the centre/Vihara and brings the centre/Vihara's ethos to life. This kind of 'working practice' – cultivating mindfulness, applying wisdom, and practising compassion and generosity with everyone in all sorts of circumstances as an expression of faith – is something that only a practising Buddhist can do. There is also the intention to make the job of running the centre/Vihara into a spiritual practice, by working in a team of other practitioners with shared aspirations. Moreover, the centre/Vihara has another consideration. In many situations the person filling this role would be entirely responsible for the representation of the organisation, its activities and spiritual tradition. This would require the postholder to be able to respond appropriately to any caller at any time, perhaps without reference to another person immediately. In other words, the job is not only about administration but more importantly about representation. Effectively, the administrator or receptionist will be the front line representative of the organisation – communicating the Buddhist ethos. This task cannot be given to a non-Buddhist.

The GOR for this job therefore is the need to be the interface between the Buddhist Centre/Vihara and the wider world, able to communicate a Buddhist perspective and values.

It is very important that the GOR is reflected in the job purpose and job description as well as the person specification. With that in mind it would be untrue to call the job an administrator. All of this should be expressed along the following lines:

- Job title: The job title should reflect the main purpose of the job – it may therefore need to be Buddhist Centre/Vihara Representative rather than Buddhist Centre/Vihara Administrator.
- Job purpose: The post holder is responsible for representing the Buddhist Centre/Vihara in the absence of the Buddhist Centre/Vihara Manager, and other Buddhist teachers.
- Task/s in the job description: Dealing with Buddhist Centre issues on behalf of the Buddhist Centre/Vihara Centre Manager and Buddhist teachers, making day-to-day decisions where appropriate.
- Person specification: Understanding of the centre/Vihara's organisational ethos – its Buddhist tradition, meditation practice and wider activities – is essential.
- Experience in dealing with Buddhist Centre/Vihara matters and relational skills is essential.
- The applicant needs to be able to communicate the centre/Vihara's activities in ways which interest and encourage newcomers to visit the centre/Vihara.
- The applicant also needs to be able to relate to people of different ages, from different backgrounds, and with different needs.

Community Outreach Worker

The appointment of the centre/Vihara representative has borne fruit. Let us now assume that the centre/Vihara is in the position of wanting to strengthen the community of people visiting and participating in its activities. At the same time, the centre/Vihara wants to widen its appeal by reaching out to the local community in new and exciting ways. The Buddhist Centre/Vihara has decided it wishes to recruit a Community Outreach Worker to act as the point of contact both with those active in the Sangha and to work on outreach activities with the local community at large. The main purpose of the role is to help practitioners develop their meditation practice and understanding of Buddhism, as well as to encourage others who are not yet involved in the Buddhist Centre/Vihara to explore a spiritual path. The role is made up of the following aspects:

- Operate the drop-in meditation classes in the Buddhist Centre/Vihara on two nights a week, encouraging people to attend;
- Initiate outreach activities (potentially working with others at the centre/Vihara as well as outside partners) to encourage people to attend the classes;
- Manage a team of volunteers to ensure that tea and refreshments are available during the classes and courses;
- Review and develop the centre/Vihara's programme of activities (in liaison with the centre/Vihara management and other team members) and consider other options (e.g. meditation for stress management, for depression, for children, etc.);
- Undertake administration e.g. rotas, bookings for the Buddhist Centre/Vihara as required.

The requirements for the job therefore is wide-ranging. Some skills – like administration – are quite generic. But the core defining purpose is the need to understand and communicate the organisation's activities and the Dharma to as broad an audience as possible, and in a variety of contexts.

It is very important that the GOR is reflected in the job purpose and the job description as well as the person specification and expressed along the following lines:

- Job purpose: Help people relate to and develop their involvement with the centre/Vihara through participation in meditation and Buddhist courses, and other activities, and to increase their awareness and understanding of Buddhist activities.
- Task/s in the job description: Lead outreach activities with the local community and run the drop-in centre at the Buddhist Centre/Vihara as part of broader community outreach activities bringing meditation and Buddhism to a wide audience, e.g. open days, new courses, etc.
- Person specification.
- The applicant needs to practise meditation, and understand Buddhist ethics and practice.
- Ability to communicate the centre/Vihara's activities, and the value of meditation, and Buddhism to people's everyday life, in ways which encourage, interest and stimulate growth is essential – if the applicant is also needed to practise a particular Buddhist tradition then this also needs to be spelt out.
- In particular, the applicant should have a commitment to his/her own spiritual practice – with a commitment to the Three Jewels –

Buddha, Dharma, Sangha – and to be able to communicate this effectively.

• The applicant needs to be able to relate to people of different ages, backgrounds, and with varying needs.

Café Manager

The Buddhist Centre/Vihara is committed to spreading the message of the Dharma, and it has set up a subsidiary enterprise, a Buddhist vegetarian café, which is applying the Buddha's teachings on right livelihood more fully. A decision has been made to expand the café, and try out a broader menu to encourage more customers, and increase income. The profits will be invested in spreading the Dharma more broadly. The café is situated in an area where there are few meeting places and where there is a wide range of social needs. It will be open through the day and in the early evening, acting as a social drop-in place where the spirit of Sangha can be nurtured. At the same time, the café enables the centre/Vihara to meet broader social aims by providing a service for the local community, many of whom will not be Buddhist. The centre/Vihara cannot easily rely on its network of volunteers to develop the operation effectively and the current team is in need of fresh energy and more business acumen to help them to go the next level. A decision has been made to employ a café manager to supervise and run the café with the current team.

The task of running a café could of course be carried out by a non-Buddhist as well as a Buddhist but the Buddhist Centre/Vihara wants to recruit a Buddhist because the café is a key part of their outreach to the community. While the occupational skills and job requirements might be clear in terms of what the Buddhist Centre/Vihara wants the person to do (to manage and run the café), it also needs to be clear what makes this café a Buddhist café. If this is not clear the Buddhist Centre/Vihara will find it difficult to identify the GOR (the requirement for a Buddhist) in the job description and person specification and could become liable to a legal challenge on the grounds of its employment policy. The distinctively Buddhist characteristic of the café is its fundamental purpose – to serve refreshments and vegetarian food to all in a Buddhist context, according to Buddhist ethics. The café intends to be a tangible expression of Buddhist values. The distinctively Buddhist aspect of this café is the motivation behind the whole operation, and the staff work co-operatively as a team, making their task a spiritual practice. Equally important, this right livelihood enterprise is a way of helping to finance the centre/Vihara's activities and to bring the Dharma to a wider range of people by modelling Buddhist values. Anybody joining the café team therefore needs to be committed to Buddhism and specifically to right livelihood as one element of their spiritual path. If the explicit Buddhist ethos, and purpose of the café, is not clarified, and the GOR to be a Buddhist is not spelt out, the enterprise could run the risk of a legal challenge. It is important to understand this, and to spend some time clearly communicating both the Buddhist purpose of the enterprise, and its organisational ethos. The GOR for this job therefore is the need to model Buddhist values in the day-to-day operations of the café – to prepare and provide food in ways that do not cause suffering to living beings; to reach out to the community and the individuals using the café with awareness and care, and to exemplify the qualities of compassion and generosity, which the Buddha's teachings encourage.

The job purpose should therefore be expressed along the following lines:

- Job purpose: This job is a way of expressing the Buddha's teachings by modelling Buddhist values such as generosity, compassion and mindfulness in all its dealings with people. Its vegetarian ethos is also a way of expressing the Buddhist commitment to not harming living beings. In addition, the job provides the post holder with the opportunity to deepen their spiritual practice, and apply Buddhist ethics through the experience of right livelihood.
- Task/s in the job description: To exemplify hospitality, serving customers with mindfulness, generosity and kindness, and welcoming all those who drop in; working co-operatively alongside other Buddhist practitioners.
- Person specification: Ability to relate to different types of people, particularly the vulnerable and disadvantaged, experience of the Buddha's teachings on ethics, compassion, mindfulness, right livelihood, as well as participation in Buddhist activities and a commitment to making work a spiritual practice.

Possible Christian GORs

Youthworker
The church wishes to recruit a youthworker to work both with the young people of the church and on outreach projects in the local community. The main purpose of the role is to help young people attached to the church to grow in their faith and to help others who are not yet involved in the church begin to explore and understand their spirituality. The role is made up of the following aspects:

- To operate the young people's drop-in centre in the church rooms on two nights a week, encouraging all young people to attend.
- To undertake some administration e.g. rotas, bookings for the church rooms.

The GOR for the job therefore is the need to relate the Christian faith, in a variety of contexts, to young people both in and outside the church.

It is very important that the GOR is reflected in the job purpose and the job description as well as the person specification and expressed along the following lines:

- Job purpose: Help young people to relate to and develop in their faith and Christian spirituality.
- Task/s in the job description: Lead projects in the community and run the drop-in centre in the church rooms as part of the church's outreach e.g. holiday clubs, fun days, etc.
- Person specification: To be able to relate to young people with different needs and to explain the Christian faith in ways which encourage interest and stimulate growth.

Church Administrator

The church has a number of activities, led by volunteers, which run from its premises – a parent/toddler group, a community support group, etc. There is only one church minister and it has been decided that support is required to off-load some of the admin work. The support role involves general administration – room bookings, clerical duties and some diary management for the minister, telephone/email enquiries, etc. At one level it is possible to conclude that this job could be carried out by a Christian or a non-Christian – it could easily be argued that at a functional level an employee of any faith or no faith at all could do this work. However, the church wishes to recruit a Christian because in many situations the person filling it would be entirely responsible for the representation of the church. This would require the postholder being able to make an appropriate response to any caller at any time, perhaps without reference to another person immediately. In other words, the job is not only about administration but more importantly about representation. The GOR for this job therefore is the need to be the interface between the church and the outside world, able to represent a church view, make a Christian response and reflect Christian values.

It is very important that the GOR is reflected in the job purpose and job description as well as the person specification. With that in mind it would be untrue to call the job an administrator. All of this should be expressed along the following lines:

- Job title: The job title should reflect the main purpose of the job – it may therefore need to be Church Representative rather than Church Administrator.
- Job purpose: This job is responsible for representing the church in the absence of the minister.
- Task/s in the job description: Dealing with church issues on behalf of the minister, making decisions where appropriate.

- Person specification: Experience in dealing with church matters and pastoral/ relational skills are essential.

Coffee Bar Supervisor
The church wishes to set up a coffee bar. It is situated in an area where there are few meeting places and where there is a wide range of social needs. It will be open through the day and for part of the evening for young people. The church is a small church, not many volunteers, and so to develop this operation effectively it has been decided to employ a part-time worker to supervise and run the coffee bar. The tasks of running a coffee bar could be carried out by a non-Christian as well as a Christian but the church wants to recruit a Christian because the coffee bar is a key part of their outreach to the community.

While it might be clear what the church wants the person to do in order to supervise and run the coffee bar, it needs to be clear what makes this coffee bar a Christian coffee bar. If this is not clear the church will find it difficult to identify the GOR (the requirement for a Christian) in the job description and person specification. The distinctively Christian characteristic of the coffee bar is its fundamental purpose – it is there to serve coffee to those who drop in but, in doing so, its wider purpose is to be a tangible expression of the Kingdom of God and its values such as love, hospitality, compassion, mercy, forgiveness and so on. The distinctively Christian aspect of this coffee bar is the motivation with which the whole operation is put together and carried out.

If the main purpose of the job is to reach out to the community it is therefore important to call the job an outreach worker rather than a coffee bar supervisor. The GOR for the job is the need to represent and live out the Christian purpose of the coffee bar in the day-to-day operation – to reach out in love, with compassion, in mercy, with grace, in a forgiving spirit, etc., expressed along the following lines:

- Job title: In accordance with the purpose of the job, the job title should be Outreach Worker.
- Job purpose: This job is a way of expressing God's love to the world by modelling Christian values in all its dealings with people.
- Task/s in the job description: To welcome all those who drop in, showing Christian hospitality.
- Person specification: Ability to relate to different types of people, experience of dealing with the needs of the young and disadvantaged, exercising Christian spirituality.

Possible Sikh GORs

Post of Granthi

A gurdwara wishes to recruit a granthi (person who reads the Guru Granth Sahib during Sikh services) to work in the gurdwara and with the Sikh community. The main purpose of the role is to lead and support the spiritual life of the community, to read, interpret and explain the Guru Granth Sahib and conduct acts of worship and prayer times.

Additional duties: Perform all ceremonies such as marriage, naming and death. Other ceremonies as required by the members of the community, such as amrit chhakna, celebrations of birthdays, marriage and death anniversaries. Take part in Sikh festivals. Teach Punjabi, kirtan, Sikh history and basic principles of Sikh religion as written in the Guru Granth Sahib and developed by the 10th Guru Gobind Singh.

See to the spiritual needs of the community members and visit homes to conduct services if and when required. The granthi is to work in the gurdwara all seven days a week ensuring prayers are conducted according to the times defined by the management committee.

A granthi is to ensure that all prayers and ceremonies are conducted according to Sikh teachings and any non-Sikh practices are forbidden. The granthi needs to be fluent in Punjabi so that s/he can speak, read, and write Punjabi fluently and understand Punjabi culture such as food habits, expectations of elderly of respect from young people and how an extended family works among Sikhs.

The GOR for the job therefore is the need to relate to Sikh faith, in a variety of contexts both in and outside the gurdwara.

Other people who work in the gurdwaras are: Ragis, Sewadars, Youth Worker, Women's Support Worker, Senior Citizens' Co-ordinator, Gurdwara Administrator, Langar supervisor, Teachers for Punjabi, Sikh religion and Sikh history. To find out whether there is a GOR in place to recruit a Sikh in any of these posts, the employer needs to consider what the actual purpose of the job is and whether this requires a Sikh to carry out the job.

Possible Jewish GORs

Youth Director

The United Synagogue wishes to recruit a youth director to work with young people within the community. The main purpose of the role is to run appropriate synagogue activities for young people which promote their involvement in synagogue life and inspire them to follow Jewish laws and practices and feel a sense of belonging within the community. The GOR for the job therefore is the need for a practising Jew whose knowledge and experience of the laws and customs of Judaism make him/her an authentic role model for young people.

Sample Job Description

Job Title: Youth Director : Responsible to: The Board of Management, through a nominated individual from the Children and Youth Sub-committee, with frequent liaison with the Rabbi and Tribe (young united synagogue).

Job Purpose: To act as a focus for the synagogue activities of the older children and youth of the community, inspiring young people to embrace the laws and customs of Judaism. To promote involvement in religious, social, educational and cultural activities within the synagogue, particularly among the 2–9 age group.

Job Tasks:

- Set up a regular youth service for post-barmitzvah teenagers, possibly in people's homes. Initially this would operate on a (bi-) monthly basis and on the High Holydays.
- Facilitate the involvement of teenagers, as appropriate, in leading elements of the youth service, for example encouraging their participation in leading the davening, layning, giving a devar Torah, etc.
- Lead the 9–12s service on at least a fortnightly basis and help with other children's services as required, providing content input, ensuring continuity from one to the next, encouraging attendance.
- Entertain children of different ages on a regular basis for lunch/tea on Shabbat either in shul or at other accommodation provided by the synagogue; organise a quarterly Shabbaton for youths.
- Challenge 12/13 and Rayder – be present to help out where needed (maybe Hebrew reading, to cover for a teacher or to take one of the Challenge sessions) to build up a rapport with participants.
- Operate a midweek club for ages 9–10 and 11–12 (leading up to BBYO age) on alternate weeks and incorporate a tuck shop, table tennis, snooker, etc. Helpers could be recruited from our 6th formers in return for payment.
- Help out on one/two evenings a week with informal learning sessions such as Rabbi's current Coke & Chat class.
- Arrange termly outings initially for the following age groups: 9/10, 11/12, 12+.
- Identify ways to enhance the frequency and effectiveness of communication between the shul and the youth and older children using a variety of media (e.g. texting, email, newsletter, etc).
- Provide information to the Board Administrator to enable communications material to be prepared and disseminated about the above (e.g. posters, flyers, information for e- and paper-based circulars).

- Ensure that information about events and activities is provided to the Board Administrator to enable the synagogue events diary to be kept up to date.
- Provide suggestions to the Board, via the Children and Youth Subcommittee, on ways to improve the activities for youth and children in the community and to encourage participation in the same.
- Attend Children & Youth Subcommittee meetings.
- Attend Tribe seminars and meetings, where appropriate.

Person Specification:

- Conversant in key aspects of the principles and practice of Judaism, together with ability to explain them in ways which encourage and interest young people.
- As a role model for young Jewish people, the jobholder will need to be a practising Jew.
- Youth leadership training and/or experience.
- Confident dealing with children of all ages and their parents.
- Common sense, maturity and a flexible approach to work.
- Organisational skills.
- High level of self-motivation.

Chevra Kadisha (Funeral Bearer)

The United Synagogue wishes to recruit a Chevra Kadisha (Bearer at a funeral) to ensure that funerals are conducted on schedule and attend to the deceased from collection to burial, in keeping with the religious obligations required by the laws of Judaism.

The GOR for this job is the religious requirement in Jewish law for a practising Jew to accompany the body until burial and make Tahara (ritual preparation of body for burial). Whilst the requirement to read and write Hebrew could be fulfilled by a non-Jew with this ability, the religious requirement could not.

Job Description

Job Title: Chevra Kadisha

Responsible to: Burial Office Manager

Job Purpose: To ensure that funerals are conducted on schedule, with respect and in strict adherence to the laws and byelaws of the United Synagogue and Halacha by attending to the deceased person from collection to burial.

Job Tasks:

- Ensure the funeral is conducted at the arranged time and in keeping with the byelaws and religious obligations by:

- Collecting the deceased person from nursing home, hospital or family member's home and taking them to the cemetery for the Tahara or any other location as instructed.
- Checking that the correct person is being taken to the correct cemetery and buried in the correct grave.
- Making Tahara on a deceased male and to assist the ladies to encoffin a deceased female.
- Placing the coffin on the bier and moving it when instructed to the appropriate hall.
- Distributing prayer books and offering help and assisting with the burial service in the absence of a Superintendent.
- Conveying the coffin to the grave side and lowering the coffin into the grave.
- Checking the availability of sheets prior to a pick up.
- Checking the name on the board matches the deceased person.
- Checking that there are adequate supplies in the mortuary and notifying the Burial Manager when supplies are low.
- Any further duties as the Honorary Officers of the United Synagogue or line managers may from time to time direct.

Person Specification:

- Ability to communicate in a compassionate manner with members of the public including mourners.
- Ability to lift deceased persons and lower coffins in a safe manner.
- Knowledge and skill to make Tahara (prepare body for burial) in accordance with Halacha (Jewish law).
- Ability to follow detailed instructions and procedures.
- Knowledge of the laws and byelaws of the Burial Society and the Jewish laws, customs and traditions regarding funerals.
- Maintaining a positive attitude in spite of the stressful nature of the work.
- Ability to establish and develop effective relationships.
- Ability to display a common sense, calm, patient, sympathetic, polite manner to the public and team members detached from emotion.
- Ability to read and write Hebrew.
- Complying with the dress code by always wearing the clothing provided in an appropriate manner.
- Through effective time management ensure that they are not responsible for delaying a funeral and that they are available to assist female voluntary chevrot.
- Ability to stand in as a Superintendent at the time of a funeral or consecration, if so instructed by the Burial Office Manager.

Jewish law requires the jobholder to be a practising Jew.

It is important to note that, whilst a job specification may mention qualities such as love, hospitality, compassion, mercy, forgiveness, generosity, honesty, integrity, etc., as requirements of an office holder, these are personal qualities which would be regarded by a tribunal as being religiously neutral and which do not, in themselves, justify a GOR being applied to a post. Most religions aspire to high personal and moral qualities and hope to inspire them in their members but no religion can honestly claim that these qualities are found only amongst its own believers. For example, in deciding on the qualities required for a particular position a Muslim organisation might decide 'for this post we require a woman who is modest, and chaste in her dress and behaviour', but it cannot go on to say 'and therefore the post must be filled by a Muslim woman', since modesty and chastity are not virtues which are unique to Muslim women, nor are they virtues which are guaranteed to exist merely because an applicant is a Muslim woman. If the post is to qualify for a GOR, more will be required.

Of course, no two jobs are the same, just as no two organisations are the same, but as a general principle for a job to qualify for a GOR it must help the organisation achieve its religious function and there must be a reasoned justification why the job should be restricted to members of one religion. All religions do have a tendency to metaphysical ways of expression which can descend into platitudes and waffle and, whilst this is maybe unavoidable in low level theology, it should be avoided in drafting a job specification which may eventually be looked at by a hard-nosed employment tribunal. For an employer to establish that a GOR exists, it must show, first, that it has an ethos based on religion or belief and, second, that the post involves real involvement in that religion or belief; for example, actions such as:

- Leading the organisation, setting out its vision and strategy, understanding and articulating its theology or motivation.
- Leading the development of or delivering the main activity/ies of the organisation.
- Representing the purpose of the organisation, speaking, preaching, advocating on behalf of the organisation.
- Being a face to face contact between the organisation and the public, or those who the organisation exists to serve.
- Being the 'voice' of the organisation, representing the organisation to enquirers, being the point of contact about the organisation.
- Being responsible inside the organisation for representing, promoting, maintaining and ensuring the transference of its ethos.
- Leading or supporting the spiritual life of the organisation, including conducting acts of worship, prayer times, retreats, and spiritual development.

Victimisation

Regulation 4 prohibits discrimination by way of victimisation:

4.—(1) For the purposes of these Regulations, a person ('A') discriminates against another person ('B') if he treats B less favourably than he treats or would treat other persons in the same circumstances, and does so by reason that B has—

(a) brought proceedings against A or any other person under these Regulations;

(b) given evidence or information in connection with proceedings brought by any person against A or any other person under these Regulations;

(c) otherwise done anything under or by reference to these Regulations in relation to A or any other person; or

(d) alleged that A or any other person has committed an act which (whether or not the allegation so states) would amount to a contravention of these Regulations, or by reason that A knows that B intends to do any of those things, or suspects that B has done or intends to do any of them.

(2) Paragraph (1) does not apply to treatment of B by reason of any allegation made by him, or evidence or information given by him, if the allegation, evidence or information was false and not made (or, as the case may be, given) in good faith.

The wording is similar to provisions in s 3 of the Race Relations Act 1976 and s 5 of the Sex Discrimination Act 1975 and the case law under those provisions will be relevant in interpreting reg 4. The acts described in reg 4(1)(a)–(d) are commonly described as 'protected acts', because an employee is protected if he does any of them. For discrimination by way of victimisation to have taken place, B needs to have been less favourably treated than 'other persons in the same circumstances' for doing, intending to do, or being suspected of doing a protected act. What constitutes less favourable treatment is anything a reasonable worker would think is a disadvantage and includes dismissal, failure to give promotion, or acts of harassment.

Defining the protected acts under reg 4(1)(a)–(c) is relatively straightforward. That in reg 4(1)(a) occurs where B has brought any proceedings under the regulations against A, or against any other person. For example, where an employee has brought a complaint in the employment tribunal alleging that he has been discriminated against by co-workers contrary to the regulations, and his employer subsequently transfers him to a job with a less favourable environment then that would constitute unlawful victimisation.

The protected act in reg 4(b) occurs where B has given evidence or information in connection with proceedings brought by any person against A or any other person under the regulations. As with reg 4(a), this relates to proceedings brought not only against A but also against any other person. For example, if B has given evidence in an employment tribunal for his friend, an applicant C who is bringing a claim of discrimination under the regulations against his employer, D; if A is unhappy about this, possibly because D is a good customer, and A subsequently dismisses B, then that would constitute victimisation contrary to reg 4(1)(b).

Regulation 4(d) concerns situations where B has alleged that A or any other person has committed an act which 'whether or not the allegation so states' amounts to a contravention of the regulations. For example, if B tells his supervisor that he thinks the employer's dress code is unfair to a Muslim employee, and B is then not promoted to become a supervisor because he is considered a 'troublemaker', then that would be victimisation contrary to reg 4(1)(d). It is not necessary that the employee brought, was bringing, or was even contemplating proceedings under the regulations, nor is it necessary that the allegation he made would constitute a breach of the regulations if it was true. The question is whether it was an allegation of conduct that could amount to a breach of the regulations and whether there has been victimisation in consequence of the allegation being made.

The victimisation may occur even if A and B are members of the same religion. For example, A is an Evangelical Christian and harasses C because C is an atheist and B, who is also an Evangelical Christian, threatens to give evidence on behalf of C in an employment tribunal unless A stops his harassment of C. If A then started to discriminate against B, that would be victimisation contrary to reg 4.

Naturally, B must establish that the less favourable treatment is as a result of the protected act, A's knowledge that B intends to do a protected act, or A's suspicion that B has done, or intends to do, a protected act. Thus, B must establish a causal link between his act and A's alleged victimisation of him even though there may be mixed motives for the less favourable treatment. When there are mixed motives, then, so long as the unlawful motive has 'sufficient weight', the conduct will be victimisation: *O'Donoghue v Redcar and Cleveland BC* [2001] EWCA Civ 701.

Employers' liability

Under reg 22, employers and others may be liable for acts of discrimination by their employees or agents:

> 22.—(1) Anything done by a person in the course of his employment shall be treated for the purposes of these Regulations as done by his

employer as well as by him, whether or not it was done with the employer's knowledge or approval.

(2) Anything done by a person as agent for another person with the authority (whether express or implied, and whether precedent or subsequent) of that other person shall be treated for the purposes of these Regulations as done by that other person as well as by him.

(3) In proceedings brought under these Regulations against any person in respect of an act alleged to have been done by an employee of his it shall be a defence for that person to prove that he took such steps as were reasonably practicable to prevent the employee from doing that act, or from doing in the course of his employment acts of that description.

These provisions follow well-established principles in race and sex discrimination law and often the only important argument is whether the acts complained of occurred 'in the course of employment'. The case law on race and sex discrimination states that ' "in the course of [his] employment" should be given a broad interpretation': *Jones v Tower Boot Co Ltd* [1997] IRLR 168. Therefore, conduct outside the working hours and away from work premises may still be in the course of employment in certain circumstances; for example, an employer could be liable for religious abuse during a works Christmas party organised by the employer and attended mostly by employees.

Conduct in the workplace will, of course, take place 'in the course of employment' so, for example, if an employee is subjected to abuse in the work canteen, during his lunch hour, the employer would be liable even though the employer may not have known of, and would not have approved of the conduct. Under reg 22(3) an employer has a defence if he can show he took 'such steps as were reasonably practicable' to prevent the employee responsible for the acts of discrimination or harassment from doing the acts complained of. Having a comprehensive equal opportunities policy, anti-harassment procedures, and proper disciplinary and grievance procedures that make clear that employees are prohibited from discrimination and harassment are important ways for employers to demonstrate they have taken steps to prevent discrimination. Equal opportunities and anti-harassment policies will need to ensure that discrimination and harassment on grounds of religion or belief will not be tolerated. However, the existence of paper policies on their own is not enough; the employer must also be able to demonstrate that he has taken steps to inform the employees of those policies, and has provided adequate training in them. Naturally, where the employee responsible for the discrimination or harassment occupies a managerial or supervisory position within the employer's undertaking, it will be more difficult for the employer to rely on the reg 22 defence, particularly where there is evidence of a record of similar behaviour by, or allegations against, the employee responsible.

Generally, where an employee has made previous complaints, whether formal or informal, about discrimination and harassment, and the employer has not taken reasonable steps to resolve those complaints, it will be difficult for the employer to rely on the defence in reg 22(3). In terms of the quality of the employer's procedures and training, the larger the employer, the greater the scrutiny an employment tribunal can be expected to put them under. What is reasonably practicable for a small or family business will be different from what is reasonably practicable for a large business.

Regulation 22(2) extends the same regime of vicarious liability that applies to employers and employees to principals and agents and a principal will be liable for the discriminatory acts of his agent when the agent is acting with the 'express or implied authority' of the principal 'whether precedent or subsequent': *Lana v Positive Action Training in Housing (London) Ltd* [2001] UKEAT 245_00_1503, para 31. Thus, where one agency worker discriminates against another, the principal will be liable for the discrimination if the discriminating agency worker is acting with the principal's express or implied authority. It does not mean the principal authorised the specific act of discrimination, rather that he authorised the agent's act which was then carried out in a discriminatory way. Regulation 23 provides that it will be unlawful for a person to 'knowingly aid' another person to do an act which is unlawful under the regulations. The words 'knowingly aid' also appear in the Race Relations Act and the Sex Discrimination Act and in respect of the Race Relations Act the House of Lords held in *Anyanwu v South Bank Students' Union* [2001] UKHL 14, para 5:

> A person aids another if he helps or assists him. He does so whether his help is substantial and productive or whether it is not, provided the help is not so insignificant as to be negligible.

Enforcement

Any claim alleging a breach of the regulations must be brought in an employment tribunal and there are strict time limits. Under s 34, any claim must be brought within three months of the act of discrimination which is complained of or, if there are a series of discriminatory acts, the case must be brought within three months of the last act of discrimination. These time limits are standard in discrimination claims brought before employment tribunals. A tribunal can allow a claim to be made after the expiry of three months but it is a matter of discretion and it is unlikely that an extension of time will be allowed unless there is a very good explanation for the delay. Under reg 30(1) a tribunal can also award compensation if it considers that it is 'just and equitable' to do so and in addition, or alternatively, it can order that the employer take action to end the practice which led to the claim of discrimination.

Under reg 29 there is a reverse burden of proof so that:

(2) Where, on the hearing of the complaint, the complainant proves facts from which the tribunal could, apart from this regulation, conclude in the absence of an adequate explanation that the respondent—

(a) has committed against the complainant an act to which regulation 28 applies; or

(b) is by virtue of regulation 22 (liability of employers and principals) or 23 (aiding unlawful acts) to be treated as having committed against the complainant such an act,

the tribunal shall uphold the complaint unless the respondent proves that he did not commit, or as the case may be, is not to be treated as having committed, that act.

This change in the normal rules of evidence and burden of proof has been adopted in all varieties of discrimination law over the past few years but a claimant would be foolish to rely on it too much. Whatever the regulations say, tribunals will still want solid evidence before they decide that an employer is guilty of unlawful discrimination.

Regulation 33 allows a claimant, or potential claimant, to serve on the defendant a questionnaire specified in Sched 2 to the regulations and a form for responding to such a questionnaire is set out in Sched 3. If such a questionnaire is sent by a claimant, or potential claimant, then the response, or lack of response, to the questionnaire can be used as evidence in any tribunal case and a tribunal will be able to draw inferences if a defendant has refused to answer a question or has given an evasive or equivocal answer. Once again, this procedure is standard in all discrimination cases.

Chapter 5

Religious discrimination in education

According to the European Court of Human Rights in *Cosans v UK* ECtHR 25 February 1982: 'the education of children is the whole process whereby, in any society, adults endeavour to transmit their beliefs, culture and other values to the young' and the fundamental nature of this task means that education is inevitably a source of both political and legal controversy. The more diverse a society is, the more the law attempts to accommodate diversity, the more difficult it is to establish exactly what are the 'beliefs, culture and other values' which need to be transmitted to the young and the more vital the task is. As was noted by Baroness Hale in *Begum v Denbigh High School* [2006] UKHL 15, para 97:

> . . . schools are different. Their task is to educate the young from all the many and diverse families and communities in this country in accordance with the national curriculum. Their task is to help all of their pupils achieve their full potential. This includes growing up to play whatever part they choose in the society in which they are living. The school's task is also to promote the ability of people of diverse races, religions and cultures to live together in harmony.

However, this responsibility for developing a harmonious and unified school community may find itself in conflict with the desires of individual pupils or parents to manifest their religion or to follow specific patterns of religious belief which may conflict with general school policies and priorities. Both Parliament and the courts have attempted to resolve these tensions with varying degrees of success.

Exemptions for educational establishments

In Britain, rightly or wrongly, religions are heavily involved in education and for that reason in both the Equality Act 2006 and the Employment Equality (Religion or Belief) Regulations 2003 special exemptions have been given to schools in particular with regard to exemptions for faith schools. These provisions are set out in ss 49–51, 59 and 61 of the Equality Act 2006 and in regs 20 and 39 of the Employment Equality (Religion or Belief) Regulations 2003 (see Appendix D).

Equality Bill 2006

The Equality Act 2006 is considered in detail in Chapter 3 but when the Bill was passing through Parliament, exemptions for faith schools were the subject of particular debate and government spokesmen were at pains to emphasise that the religious discrimination provisions in the Act should not be used to challenge existing educational practices or school status. Home Office Minister Baroness Scotland said (Hansard, 13 July 2005, col 1136):

> I know that some people would like to use this Bill as an opportunity to pursue a separate agenda to do with the existence of faith schools and their place in a largely secular society. Others here are deeply engaged in and committed to faith-based education. For that purpose, I should declare my own interest as a practising Catholic whose son attends a faith-based school. I need to make it clear that the Government are firmly of the view that faith-based schools make an important contribution to the diversity of our education provision. Therefore we do not intend this Bill to affect the status quo in terms of their continued existence and their ability to operate in accordance with their particular ethos.

Similarly, Home Office Minister Paul Goggins said (Hansard, 6 December 2005, col 171):

> We do not want individuals who argue that something is of detriment to them to be able to challenge the school and embroil it in all kinds of legal challenge, debate and argument in an unfair and burdensome way. We want to make it clear that we do not want individuals to pursue legal action along those lines . . . The Government have no intention under the Bill of reopening the role of faith schools. Faith schools have a right to operate effectively and they must be free to discriminate in certain respects on religious grounds.

Private fee paying schools, as well as publicly funded schools, are governed by s 49(1) of the Equality Act 2006, which makes it unlawful for a school to discriminate on religious grounds against a person:

(a) in the terms on which it offers to admit him as a pupil,
(b) by refusing to accept an application to admit him as a pupil, or
(c) where he is a pupil of the establishment—

(i) in the way in which it affords him access to any benefit, facility or service,

(ii) by refusing him access to a benefit, facility or service,

(iii) by excluding him from the establishment, or

(iv) by subjecting him to any other detriment.

However, s 50 then goes on to list various exemptions to this general prohibition. Subsections 49(1)(a), (b), (c)(i) and (ii) do not apply to a school designated under s 69(3) of the School Standards and Framework Act 1998, nor do they apply to a school listed in the register of independent schools for England or for Wales where the entry in the register records that the school has a religious ethos; the register itself being authorised by s 158 of the Education Act 2002.

Whether a school is designated under s 69, or is on the register, is a matter of fact and where it applies it will provide a complete defence to any claim of discrimination under s 49(1)(a), (b), (c)(i) or (ii). However, it is worth noting that s 50 does not provide any defence to a claim under s 49(c)(iii) or (iv), namely actions of discrimination involving:

(iii) by excluding him from the establishment, or

(iv) by subjecting him to any other detriment.

What this means is that whilst a faith school can discriminate against a child on religious grounds, in deciding not to offer him a place in the school, they cannot afterwards exclude him if he, or his parents, subsequently change or lose their faith. The phrase 'any other detriment' is also somewhat open-ended. As is discussed in Chapter 6, the same phrase, in the Race Relations Act 1976 and the Sex Discrimination Act 1975, was used to develop the concept of sexual and racial harassment, even though this was not laid down in the legislation itself and therefore, despite Paul Goggins' views, it could well be that 'any other detriment' could be used as a Trojan Horse to mount a variety of legal challenges to the practices of faith schools.

This danger is partly taken care of by s 50(2), which says that:

(2) Section 49(1)(c)(i), (ii) or (iv) shall not apply in relation to anything done in connection with—

(a) the content of the curriculum, or

(b) acts of worship or other religious observance organised by or on behalf of an educational establishment (whether or not forming part of the curriculum).

In Hansard (13 July 2005, col 1140) Baroness Scotland said of this provision:

. . . parents are, of course, entitled to their views, but we do not intend to let them use this legislation to impose those views on the majority . . . Some religiously conservative groups or sects within religious groups may object to mixed-sex classes or to sports activities. Some religiously conservative groups also object to sports provision for girls. Some groups may attempt to undermine the very diversity which the curriculum seeks to maintain and which the legislation seeks to protect. Schools need to be confident that they can follow the curriculum without being challenged. No subject should be squeezed out of the curriculum because schools feel vulnerable under the Bill. They should not be required to justify practices which might constitute indirect discrimination on harassment merely because they are properly abiding by education law and following a reasonable and balanced approach to the curriculum.

Paul Goggins made a similar point in Hansard (6 December 2005, col 171):

We do not believe that the concept of individual rights should be used by those who may not agree with particular aspects of the curriculum in our schools as a means of challenging existing school policies of inclusiveness and diversity in the curriculum that are set out in statute. The Education Act 2002 provides for a basic curriculum that every main-tained school is required to follow. There would be considerable concern if there were a suggestion that the way in which dancing, singing, music, physical education or even science lessons were taught should be changed to avoid challenge on the grounds of the religion or belief of certain children or their parents. That would clearly be unacceptable.

Whilst in *Begum v Denbigh High School* [2006] UKHL 15, para 97, Baroness Hale said:

Like it or not, this is a society committed, in principle and in law, to equal freedom for men and women to choose how they will lead their lives within the law. Young girls from ethnic, cultural or religious minorities growing up here face particularly difficult choices: how far to adopt or to distance themselves from the dominant culture. A good school will enable and support them.

Therefore, it seems clear, both politically and legally, that schools should not be required to change their policies or practices so as to accommodate particular religious views or practices that are in conflict with the general practices of the school and the national curriculum.

In deciding whether a school rule or practice, which is alleged to be dis-criminatory, can be reasonably justified for the purposes of s 45(3)(d) a court is entitled to take account of the age of the pupils and the fact that adults do have both the right, and the obligation, to take decisions on their behalf. In *Dahlab v Switzerland* ECmHR Application No 42393/98 15 February 2001 the European Commission on Human Rights noted, with regard to a teacher wearing a jilbab:

> The Court accepts that it is very difficult to assess the impact that a powerful external symbol such as the wearing of a headscarf may have on the freedom of conscience and religion of very young children. The applicant's pupils were aged between four and eight, an age at which children wonder about many things and are also more easily influenced than older pupils. In those circumstances, it cannot be denied outright that the wearing of a headscarf might have some kind of proselytising effect.

Whilst in *Begum v Denbigh High School* [2006] UKHL 15, para 93, Baroness Hale said:

> Important physical, cognitive and psychological developments take place during adolescence. Adolescence begins with the onset of puberty; from puberty to adulthood, the 'capacity to acquire and utilise knowledge reaches its peak efficiency'; and the capacity for formal operational thought is the forerunner to developing the capacity to make autonomous moral judgments. Obviously, these developments happen at different times and at different rates for different people. But it is not at all surprising to find adolescents making different moral judgments from those of their parents. It is part of growing up. The fact that they are not yet fully adult may help to justify interference with the choices they have made. It cannot be assumed, as it can with adults, that these choices are the product of a fully developed individual autonomy.

That does not of course mean that schools can ignore the views of pupils or parents with impunity, nor that they cannot adapt their practices so as to accommodate parental or pupil wishes, but any such accommodation must itself be non-discriminatory. For example, if a school had a policy of having mixed changing rooms for PE and mixed PE classes, many parents might object either on religious or personal grounds. A school would be entitled to respond to those concerns by switching to separate changing rooms or indeed separating boys' and girls' PE lessons, but it would have to apply any such policy equally. Deciding, for example, that only Muslim girl pupils could have separate PE lessons would be direct discrimination against those girl pupils who were not Muslims; similarly, leaving it as a personal choice for parents or pupils could constitute indirect discrimination; after all, one does not have to be a Muslim girl to find undressing in front of boys either distressing or offensive.

School uniforms and religious symbols

Whilst not specifically dealt with in the Equality Act 2006, the subject of school uniform and its conformity with religious beliefs and obligations is a controversial subject, as was shown by the case of *Begum v Denbigh High School*, which dealt with the demand by a Muslim girl that she should be allowed to wear the jilbab (a long garment covering arms, legs and hair) in defiance of the schools rules relating to uniform. The case went through the High Court [2004] EWHC 1389 (Admin), Court of Appeal ([2005] EWCA Civ 199), and House of Lords ([2006] UKHL 15) and even though it was brought under Art 9 of the European Convention on Human Rights (Chapter 2), its principles are applicable to cases brought under the Equality Act 2006.

Any uniform that was laid down by a school would not constitute direct discrimination but could be argued to constitute indirect discrimination contrary to s 45(3), but any such indirect discrimination is permissible if the school can 'reasonably justify' it (s 45(3)(d)). In *Begum* the court noted that schools had the right to decide on their own policies regarding school uniform and that courts were not qualified to interfere with the fine judgments which might need to be made. Lord Bingham said (para 34):

> It [the school] had taken immense pains to devise a uniform policy which respected Muslim beliefs but did so in an inclusive, unthreatening and uncompetitive way. The rules laid down were as far from being mindless as uniform rules could ever be. The school had enjoyed a period of harmony and success to which the uniform policy was thought to contribute. On further enquiry it still appeared that the rules were acceptable to mainstream Muslim opinion. It was feared that acceding to the respondent's request would or might have significant adverse repercussions. It would in my opinion be irresponsible of any court, lacking the experience, background and detailed knowledge of the head teacher, staff and governors, to overrule their judgment on a matter as sensitive as this. The power of decision has been given to them for the compelling reason that they are best placed to exercise it, and I see no reason to disturb their decision.

The House of Lords also accepted that a school was entitled to rely on the fact that its rules regarding uniform had been accepted by the girl's parents before she joined the school. As Lord Hoffmann said (para 50):

> Her family had chosen that school for her with knowledge of its uniform requirements. She could have sought the help of the school and the local education authority in solving the problem. They would no doubt have advised her that if she was firm in her belief, she should change schools.

That might not have been entirely convenient for her, particularly when her sister was remaining at Denbigh High, but people sometimes have to suffer some inconvenience for their beliefs.

The tests of reasonableness and proportionality under Art 9(2) are, in essence, the same as the tests under s 45(3)(d).

Religious symbols

It is important for any rules on school uniform or religious symbols to be applied consistently and in a non-discriminatory way. A school therefore could decide to ban all religious symbols but, unless it is a faith school, it cannot pick and choose which religious symbols to ban. For example, if school teachers and/or pupils are banned from wearing crosses, then other religious symbols must be banned also, including Sikh turbans and Muslim hijabs and if the school does not do this then it will be guilty of discrimination.

In *Dahlab v Switzerland* ECmHR Application no 42393/98 15 February 2001 the European Commission on Human Rights held that the Islamic hijab was 'a powerful external symbol [of religious belief]' and on that basis if a pupil, or teacher is allowed to wear a hijab then other pupils, and teachers, must similarly be allowed to wear religious symbols of their choice, such as a cross. There have been reports of some schools banning the wearing of crosses by pupils whilst permitting the wearing of hijabs and Sikh jewellery, but when the Equality Act 2006 comes into force any such uniform rules would constitute unlawful discrimination. There have been attempts to justify such policies on the grounds that wearing a hijab is compulsory in Islam but wearing a cross is not compulsory in Christianity, but this is a theologically questionable opinion, and in any event, it is not the role of a secular authority, such as a school, to decide what are or are not the compulsory requirements of a religion: *R (Williamson) v Secretary of State for Education and Employment* [2005] UKHL 15, para 22.

Because faith schools are exempt from s 49, they are allowed to have uniform rules which are discriminatory; for example, a Muslim school could require all its girl pupils and/or female teachers to wear a jilbab regardless of their religion and a Christian school could decide to ban both the jilbab and the hijab whilst still permitting the wearing and/or display of crosses.

Employment Equality (Religion or Belief) Regulations 2003

The Employment Equality (Religion or Belief) Regulations 2003 are discussed in detail in Chapter 4.

Regulation 20 applies the regulations to admission as a student in a university or further education college and in general terms it is illegal for either of these institutions to discriminate on religious grounds in admitting people as students or discriminating against them once they are admitted. Regulation 20(3), however, says:

> (3) Paragraph (1) does not apply if the discrimination only concerns training which would help fit a person for employment which, by virtue of regulation 7 (exception for genuine occupational requirement), the employer could lawfully refuse to offer the person in question.

Genuine occupational requirements (GORs) are discussed in detail in Chapter 4 but reg 20(3) clearly allows discrimination with regard to vocational training required for a particular religious post. For example, a university which was offering a Doctor of Divinity course could give preference to applicants who were planning to join the priesthood and who required a DD qualification in order to enter a seminary; similarly a catering college could reserve places for Muslims in a course on halal butchery, since only a practising Muslim can actually work as a halal butcher. However, a college that was offering a course on the history and theology of Islam could not discriminate, directly or indirectly, in favour of Muslim students, since both Muslims and non-Muslims would have valid grounds for studying the subject.

Regulation 39 states:

> (1) These Regulations are without prejudice to—
>
> (a) sections 58 to 60 and 124A of the School Standards and Framework Act 1998 (appointment and dismissal of teachers in schools with a religious character etc); and
> (b) section 21 of the Education (Scotland) Act 1980 (management of denominational schools).

These provisions were inserted because, as was stated by Paul Goggins in the House of Commons debate on 6 December 2005, the government believe that 'Faith schools have a right to operate effectively and they must be free to discriminate in certain respects on religious grounds' and, as was stated by Baroness Scotland on 13 July 2005, the government 'are firmly of the view that faith-based schools make an important contribution to the diversity of our education provision'.

In effect, the legislation set out in reg 39(1)(a) allows discrimination by faith schools in order to ensure that they retain their religious character. In particular, s 60 of the School Standards and Framework Act 1998 permits preference in employment, promotion, etc. to be given to teachers:

(i)   whose religious opinions are in accordance with the tenets of the religion or religious denomination specified in relation to the school under section 69(4), or

(ii) who attend religious worship in accordance with those tenets, or

(iii) who give, or are willing to give, religious education at the school in accordance with those tenets; and . . .

whilst disciplinary action may also be taken against a teacher for:

any conduct on his part which is incompatible with the precepts, or with the upholding of the tenets, of the religion or religious denomination so specified [i.e. the religion sponsoring the school].

Similarly, ss 124A and 124B of the School Standards and Framework Act 1998 were added to that Act in response to the bringing in of the Employment Equality (Religion or Belief) Regulations 2003 in order to allow independent schools with a religious character to give preference in employment, promotion or remuneration to teachers:

(a) whose religious opinions are in accordance with the tenets of the religion or the religious denomination specified in relation to the school under section 124B(2), or

(b) who attend religious worship in accordance with those tenets, or

(c) who give, or are willing to give, religious education at the school in accordance with those tenets.

The end result is that whilst the 2003 regulations are relatively straightforward to apply to cases of employment in 'ordinary' state schools, they are far more complex in situations involving teachers in faith schools. The exact situation will depend on the precise status of the school in question and the exact role and duties of the teacher.

Human rights

Articles 9 and 10 of the European Convention on Human Rights have been considered in detail in Chapter 2 and both articles apply to schools and education authorities. In addition, there is Art 2 of the First Protocol to the Convention, which deals with the 'right to education':

No person shall be denied the right to education. In the exercise of any functions which it assumes in relation to education and to teaching, the State shall respect the right of parents to ensure such education and teaching in conformity with their own religious and philosophical convictions.

In the cases of *Begum v Denbigh High School* [2006] UKHL 15 and *Sahin v Turkey* ECtHR Application No 4477/98 10 November 2006 the applicants in each case relied on Art 2 as well as Art 9. Both cases had similarities, since they both involved Muslim females excluded from their place of education (Denbigh High School for Begum, Istanbul University for Sahin) because of their insistence on wearing Islamic dress. In both cases the court (House of Lords for Begum, European Court of Human Rights for Sahin) decided that the questions in the case revolved around Art 9 and that in practice Art 2 added nothing to the arguments advanced by the parties involved. This is likely to be the case in most cases involving allegations of religious discrimination by schools. If the actions of the school can be objectively justified either by reference to Art 9(2) or by reference to any exemptions for religious discrimination in the Equality Act 2006 then it is unlikely that a school would be guilty of 'denying' the pupil their Art 2 right to an education.

Universities are also covered by the European Convention on Human Rights including Art 10 (freedom of expression). However, in addition to Art 10, universities have to comply with s 43 of the Education (No 2) Act 1986, which states that:

(1) Every individual and body of persons concerned in the government of any establishment to which this section applies shall take such steps as are reasonably practicable to ensure that freedom of speech within the law is secured for members, students and employees of the establishment and for visiting speakers.

and therefore goes further than Art 10 because it lays a positive obligation on universities to ensure the right to freedom of speech, whilst Art 10 merely prevents a university interfering with freedom of speech.

Section 43(3) requires a university to have a code of practice regulating:

(a) the procedures to be followed by members, students and employees of the establishment in connection with the organisation:

    (i)   of meetings which are to be held on premises of the establishment and which fall within any class of meeting specified in the code; and

    (ii) of other activities which are to take place on those premises and which fall within any class of activity so specified; and

(b) the conduct required of such persons in connection with any such meeting or activity; and dealing with such other matters as the governing body considers appropriate.

In *Sahin v Turkey* ECtHR Application No 4477/98 10 November 2006 the European Court of Human Rights accepted that regulations laid down by the University of Istanbul regarding the conduct of students in the university were rules 'prescribed by law' for the purpose of Art 9(2) and on the same basis a code of practice laid down by a university under s 43(3) would be regarded as rules 'prescribed by law' for the purposes of Art 10(2).

Under s 43(2):

> (2) The duty imposed by subsection 1 of above includes (in particular) the duty to ensure, so far as is reasonably practicable, that the use of any premises of the establishment is not denied to any individual or body of persons on any ground connected with:
>
> (a) the beliefs or views of that individual or any member of that body; or
> (b) the policy or objectives of that body.

This means, amongst other things, that a university cannot close down or restrict the activities of a student religious organisation merely because such an organisation may have views, for example on homosexuality, which the university or Students' Union may disagree with, and it must also ensure that the right to free speech by members of such an organisation is not interfered with.

A student religious organisation would, incidentally, be classified as an 'organisation relating to religion or belief' for the purposes of s 57 of the Equality Act 2006 and therefore, if it were to restrict its membership to believers in a particular religion, such a restriction would be lawful and thus could not be prohibited by the university. If a university did attempt to interfere in such a way with a students' religious organisation then it would be interfering with the students' rights under Art 9 (freedom of religion) and Art 11 (freedom of association) of the European Convention on Human Rights.

Chapter 6

Religious harassment

General background

There are two main ways in which harassment on the grounds of religion is dealt with by the law. Where there is religious harassment of an employee in connection with their employment then a claim can be brought under reg 5 of the Employment Equality (Religion or Belief) Regulations 2003; in all other cases a claim can be brought under the Protection from Harassment Act 1997.

When the government initially introduced the Equality Bill into Parliament, cl 47 of the Bill proposed a general tort of religious harassment, based on reg 5; cl 47 was, however, removed by the House of Lords and the government accepted the removal. It was common ground in the debate on cl 47 that all forms of religious harassment could already be dealt with by means of a claim for damages and/or an injunction, under the Protection from Harassment Act 1997 and for that reason both reg 5 and the 1997 Act are considered in this chapter.

Claims of harassment contrary to reg 5 must be brought in the employment tribunal within three months of the last incident of harassment complained of (see Chapter 4 for tribunal procedure); civil claims under the Protection from Harassment Act 1997 can be brought in either the High Court or the county court and must be brought within six years of the last incident of harassment complained of (s 6 of the Act); criminal charges under s 2 of the Act must be brought within six months of the last incident of harassment complained of: *DPP v Baker* [2004] EWHC 2782 (Admin).

Regulation 5

When the Employment Equality (Religion or Belief) Regulations 2003 were brought into force, the concept of harassment in the workplace had been well established for a number of years. Racial harassment was recognised as being contrary to the Race Relations Act 1976 and sexual harassment as contrary to the Sex Discrimination Act 1975. However, though the phrases 'racial harassment' and 'sexual harassment' have been widely used in cases under these Acts, there was, until 2003, no specific definition of harassment in either of the two acts. Claims alleging harassment were brought under s 6(2)(b) of the Sex Discrimination Act 1975 or s 4(2)(c) of the Race Relations Act 1976, both of which prohibited employers from subjecting employees to discrimination or to 'any other detriment'. Harassing behaviour was regarded by courts and tribunals to be behaviour which constituted a 'detriment'.

Throughout the EU sexual harassment at work was dealt with differently by the laws in each Member State and this was considered by some to be undesirable. Therefore, as part of its goal to ensure common working standards throughout the EU, the following definition of harassment was adopted by the EU in Council Directive 2002/73/EC and EU Council Directive 2000/78/EC:

> Unwanted conduct with the purpose or effect of violating the dignity of a person and of creating an intimidating, hostile, degrading, humiliating or offensive environment.

It was decided by the British Government to adopt this definition virtually unchanged as the definition of harassment for all forms of discrimination. The only significant change being that, in place of the EU wording 'and of creating' the UK definition is 'or of creating'; the government taking the view that it was impossible to conceive of a situation where harassment occurred which violated the dignity of a person but which did not create an intimidating, hostile, degrading, humiliating or offensive environment. Whether that view is correct is perhaps debatable, but the new definition must be considered on its own merits, since reg 2(3) states that ' "detriment" does not include harassment within the meaning of regulation 5'; therefore, claims of religious harassment in the workplace must be brought under reg 5 and cannot be claimed as 'harassment and/or detriment'. For reasons which seem difficult to understand, the government did not adopt the new definition of harassment on the same date for all forms of discrimination but instead introduced it for racial harassment on 19 July 2003 in the Race Relations Act 1976 (Amendment Regulations) 2003 SI 2003/1626, for disability harassment on 1 October 2004 in the Disability Discrimination Act 1995 (Amendment) Regulation 2003 SI 2003/1673, and for sexual harassment on 1 October 2005 in the Employment Equality (Sex Discrimination) Regulations 2005 SI 2005/2467, whilst reg 5 of the Employment Equality (Religion of Belief) Regulations 2003 came into force on 2 December 2003. Because of the adoption of this new statutory definition of harassment, old cases where tribunals decided that particular types of behaviour did not constitute sexual or racial harassment should be approached with caution and may well be overruled by the new definition of harassment. However, it does seem that behaviour which would have been considered as harassment under the 'any other detriment' case law will continue to be regarded as harassment under the new statutory definition.

Requirements of reg 5

(1) For the purposes of these Regulations, a person ('A') subjects another person ('B') to harassment where, on grounds of religion or belief, A engages in unwanted conduct which has the purpose or effect of—

(a) violating B's dignity; or
(b) creating an intimidating, hostile, degrading, humiliating or offensive environment for B.

(2) Conduct shall be regarded as having the effect specified in paragraph (1)(a) or (b) only if, having regard to all the circumstances, including in particular the perception of B, it should reasonably be considered as having that effect.

Therefore, in order for conduct by A to constitute harassment it must either:

(a) have the purpose of violating B's dignity; *or*
(b) have the purpose of creating an intimidating, hostile, degrading, humiliating or offensive environment for B; *or*
(c) have the effect of violating B's dignity; *or*
(d) have the effect of creating an intimidating, hostile, degrading, humiliating or offensive environment for B.

In order to prove a claim of religious harassment contrary to reg 5, the alleged harasser (A) must engage in 'unwanted conduct' and must do so 'on grounds of religion or belief'. Whether conduct is unwanted will be a matter of fact for a tribunal to determine but, for example, if employees are engaging in mutual banter about religion, it may be rather difficult for one employee who is participating in that banter suddenly to take offence at a particular thing that is said and to claim that as harassment unless what was said was so beyond the bounds of the general banter that it could be considered as clearly unwanted. Whether conduct is unwanted is usually a question of fact varying from case to case; if someone asks that particular behaviour should stop then it is obvious that the conduct is 'unwanted' from that moment on, but it is not essential that the victim state that they dislike particular behaviour in order for it to be unwanted; a degree of common sense must be applied. In *Reed v Stedman* [1999] IRLR 299, where the defendant made a sexually suggestive remark and attempted to look up the complainant's skirt, the Employment Appeal Tribunal said (at para 30):

... it seems to be the argument that because the Code [the ACAS Code] refers to 'unwanted conduct' it cannot be said that a single act can ever amount to harassment because until done and rejected it cannot be said that the conduct is 'unwanted'. We regard this argument as specious. If it were correct it would mean that a man was always entitled to argue that every act of harassment was different from the first and that he was testing to see if it was unwanted; in other words it would amount to a licence for harassment . . . The word 'unwanted' is essentially the same as 'unwelcome' or 'uninvited'. No one other than a person used to engaging in loutish behaviour could think that the remark made in this case was other than obviously unwanted.

Similarly, in *Heads v Insitu Cleaning Co* [1995] IRLR 4, when a women employee was greeted with the words 'Hiya, big tits' as she walked into a meeting, that remark was accepted as being obviously unwanted.

Therefore, if a Mormon employee was to be greeted each day with the words 'Oh God it's holy Joe Smith' or 'are you wearing your temple undies today', then that type of behaviour would constitute 'unwanted' conduct without the victim needing to object to it first. But evidence of mutual banter, or the fact that an exchange was initiated by the alleged victim, might mean that remarks which would otherwise constitute harassment would not be harassment in that particular situation. For example, if a religious member of staff said that he was going on pilgrimage to 'pray for all you sinners' then a response 'don't bother praying for me, religion is just a load of rubbish' would probably not constitute harassment even though it might be regarded as an unnecessarily aggressive response.

Secondly, the unwanted conduct must be engaged in by A 'on the grounds of religion or belief'. It is unclear from the wording of reg 5 whether the conduct must be on the grounds of religion or belief of A himself or on the grounds of religion or belief of B, but para 1.4 of the ACAS guidelines on the regulations (Appendix C–2) indicate that reg 5 could cover either situation. The ACAS guidelines also consider that reg 5 covers harassment directed not just at the religion or belief of the victim but also at the religion or belief of any person with whom the victim associates and it is likely that tribunals will agree with and adopt the wide-ranging ACAS definition which is consistent with the way other types of discrimination law have been interpreted. Provided that the harassment is on 'on the grounds of religion or belief', it will be irrelevant whether it is on the grounds of religion or belief of A, or of B or of someone with whom B associates.

It is, however, essential that the conduct is engaged in by A 'on the grounds of religion or belief'. Merely because A engages in conduct to which B objects 'on the grounds of religion or belief', that will not be sufficient to constitute harassment of B contrary to reg 5 unless the conduct is engaged in by A 'on the grounds of religion or belief'. For example, there have been media reports that some workplaces have been telling staff to remove mugs which contain pictures of pigs and not to have any items on their desk etc. which relate to pigs, the reason for these instructions being concern that such references to pigs might harass Muslims; however, it is doubtful whether employers can justify such instructions if the mugs etc. are not introduced for the purpose of causing harassment to Muslims etc. but are merely personal items which the employee has with them anyway. If a new employee, who is Muslim, starts in an office and one of their co-workers then brings in a mug with a pig picture on it or puts a model of a pig on their desk, then it might not be too difficult to establish that such behaviour was done 'for the purpose' of 'creating an intimidating, hostile, degrading, humiliating or offensive environment' for the Muslim employee. However, if a co-worker merely happens to possess a pig mug or model because, for example, they bought it on a visit to a farm or nature reserve or it was given to them by a son or daughter and has sentimental value, then there is no reason why they should be asked to remove it. The mug etc. is not in their possession 'on grounds of religion or belief' and therefore cannot constitute harassment, albeit that a Muslim worker, for their own personal reasons, might find it offensive. Similarly, a display of the St George flag might be objected to by some Muslims on the basis that it is a 'Crusaders' flag but if the St George flag is being displayed for reasons of patriotism or, more probably, out of support for the England football team, then it is not being displayed 'on grounds of religion or belief' and therefore would not constitute harassment under reg 5.

For the purpose of reg 5 it is irrelevant whether the person doing the harassment is a member of the same religion as the victim of the harassment. For example, two women, A and B, work in a Catholic book shop. Wherever she can, B goes to a Catholic church where there is a celebration of the Tridentine (traditional Latin) Catholic Mass, whilst A goes only to churches where the Mass is in the new modern form in English, and A makes regular sarcastic comments to B about 'out of date' Catholics hanging on to 'mumbo jumbo Latin'. Even though both A and B are members of the same religion, A would still be guilty of harassment of B because her comments would be made 'on grounds of religion or belief'.

Where the conduct complained of is engaged in with the 'purpose' of violating dignity etc., then that should be capable of proof through evidence of the actions or words of A. For example, if Muslim employee B had stated in a conversation with co-worker A that, for religious reasons, B found pictures of pigs offensive and the next day A put a picture of a pig on his desk, then that might well be good evidence that A put the picture on his desk with 'the purpose' of 'creating an offensive environment' for B. Similarly, if a Christian employee was to ask his colleagues to stop using the words 'Jesus Christ' as a swear word in his presence and they did not stop doing so, then it would seem likely that they were engaging in that conduct 'for the purpose' of creating an offensive environment for their Christian colleague.

Where a tribunal is satisfied that particular behaviour was engaged in for 'the purpose' of causing harassment then that will usually be sufficient to prove the case. More difficult problems arise where the harassment has the 'effect' of violating dignity etc. but it is not proved that that was its 'purpose'. When this is the situation, tribunals and employers will have to consider reg 5(2):

> (2) Conduct shall be regarded as having the effect specified in paragraph (1)(a) or (b) only if, having regard to all the circumstances, including in particular the perception of B, it should reasonably be considered as having that effect.

Regulation 5(2) therefore requires tribunals to apply an objective 'reasonableness' test to allegations that conduct has had the 'effect' of violating dignity etc. It is, however, a reasonableness test that is somewhat skewed in favour of the subjective point of view of the victim. Questions will arise over the clause that the tribunal should have regard to all the circumstances including 'in particular the perception of B'. Does 'in particular' mean that the perception of B overrides other circumstances and other points of view? The proper interpretation of reg 5(2) would seem to be that the perception of B is merely one of the factors that a tribunal must have regard to, even though it is clearly a very important factor; if all other factors are equal, then the perception of B becomes the dominant fact on which the tribunal should base its decision but the perception of B cannot override all other circumstances. Therefore, if A is doing something which is in accordance with his own religion, and is otherwise lawful, then even though B may dislike those actions, that would not be sufficient for them to qualify as harassment. For example, if A is a Muslim woman who wears a niqab (a veil covering the lower part of her face) then many of her fellow workers may find that offensive but that would not mean that the wearing of the niqab constituted harassment. As Baroness Hale said in *Begum v Denbigh High School* [2006] UKHL 15, para 96:

> ... the sight of a woman in full purdah may offend some people, and especially those western feminists who believe that it is a symbol of her oppression, but that could not be a good reason for prohibiting her from wearing it.

In determining whether behaviour is reasonable a tribunal should have regard to the judgment of the EAT in *Driskel v Peninsular Business Services Ltd* (2000) IRLR 151, where the EAT laid down that in determining whether sexual harassment took place the tribunal must look at all the facts and not fall into the error of looking at each individual incident in isolation. In para 3 of the judgment, the EAT said:

There is a tendency, however, where many evidentiary incidents or items are introduced, to be carried away by them and to treat each of the allegations, incidents or items as if they were themselves the subject of a complaint. In the present case it was necessary for the Tribunal to find the primary facts about those allegations. It was not, however, necessary for the Tribunal to ask itself, in relation to each such incident or item, whether it was itself explicable on 'racial grounds' or on other grounds. That is a misapprehension about the nature and purpose of evidentiary facts. The function of the Tribunal is to find the primary facts from which they will be asked to draw inferences and then for the Tribunal to look at the totality of those facts (including the respondent's explanations) in order to see whether it is legitimate to infer that the acts or decisions complained of in the originating applications were on 'racial grounds' . . . The process of inference is itself a matter of applying common sense and judgment to the facts, and assessing the probabilities.

The EAT, in para 4, quoted with approval the words of an American judgment: '. . . the trier of fact must keep in mind that each successive episode has its predecessors, that the impact of the separate incidents may accumulate'. Therefore, an incident which in itself seems trivial may be significant because it is part of a pattern of incidents directed towards B which, looked at as a whole, demonstrate behaviour which a reasonable person would regard as 'violating B's dignity; or creating an intimidating, hostile, degrading, humiliating or offensive environment for B'. For example, if a Muslim woman chose not to wear a hijab it would not, in itself, be harassment for her Muslim co-workers to ask her about this decision or to disagree with her interpretation of the Koran regarding what is acceptable clothing for a Muslim woman. However, if her co-workers were to make constant comments about 'so-called Muslim women' who refused to dress properly or refused to talk to her or acknowledge her existence then even though the individual incidents may each be trivial in themselves, their total effect would constitute harassment contrary to reg 5.

Employers are under an obligation to protect their employees from harassment and for that purpose they are entitled to issue instructions that particular religious symbols, pictures, objects, etc. are removed from the workplace; however, it is important that any such instructions are fair and do not in themselves constitute harassment or discrimination. For example, if an employer were to order a Christian employee to remove an icon she habitually kept on her desk and they did so on the basis that an icon is a religious symbol which might create an offensive environment for non-Christians, then that instruction would be lawful provided the employer required all employees to refrain from displays of religious symbolism and hence banned Muslim employees from wearing hijabs and banned Sikh employees from wearing turbans, both of which are religious symbols. To order a Christian employee to remove her religious symbols whilst allowing other employees to retain their religious symbols could be said to constitute harassment of the Christian employee because it would either 'violate her dignity' or 'create a hostile, degrading, humiliating environment' for her. This is the essence of the problem of religious harassment: one person's harassment may be another person's manifestation of religious belief.

In considering an allegation of religious harassment brought against an employer which was a religious organisation, a tribunal would have to have regard to the fact that the employer was a religious organisation as being part of 'all the circumstances'. For example, if an atheist was employed by a Catholic school, he could not complain that he found the various religious items in the school such as crucifixes, statues, etc. 'offensive' and thereby claim to be harassed because 'all the circumstances' would include the fact that the school was a church school.

It is important, however, to note that harassment stands on its own and is separate from discrimination, which means that the exemptions from the regulations, discussed in Chapter 4, do not apply to allegations of harassment and, in particular, the 'genuine occupational requirement' (GOR) defence in reg 7 does not provide any defence to a claim for harassment. Once an employee is employed, he is entitled not to be subjected to religious (or indeed any other form of) harassment. For example, an atheist might be employed as an accountant by a Catholic school on the basis that mathematics is religiously neutral and therefore there was no GOR for the accountant to be a Catholic or indeed a believer of any sort. Though the atheist would not be entitled to complain about the use of religious symbolism in the school, he would be entitled to bring an action for harassment under reg 5 if he is subjected by staff members, or pupils, to critical references regarding his lack of belief or regular warnings about his fate in the afterlife.

Under reg 6(3): 'it is unlawful for an employer in relation to employment by him at an establishment in Great Britain, to subject to harassment a person whom he employed or has applied to him for employment'. The words 'subject to harassment' have a number of different meanings. First, it is, of course, unlawful for the employer himself personally to harass an employee; second, it is unlawful for fellow employees to subject another employee to harassment or for customers or persons working or having dealings with the employee to do so. These principles are common to all forms of discrimination law and have been defined in a number of employment cases which, in general terms, can be summarised as follows. Once an employer is informed by an employee that other employees are making harassing remarks, comments, etc., then the employer is fixed with that knowledge and is obliged to take some action to deal with it. If he is aware that customers etc. of the employer are subjecting his employees to harassment then he is obliged to take some action, once again, to prevent that. Simply telling the employee 'to put up with it' is not acceptable.

Though previous case law may not always be relevant in determining the meaning of the new definition of harassment, the case of *Vento v Chief Constable of West Yorkshire Police* [2002] EWCA Civ 1871, para 65, certainly will. In this case the Court of Appeal laid down guidelines for tribunals in assessing the damages that should be awarded in cases of racial or sexual harassment and the same guidelines will also be applied to the assessment of damages for claims of religious harassment under reg 5:

> The top band should normally be between £15,000 and £25,000. Sums in this range should be awarded in the most serious cases, such as where there has been a lengthy campaign of discriminatory harassment on the ground of sex or race. This case falls within that band. Only in the most exceptional case should an award of compensation for injury to feelings exceed £25,000.
>
> The middle band of between £5,000 and £15,000 should be used for serious cases, which do not merit an award in the highest band.
>
> Awards of between £500 and £5,000 are appropriate for less serious cases, such as where the act of discrimination is an isolated or one-off occurrence. In general, awards of less than £500 are to be avoided altogether, as they risk being regarded as so low as not to be a proper recognition of injury to feelings.

Equality Bill, cl 47

As has been indicated, a proposed tort of religious harassment in cl 47 of the Equality Bill was removed by the House of Lords. Unlike reg 5, the proposed cl 47 could have been used as the basis for obtaining an injunction as well as a basis for a claim for damages and concern was expressed in the House of Lords that cl 47 could be used by various religious groups in order to apply for injunctions to stop other religions staging events, or discussions, which they considered offensive. This concern was based in large part on the case of *Islamic Council of Victoria v Catch the Fire Ministries Inc* [2004] VCAT 2510, where 'religious vilification' legislation, in Victoria, Australia, was used by an Islamic association in order to obtain an injunction against an Evangelical Christian church and its preachers. For those who may be interested, the proposed wording of cl 47 is given below and provides an interesting comparison to reg 5:

47 Harassment

(1) For the purposes of this Part a person ('A') harasses another ('B') if on grounds of religion or belief A does anything which has the purpose or effect of—

  (a) violating B's dignity, or

(b) creating an intimidating, hostile, degrading, humiliating or offensive environment for B.

(2) In subsection (1)—

(a) 'religion or belief' means a religion or belief of B or of any other person except A, and

(b) a reference to a person's religion or belief includes a reference to a religion or belief to which he is thought to belong or subscribe.

(3) Action by A shall be regarded as having the effect described in subsection (1)(a) or (b) only if it should reasonably be regarded as having that effect having regard to—

(a) B's perception, and

(b) all the other circumstances.

(4) Where B wants A to do something, it is not harassment for the purposes of subsection (1).

Protection from Harassment Act 1997

Whilst reg 5 applies only to religious harassment in the workplace, the Protection from Harassment Act 1997 covers all forms of harassment, whether religious harassment or otherwise, and regardless of whether the harassment occurs in the workplace or outside it. The Act was primarily passed in order to deal with the problem of stalking and is indeed often referred to in the media as the 'stalking law'; however, it has been used in a number of other ways and, following the creation of racially and religiously aggravated harassment offences in s 32 of the Crime and Disorder Act 1998 (Chapter 7), it is apparent that the Act does not merely cover stalking. This was also recognised in the case of *DPP v Moseley* (1999) Times 23 June, where Collins J said: 'Whatever may have been the purpose behind the Act its words are clear, and it can cover harassment of any sort.' In the case of *Thomas v News Group Newspapers Ltd* [2001] EWCA Civ 1223 the Court of Appeal decided that the Act could be used to sue a newspaper over two articles it had published, and in *Majrowski v Guys and St Thomas's NHS Trust* [2006] UKHL 34 the House of Lords accepted that the Act could also be used to claim damages for bullying in the workplace.

Under the Act only individuals can be harassed and not organisations (*DPP v Dziurzynski* [2000] EWHC 1380 (Admin)), and therefore a church or religious organisation cannot claim that it has been harassed. However, claims under the Act could be brought by a church or other religious organisation in order to protect its members from harassment. Claims can also be brought by an individual, or a group of individuals, who have been, or might be, harassed because of their religion or belief and any injunction which was granted could protect not just the specific claimants but also any other person who shares their religion.

The basic principles behind the Protection from Harassment Act 1997 are laid down in ss 1 and 7:

1 Prohibition of harassment

(1) A person must not pursue a course of conduct—

    (a) which amounts to harassment of another, and

    (b) which he knows or ought to know amounts to harassment of the other.

(1A) A person must not pursue a course of conduct—

    (a) which involves harassment of two or more persons, and

    (b) which he knows or ought to know involves harassment of those persons, and

    (c) by which he intends to persuade any person (whether or not one of those mentioned above)—

        (i) not to do something that he is entitled or required to do, or

        (ii) to do something that he is not under any obligation to do.

(2) For the purposes of this section, the person whose course of conduct is in question ought to know that it amounts to or involves harassment of another if a reasonable person in possession of the same information would think the course of conduct amounted to or involved harassment of the other.

(3) Subsection (1) or (1A) does not apply to a course of conduct if the person who pursued it shows—

    (a) that it was pursued for the purpose of preventing or detecting crime,

    (b) that it was pursued under any enactment or rule of law or to comply with any condition or requirement imposed by any person under any enactment, or

    (c) that in the particular circumstances the pursuit of the course of conduct was reasonable.

7 Interpretation of this group of sections

(1) This section applies for the interpretation of sections 1 to 5.

(2) References to harassing a person include alarming the person or causing the person distress.

(3) A 'course of conduct' must involve—

    (a) in the case of conduct in relation to a single person (see section 1(1)), conduct on at least two occasions in relation to that person, or

     (b) in the case of conduct in relation to two or more persons (see section 1(1A)), conduct on at least one occasion in relation to each of those persons.

(3A) A person's conduct on any occasion shall be taken, if aided, abetted, counselled or procured by another

     (a) to be conduct on that occasion of the other (as well as conduct of the person whose conduct it is); and

     (b) to be conduct in relation to which the other's knowledge and purpose, and what he ought to have known, are the same as they were in relation to what was contemplated or reasonably foreseeable at the time of the aiding, abetting, counselling or procuring.

(4) 'Conduct' includes speech.

(5) References to a person, in the context of the harassment of a person, are references to a person who is an individual.

Breach of either s 1(1) or (1A) is a criminal offence punishable with up to six months' imprisonment (s 2) and in its religiously aggravated form (see Chapter 7) with up to two years' imprisonment; breach of s 1(1) or (1A) of the Act also constitutes a civil tort for which damages may be awarded and/or an injunction made (ss 3 and 3A). Breach of an injunction made under the Act is a criminal offence punishable by five years' imprisonment and this makes injunctions under the Act unusually powerful because police officers can arrest anyone whom they reasonably suspect of breaching an anti-harassment injunction, whilst the police have no power to enforce most types of injunctions.

This requirement for there to be a 'course of conduct' is the most funda-mental aspect of the Act and the area that has created the largest number of criminal appeals. Course of conduct is defined in s 7(3) as involving 'conduct on at least two occasions' and one incident of harassment, however serious it may be, is not enough to justify either a claim for damages or a prosecution under the Act. However, under s 3(1): 'An actual or apprehended breach of section 1 may be the subject of a claim in civil proceedings' and therefore an injunction may be applied for under the Act even if the claimant has not yet been the victim of a course of conduct by the defendant. All that is necessary is that there is some evidence that the claimant 'apprehends' that the defendant will pursue a course of conduct at some time in the future. For example, if someone (A) has left a religious cult and knows that the last person to leave was subjected to harassment by various members of the cult then that knowledge would probably be sufficient to justify an application for an injunction against members of the cult; A would not have to wait until he was harassed.

In order to establish a case under the 1997 Act a defendant must pursue a course of conduct, the course of conduct must amount to harassment of the claimant and the defendant must 'know or ought to know' that the course of conduct amounted to harassment of the claimant. Course of conduct is defined in s 7(3) as involving 'conduct on at least two occasions' and therefore any claim for damages will have to involve two incidents. This requirement for there to be a course of conduct for claims under the Act is in contrast to claims of harassment under reg 5, where one act of harassment can be sufficient to justify a claim. However, even though the course of conduct must involve two incidents, there is no requirement that the incidents have to be the same or even similar each time; for example, deliberately ripping up a holy picture on a Monday followed by deliberately offensive remarks about Christianity on a Wednesday could constitute a course of conduct even though the conduct was different on each occasion.

One point that must be borne in mind is that though a course of conduct must involve conduct on at least two occasions, that is still a bare minimum. If the actions complained of are clearly harassing in themselves then two occasions on their own should be sufficient to form the basis for a case but if the actions are not harassing of their nature then much more will be required than merely two incidents. For example, if a Mormon is offered tea on one day and politely declines and then is offered coffee a few days later that could technically constitute a course of conduct but a court would probably want more evidence before it found the case proved. Merely because there have been two incidents involving the same defendant and the same victim, that does not of itself necessarily prove that there has been a course of conduct. There must be some nexus between the incidents, something which shows a continuity of purpose. The distance in time between the two incidents is also relevant and the longer the length of time between incidents or the more dissimilar the incidents the less likely they are to constitute a course of conduct. This was accepted by the Divisional Court in the case of *DPP v Lau* [2000] Times 29 March, where two incidents of harassment separated by over three months were held not to constitute a course of conduct but, in para 15 of the judgment Schiemann J noted that in some situations a course of conduct could involve incidents which are a long time apart:

> . . . it seems to me, the fewer the occasions and the wider they are spread the less likely it would be that a finding of harassment can reasonably be made. One can conceive of circumstances where incidents, as far apart as a year, could constitute a course of conduct and harassment . . . racial harassment taking place outside a synagogue on a religious holiday, such as the day of atonement, and being repeated each year as the day of atonement came round.

The reference to the Jewish festival of the Day of Atonement could, of course, be extended to harassment occurring at any set of religious festivals. If harassment occurred which was linked to religious observance or religious festivals then it could constitute a course of conduct even if the harassment occurred intermittently and on widely separated dates.

Under s 7(2), '[r]eferences to harassing a person include alarming the person or causing the person distress'. 'Harassment', 'alarm' and 'distress' are not defined in the Act and so need to be given their ordinary dictionary meanings but they are words used in the criminal offences of ss 4A and 5 of the Public Order Act 1986 (see Chapter 7) and have not caused the criminal courts any difficulties of definition. In *DPP v Baron* EWHC (Admin) CO/1569/00 13 June 2000 Kennedy LJ said: 'I for my part have no problem [of interpretation] with the statute which uses ordinary English words.'

The *Oxford English Dictionary* defines harassment, alarm and distress as follows:

Harassment
1   trouble and annoy continually or repeatedly.
2   make repeated attacks on (an enemy or opponent).

Alarm
1   frighten or disturb.
2   arouse to a sense of danger.

Distress
1   subject to distress; exhaust, afflict.
2   cause anxiety to; make unhappy; vex.

Sections 4A and 5 of the Public Order Act 1986 require harassment, alarm or distress to be caused by the use of 'threatening, abusive or insulting words or behaviour or disorderly behaviour or by the display of any writing sign or other visible representation which is threatening abusive or insulting', but under the Protection from Harassment Act 1997 there is no equivalent requirement for the behaviour complained of to be 'threatening abusive or insulting'. This arises because of the fact that the initial impetus behind the Act was to deal with stalkers who invariably had no intention of threatening, abusing or insulting those they were stalking. Someone who stands every day outside a house with a notice saying 'I love you' or who sends red roses to a person's place of work every day is certainly not being threatening, abusive or insulting but could still be causing harassment, alarm or distress. Depending on the facts, therefore, almost any form of activity which annoys another person could technically be defined as harassment. An Orange band playing 'The Protestant Boys' outside a Catholic church every Sunday could constitute harassment, as could standing with an Israeli flag outside a mosque or a PLO flag outside a synagogue; desecration of, or abuse towards, religious symbols could also constitute harassment.

A specific purpose of the Act was to deal with what were perceived to be inadequacies in the existing law, the main problem being that almost all criminal offences required some evidence of intent on behalf of the alleged offender. The solution adopted in s 1(2) of the Act was to consider harassment objectively in terms of what actually happened rather than subjectively in terms of what the offender intended (s 1(2)):

> For the purposes of this section the person whose course of conduct is in question ought to know that it amounts to harassment of another if a reasonable person in possession of the same information would think the course of conduct amounted to harassment of the other.

The idea of the 'reasonable man' (today the reasonable person) is an old one in English law but what exactly is 'reasonable' can differ from place to place and person to person; for example, swearing that might be accepted on a building site would be completely unacceptable in a church – everything will depend on the place, the time and the people involved.

The provision relating to 'a reasonable person in possession of the same information' could be particularly relevant in situations involving allegations of religious harassment where someone may be claiming that a defendant has acted in a way that is religiously offensive. In that situation, the first point to establish is whether the defendant knew, or ought to have known, that their behaviour was religiously offensive. For example, if a Hindu man wears a 'shikha' or small ponytail of hair, he may find that some other men make sarcastic comments about it. It could not necessarily be assumed that those comments are animated by any religious animosity, since most non-Hindus are completely unaware that a shikha has any religious, or other, significance. However, if the other men are told that the shikha is worn for religious reasons, they are in 'possession' of that information and any further comments could then be considered as harassment. By contrast, behaviour which may appear innocuous can be harassing for reasons which are related to religion and which the person knows would cause offence; for example, if a person (A) knows that another person (B) is a Mormon and that Mormons do not drink coffee, then a course of conduct of constantly offering B coffee could constitute harassment because A is in 'possession of information' which would make a reasonable person think that the behaviour would amount to harassment. Similarly, a remark 'how's your underwear today' may be harassing if it is directed towards a Mormon whom the speaker knows is a 'temple Mormon' and is thus wearing specific underwear worn by certain Mormons following Mormon temple ceremonies. The remark, which on the surface may appear innocuous, would constitute harassment because the speaker is in possession of 'information' which means that he knows, or ought to know, that the remark would be harassing.

Therefore, if a claimant can show that a defendant was in possession of particular information which meant that they would know that their actions would cause distress or alarm then that is highly relevant to any claim under the Act. For example, if the victim is, or has been, a member of a particular religious cult which uses certain esoteric symbols which represent death or damnation, then the display of those symbols or the sending of cards or letters containing these symbols could constitute harassment even though to most people, who do not know anything about the particular religious cult in question, the symbols are on the face of it either meaningless or innocuous. It is the fact that the harasser is 'in possession of the same information' which makes him guilty of harassment because he would be engaging in conduct which he knows would harass a person who understands the significance of the symbols concerned.

Collective harassment

Even though the Protection from Harassment Act 1997 was passed primarily to deal with stalking, it has been widely used against animal rights demonstrators by companies who have used it in order to obtain anti-harassment injunctions against demonstrators. Though the Act does not protect organisations from harassment (*DPP v Dziurzynski* [2000] EWHC 1380 (Admin)), companies have been allowed to apply for injunctions to protect their employees from harassment, and religious organisations whose members are subjected to harassment can use the Act in a similar way. In *Church of Jesus Christ of Latter Day Saints v Price* [2004] EWHC 3245 the Church of Jesus Christ of Latter Day Saints (the Mormon Church) obtained a High Court anti-harassment injunction against a Mr Andrew Price because of his continual harassment of Mormon missionaries and churches. The injunction banned him from contacting any Mormon missionary or from going within 30 yards of any Mormon mission, and other religious organisations which face similar harassment could be tempted to do the same.

Under s 1(1A):

A person must not pursue a course of conduct—

(a) which involves harassment of two or more persons, and
(b) which he knows or ought to know involves harassment of those persons, and
(c) by which he intends to persuade any person (whether or not one of those mentioned above)—

(i) not to do something that he is entitled or required to do, or
(ii) to do something that he is not under any obligation to do.

The practice of a religion is, of course, something a person is 'entitled' to do and leaving a religion or cult is something that a person 'is not under any obligation to do'. Therefore, injunctions under s 1(1A) could be of particular interest to minority religions or cults which may want to ban persons from attempting to lure away or 'de-program' cult members.

Section 3A allows the High Court or a county court to make injunctions for behaviour contrary to s 1(1A), but s 3A only allows an injunction to be granted and does not provide a basis for a claim for damages. Any claim for damages must be made by an individual personally and must be made under s 3 for behaviour contrary to s 1(1).

Defence of reasonableness

Under s 1(3)(c), it is a defence to either a criminal prosecution or a claim for an injunction 'that in the particular circumstances the pursuit of the course of conduct was reasonable'.

In the case of *Hirst and Agu v Chief Constable of West Yorkshire* [1987] 85 Cr App R 00 the Divisional Court noted that before an action could be reasonable it had to be 'inherently lawful' and on this basis in *DPP v Moseley* (1999) Times, 23 June the Divisional Court held that a defendant who was acting in breach of a court injunction could not claim that his actions were reasonable.

In religious harassment cases the defence of reasonableness is most likely to be argued in the context of manifesting religious belief as protected by Art 9 of the European Convention on Human Rights (Chapter 2). This was certainly the situation in *Church of Jesus Christ of Latter Day Saints v Price* [2004] EWHC 3245, where it was alleged that Price had made over 4,000 cold calls to Mormon missionaries, preached for 30 minutes at Mormons travelling on the tube, and chased them down the street. Price, however, defended his actions on the basis that they were reasonable attempts to evangelise Mormons. Beaston J, however, granted the injunction and said of Mr Price (paras 143 and 137):

> His behaviour, although undoubtedly based on sincere religious beliefs bordered on the obsessional ... I have concluded that activities the defendant describes as preaching, and the defendant describes as addressing and challenging, can accurately be described as ranting.

In the case of *R v Colohan* [2001] EWCA Crim 1251 the Court of Appeal rejected a suggestion that mental illness afforded a defence to a charge of harassment and also the suggestion that the test of 'reasonableness' depended on the personal characteristics, i.e. mental illness, of the defendant, it was a completely objective test.

Causing fear of violence

Under s 4 of the Protection from Harassment Act 1997:

(1) A person whose course of conduct causes another to fear, on at least two occasions, that violence will be used against him is guilty of an offence if he knows or ought to know that his course of conduct will cause the other so to fear on each of those occasions.

(2) For the purposes of this section, the person whose course of conduct is in question ought to know that it will cause another to fear that violence will be used against him on any occasion if a reasonable person in possession of the same information would think the course of conduct would cause the other so to fear on that occasion.

Section 4 of the Act is a more serious criminal offence than s 2 and is punishable in the Crown Court with up to five years' imprisonment or, in its religiously aggravated form (Chapter 7), with up to seven years' imprisonment.

'Course of conduct' in s 4 has the same meaning as in s 2, namely 'conduct on at least two occasions' (s 7(3)) and again 'conduct' includes speech (s 7(4)). To prove the offence it is essential that fear of violence is caused on the two occasions complained of so that if on one occasion harassment is caused rather than fear of violence then only an offence contrary to s 2 will have been committed even if a fear of violence is caused on the other occasion. As with s 2, a reasonable person in possession of the same information would have to think that fear would be caused on the two occasions and therefore most of the defences and reasoning already discussed in relation to s 2 also apply in relation to proving or defending charges under s 4.

Whilst there are obvious threats that may cause somebody to fear violence, there could be situations in religiously aggravated cases where particular words or symbols are unusually threatening. For example, to say to a Moslem convert to Christianity 'you are an apostate to Islam and should be treated as such' might appear to a non-Muslim to be nothing more than an insulting remark; however, the words may cause the victim to fear that violence will be used against them since, under Shariah law, the penalty for apostasy from Islam is death. Another example of behaviour which could cause a person to fear that violence might be used against them would be sending messages to a Hindu which contained symbols relating to Kali, goddess of death.

Chapter 7

Religious crimes

Historically, all societies have had criminal offences which relate to religion. In the Christian West, the main religious criminal offences have been blasphemy (defamation of Christianity), heresy (expression of unacceptable religious views) and desecration (damage to, or destruction of, sacred objects and buildings). However, in Britain today the only remaining element of these old offences is the crime of blasphemy and all other offences which relate to religion are, in general, dealt with under the ordinary criminal law. For example, a burglar who breaks into a church and steals a chalice would be prosecuted for the crime of burglary and the fact that his offence also involved sacrilege of a church would not involve any separate charge. However, in addition to blasphemy, some old offences involving disorder in churches or cemeteries remain on the statute book and in 2001 a new category of religiously aggravated offences was created. An offence of stirring up religious hatred was created in the Racial and Religious Hatred Act 2006 and that offence is discussed in Chapter 8.

Blasphemy

Blasphemy (technically called blasphemous libel) is a long-established offence in English common law, and in the law of many other countries. In England, for understandable historical reasons, the blasphemy law applies to protection of the Christian religion in its Anglican (Church of England) form and was defined in the following terms in article 214 of Stephen's Digest of the Criminal Law (9th edn, 1950):

> Every publication is said to be blasphemous which contains any contemptuous, reviling, scurrilous or ludicrous matter relating to God, Jesus Christ, or the Bible, or the formularies of the Church of England as by law established. It is not blasphemous to speak or publish opinions hostile to the Christian religion, or to deny the existence of God, if the publication is couched in decent and temperate language. The test to be applied is as to the manner in which the doctrines are advocated and not

as to the substance of the doctrines themselves. Everyone who publishes any blasphemous document is guilty of the [offence] of publishing a blasphemous libel. Everyone who speaks blasphemous words is guilty of the [offence] of blasphemy.

This definition was accepted by the House of Lords in the case of *Whitehouse v Gay News Ltd and Lemon* [1979] 2 WLR 281, which was the last prosecution for blasphemy in England. Being a common law offence, blasphemy is only triable on indictment, i.e. before a jury, in the Crown Court and the maximum penalty is imprisonment for life and/or a fine. In *Bowman v Secular Society Ltd* [1917] AC 406 the House of Lords held that the gist of the crime of blasphemy was not the words that were used rather it was:

> . . . their manner, their violence or ribaldry or, more fully stated, for their tendency to endanger the peace then and there, to deprave public morality generally, to shake the fabric of society, and to be a cause of civil strife.

Prosecutions for blasphemy have been rare in the twentieth century. In *R v Gott* [1922] 16 Cr. App. R 87 a publisher was successfully prosecuted for publishing a pamphlet that compared Jesus' journey to Jerusalem with 'a circus clown on a donkey' but after that case there were no further prosecutions until 1977 and the case of *Whitehouse v Gay News Ltd and Lemon* [1979] 2 WLR 281. This was a private prosecution brought against the editor and publisher of the newspaper *Gay News* for publishing a homo-erotic poem concerning Christ and the crucifixion. The Court of Appeal upheld the conviction but revoked the sentences of imprisonment on the editor, remarking that it did not consider it an appropriate case for a prison sentence.

In 1991 in *Chief Metropolitan Stipendiary Magistrate ex p Choudhury* [1991] 1 QB 429 an attempt was made to bring a private prosecution for blasphemy against the author Salman Rushdie following the publication of his book *The Satanic Verses*. It was argued in the case that the crime of blasphemy should be extended by the courts so as to cover all religions including Islam. The Court of Appeal, however, was not prepared to extend an offence for which there had only been two prosecutions in 70 years and which the Law Commission in 1985 had recommended should be abolished (Law Com 145) and the court also noted a real practical difficulty in extending blasphemy to cover every religion:

> Since the only mental element in the offence is the intention to publish the words complained of, there would be a serious risk that the words might, unknown to the author, scandalise and outrage some sect or religion.

In *Choudhury v UK* [1991] 12 HRLJ 172 the European Commission of Human Rights did not accept a claim that because the blasphemy law in England only protected Christianity it was therefore in breach of the European Convention on Human Rights.

In the case of *Corway v Independent Newspapers (Ireland) Ltd* [1999] 4 IR 484 the Supreme Court of Ireland decided that the crime of blasphemy no longer existed in Ireland. In part this was because of the wording of the Irish Constitution and its constitutional guarantees of free speech and freedom of conscience (Appendix A) but was also because the court noted that the English common law offence of blasphemy only protected the church 'by law established' which, in England, meant the Church of England. The Supreme Court was therefore doubtful whether the common law offence of blasphemy had continued to apply in Ireland once the Church of Ireland was disestablished in 1871. If this view is correct then it could mean that blasphemy is no longer a crime in Wales, since there has been no church 'by law established' in Wales since the disestablishment of the Anglican Church in Wales in 1920.

The future of the blasphemy law was examined by a committee of the House of Lords (the legislature not the court) in 2003 (HL Paper 95-I). During the evidence before that committee, views were expressed that prosecutions for blasphemy would be unlawful under the Human Rights Act 1998 because of the protection for freedom on expression in Art 10 of the European Convention on Human Rights (Chapter 2). However, the crime of blasphemy in England and similar legislation in Austria has already been considered by the European Court of Human Rights and was found to be compatible with Art 10. In 1989 the British Board of Film Classification (BBFC) denied a classification to the video of *Visions of Ecstasy* published by Redemption Films, on the ground that it was blasphemous. The film involved St Teresa of Avila, a sixteenth-century nun, and showed her experiencing erotic visions of Jesus. Following the BBFC decision, Nigel Wingrove of Redemption Films made an application to the European Court of Human Rights claiming that the ban breached Art 10 of the European Convention on Human Rights and was disproportionate. The court, however, dismissed the claim (*Wingrove v UK* [1996] 24 EHRR), and accepted that the criminal law of blasphemy in England did not infringe the right to freedom of expression under Art 10. Similarly, in the case of *Otto-Preminger-Institute v Austria* [1994] 19 EHRR 34 the court decided that Austria had not breached Art 10 when it had banned a film which satirised God, Jesus and Mary:

49. As the Court has consistently held, freedom of expression constitutes one of the essential foundations of a democratic society, one of the basic conditions for its progress and for the development of everyone. Subject to paragraph 2 of Article 10 (art. 10–2), it is applicable not only to 'information' or 'ideas' that are favourably received or regarded as

inoffensive or as a matter of indifference, but also to those that shock, offend or disturb the State or any sector of the population. Such are the demands of that pluralism, tolerance and broadmindedness without which there is no 'democratic society' (see, particularly, the Handyside v. the United Kingdom judgment of 7 December 1976, Series A no. 24, p. 23, para. 49). However, as is borne out by the wording itself of Article 10 para. 2 (art. 10–2), whoever exercises the rights and freedoms enshrined in the first paragraph of that Article (art. 10–1) undertakes 'duties and responsibilities'. Amongst them – in the context of religious opinions and beliefs – may legitimately be included an obligation to avoid as far as possible expressions that are gratuitously offensive to others and thus an infringement of their rights, and which therefore do not contribute to any form of public debate capable of furthering progress in human affairs. This being so, as a matter of principle it may be considered necessary in certain democratic societies to sanction or even prevent improper attacks on objects of religious veneration, provided always that any 'formality', 'condition', 'restriction' or 'penalty' imposed be proportionate to the legitimate aim pursued (see the Handyside judgment referred to above, ibid.).

The fact that the law of blasphemy has not been used for nearly 30 years and the fact that its continued existence is routinely criticised by certain politicians and commentators means that, in all probability, the offence can be regarded as moribund today. On the 25th anniversary of the *Gay News* case, a group gathered to perform a well-publicised public reading of the prosecuted poem and did so without being either arrested or prosecuted. In the debates over the various attempts to create a religious hatred law, the fear was often expressed that it could become a new form of blasphemy law which would prevent criticism of any religion. For example, the fact that under Islamic Shariah law criticism of the Muslim prophet Muhammad is considered a form of blasphemy was behind the well-publicised campaigns against *The Satanic Verses* and the 'Danish Cartoons' of 2005 and led to fears that new legislation could be used to prevent legitimate study, and criticism, of the life of Muhammad and the religion he established. For these reasons the options for the future of the blasphemy law seem to lie between complete repeal or an enlargement to cover all religions and both options are politically controversial. In considering options for the future, a study of legislation passed in British India can be instructive, since India was, and is, a multi-religious society which was governed by English criminal law. The important difference between the Indian Penal Code offence and the blasphemy law in English common law was that the Indian legislation required the defendant to have a 'deliberate and malicious intention of outraging religious feelings', which meant that the crime could not be committed recklessly or accidentally.

Indian Penal Code 1860
Preface to Chapter XV dealing with offences relating to religion
The principle on which this chapter has been framed is a principle on which it would be desirable that all Governments should act, but from which the British Government in India cannot depart without risking the dissolution of society: it is this, that every man should be suffered to profess his own religion, and that no man should be suffered to insult the religion of another.

Section 295 (1860) Whoever destroys, damages or defiles any place of worship, or any object held sacred by any class of persons with the intention of thereby insulting the religion of any class of persons is likely to consider such destruction, damage or defilement as an insult to their religion, shall be punished with imprisonment of either description for a term which may extend to two years or with fine or with both.

295-A (1927) Whoever with deliberate and malicious intention of outraging the religious feelings of His Majesty's subjects in India, by words, either spoken or written, or by visible representation, insults or attempts to insult the religion or the religious beliefs of that class, shall be punished with imprisonment of either description for a term which may extend to ten years, or with fine or with both.

It is noteworthy that there are similarities between s 295-A of the Indian Penal Code and s 4A of the Public Order Act 1986 (discussed below).

Religiously aggravated criminal offences

The Crime and Disorder Act 1998 created a new category of 'racially aggravated criminal offences' and s 39 of the Anti-terrorism, Crime and Security Act 2001 amended the Crime and Disorder Act 1998 so as to change the existing racially aggravated criminal offences into 'racially or religiously aggravated criminal offences'. These are defined in s 28 of the Crime and Disorder Act 1998 as follows:

Meaning of 'racially or religiously aggravated'
28.—(1) An offence is racially or religiously aggravated for the purposes of sections 29 to 32 below if—

(a) at the time of committing the offence, or immediately before or after doing so, the offender demonstrates towards the victim of the offence hostility based on the victim's membership (or presumed membership) of a racial or religious group; or

(b) the offence is motivated (wholly or partly) by hostility towards members of a racial or religious group based on their membership of that group.

(2) In subsection (1)(a) above—

> 'membership', in relation to a racial or religious group, includes association with members of that group;
> 'presumed' means presumed by the offender.

(3) It is immaterial for the purposes of paragraph (a) or (b) of subsection (1) above whether or not the offender's hostility is also based, to any extent, on any other factor not mentioned in that paragraph.

(4) In this section 'racial group' means a group of persons defined by reference to race, colour, nationality (including citizenship) or ethnic or national origins.

(5) In this section 'religious group' means a group of persons defined by reference to religious belief or lack of religious belief.

Under ss 29–32 of the Act there are a variety of offences which can be religiously aggravated: s 29 crimes of violence; s 30 criminal damage; s 31 public order offences; and s 32 harassment. In practice, the most important section is s 31, since prosecutions for public order offences can raise complex and controversial questions relating to the balance between freedom of expression and freedom from insult.

The wording of s 28(5) makes it clear that a religiously aggravated offence must be motivated by 'hostility' towards a group defined by reference to 'religious' belief or lack of religious belief'. It is a much narrower definition than the definition 'religion or belief' used in Pt 2 of the Equality Bill and Art 9 of the European Convention on Human Rights and therefore an offence motivated by hostility towards a group which is defined by non-religious beliefs or philosophies would not classify as a religiously aggravated offence. This means that in a religiously aggravated case a criminal court may have to make an independent decision as to whether a group's beliefs do constitute religious beliefs and it cannot automatically rely on decisions under the Equality Act 2006 or under Art 9. In the majority of cases the question of whether or not a victim is a member of a religious group will probably not be disputed, but in any prosecution for a religiously aggravated offence it is open to a defendant to argue that the 'group' in question is not a religion. The definition of 'religion' is considered in Chapter 1. However, it is worth noting that Buddhists would be regarded as members of a group defined by 'religious belief' even though Buddhism is more of a philosophy than a religion (*Barralet v Attorney General* [1980] 3 All ER 925) but Secularists and Scientologists would not (*Bowman v Secular Society* [1917] AC 406 and *R v Registrar General ex p Segerdal* [1970] 3 All ER 886).

The words 'lack of religious belief' can obviously mean those who do not hold any religious belief, such as atheists, but it also includes those who do not hold a particular religious belief. For example, if someone (A) was to attack another person (B) simply because B was a Jehovah's Witness, then that would obviously be a religiously aggravated assault by A; conversely, if A was a Jehovah's Witness and attacked B simply because B was not a Jehovah's Witness, then that would also be a religiously aggravated assault because in that case B would have been attacked because he was part of a group defined by 'lack of religious belief', namely everyone who was not a Jehovah's Witness. Where things may become more complicated is where both the attacker and the victim are members of the same religion but practise it, or interpret it, differently. For example, if both A and B are Muslim women but A wears the hijab and B does not, what would be the situation if A were to assault B because A regarded B as being a bad Muslim who was bringing Islam into contempt? Arguably, such a case would still constitute a religiously aggravated assault. Even though A and B would claim to be members of the same religion, the fact that B did not regard it as essential that she wear the hijab would mean that B lacked the specific religious belief, or interpretation of belief, of A.

Section 28(2) means that it is irrelevant if the offender is incorrect in their assumptions about the religion of the victim. For example, there have been a number of reports of Sikhs being attacked by persons who assumed that the Sikh turban was a Muslim symbol and in that situation, even though the attackers were incorrect about the religion of their victim, they would still be guilty of religiously aggravated assault. Similarly, someone can be the victim of a religiously aggravated offence owing to association with members of another religion, for example, if a Muslim girl had a Hindu boyfriend and was attacked by other Muslims because of her association with him that would still be a religiously aggravated assault even though both victim and attackers were members of the same religion.

It is important to note that ss 28–32 did not actually create any new offences or make anything illegal that had been legal before. What they did was to increase the possible sentence for certain existing criminal offences if they were committed in a racially or religiously aggravated way. For example, the maximum sentence for 'normal' common assault is six months' imprisonment but for religiously aggravated common assault the maximum sentence is up to two years' imprisonment. Therefore, if A, who happens to be a Mormon, was assaulted by B for reasons unconnected with A's religion, then that would be a 'normal' assault, but if A was assaulted by B because A was a Mormon and B was hostile to Mormonism, then that would be a religiously aggravated assault and B would be liable to a heavier sentence. The Court of Appeal stated in *R v Saunders* [2000] 1 Cr App R 458 and *R v Kelly* [2001] EWCA Crim 170 that for the racially aggravated form of an offence the sentence should indicate the appropriate sentence for the offence in the absence of racial aggravation and then add a further term for the racial element and the same principles apply to sentencing for religiously aggravated offences.

Besides the specific religiously aggravated offences created by ss 29–32, where a court is sentencing any offence which was motivated by religious hostility it has to regard that fact as an aggravating factor which should attract a heavier sentence. The Criminal Justice Act 2003 provides:

> 145 Increase in sentences for racial or religious aggravation
>
> (1) This section applies where a court is considering the seriousness of an offence other than one under sections 29 to 32 of the Crime and Disorder Act 1998 (c. 37) (racially or religiously aggravated assaults, criminal damage, public order offences and harassment etc)
>
> (2) If the offence was racially or religiously aggravated, the court—
>
> > (a) must treat that fact as an aggravating factor, and
> > (b) must state in open court that the offence was so aggravated.
>
> (3) Section 28 of the Crime and Disorder Act 1998 (meaning of 'racially or religiously aggravated') applies for the purposes of this section as it applies for the purposes of sections 29 to 32 of that Act.

How this works can be shown by considering the criminal offence of s 1 of the Malicious Communications Act 1988, under which it is an offence for any person to send:

> (a) a letter, electronic communication or article of any description which conveys
>
> > (i)   a message which is indecent or grossly offensive
> > (ii) a threat or
> > (iii) information which is false and known or believed to be false by the sender or
>
> (b) any article or electronic communication which is, in whole or part, of an indecent or grossly offensive nature.

If an anti-semite were deliberately to send to a rabbi a parcel which contained pork, then that would constitute an 'article' of a 'grossly offensive nature' to the rabbi and, because of s 145, it would attract a heavier sentence than might otherwise be the case, even though there is no specific offence of 'religiously aggravated malicious communications'.

Religiously aggravated assaults

There are three types of religiously aggravated assaults: 'common assault'; 'assault casing actual bodily harm (ABH)'; and 'grievous bodily harm

(GBH)'. The maximum sentence for religiously aggravated common assault is two years' imprisonment, whilst the maximum sentence for 'ordinary' common assault is only six months' imprisonment. The maximum sentence for religiously aggravated ABH or GBH is seven years' imprisonment, rather than the normal maximum of five years' imprisonment.

An assault is committed when the accused intentionally or recklessly causes another to apprehend immediate and unlawful violence, the separate offence of battery occurs when the accused intentionally or recklessly inflicts unlawful force on the victim though in practice the term 'assault' is often used in situations which technically constitute battery. The difference between the charges of common assault, ABH and GBH depends on the level of injury which occurs. For common assault there needs to be no injury whatsoever, but quite often where there are minor injuries such as graze or minor bruising the defendant will still be charged with common assault. Actual bodily harm covers any injury which is 'calculated to interfere with the health or comfort of the victim' (*R v Miller* [1954] 2 QB 282) and therefore minor cuts and bruises may be sufficient, though in practice ABH is only charged in cases involving more serious injuries such as extensive bruising, cuts, etc., which require some degree of medical treatment. GBH has been interpreted by the court as meaning 'really serious harm' (*DPP v Smith* (1961) AC 290) and is usually only charged in situations involving broken bones, extensive injuries, etc.

No offence of assault is committed if the defendant is acting in self-defence, which is defined in the Criminal Law Act 1967, s 3(1):

> A person may use such force as is reasonable in the circumstances in the prevention of crime, or in effecting or assisting in the lawful arrest of offenders or suspected offenders or of persons unlawfully at large.

However, in cases of religiously aggravated assaults, self-defence may be less likely to arise than in cases of 'ordinary' assault because if the prosecution can prove that the offender has 'demonstrated hostility towards the victim based on the victim's religion' then it will be difficult for the defendant to claim that they are acting in self-defence.

Religiously aggravated criminal damage

The definition of criminal damage is in s 1 of the Criminal Damage Act 1971:

> (1) A person who without lawful excuse destroys or damages any property belonging to another intending to destroy or damage any such property or being reckless as to whether any such property would be destroyed or damaged shall be guilty of an offence

and is not limited to permanent damage, for example smearing mud on the walls of a police cell was held to be criminal damage (*Roe v Kingerlee* (1986) Crim LR 735), where it was said: 'What constitutes criminal damage is a matter of fact and degree and it is for the justices, applying their common sense, to decide whether what occurred was damage or not.'

Though most incidents of religiously aggravated criminal damage will involve actual damage to a religious object or, quite frequently, graffiti on a religious building, any action which damaged a religious item or prevented it being used could classify as religiously aggravated criminal damage. For example, if a religious book or missal were deliberately soaked in water, that could constitute religiously aggravated criminal damage even if it could be used again once it had been dried out, because during the period in which it could not be used it was damaged. Though criminal damage can be committed both intentionally and recklessly it is likely that there will be few occasions of 'reckless' religiously aggravated criminal damage, since if the offence is committed recklessly it is unlikely to have been 'motivated by hostility'. One of the main uses of the religiously aggravated offence is likely to involve cases where there is damage or graffiti to gravestones belonging to a particular religious group. The maximum penalty for 'normal' criminal damage is ten years' imprisonment but for religiously aggravated criminal damage it is 14 years' imprisonment. However, in practice the additional sentence is less important than the fact that religiously aggravated criminal damage does not have any financial limit applied to it. Under s 22 of the Magistrates Courts Act 1980, which applies to 'ordinary' criminal damage, if the value of the damage is less than £5,000 then the charge of criminal damage can only be tried summarily and the maximum penalty is three months' imprisonment; it is only if someone is charged with criminal damage exceeding £5,000 in value that there is any danger of a sentence exceeding three months. However, this restriction does not apply in cases of religiously aggravated criminal damage and therefore it is quite possible that someone charged with religiously aggravated criminal damage of relatively small value could receive a lengthy custodial sentence. This therefore means that, in cases involving criminal damage, the question of whether the damage is religiously aggravated or not is a matter of considerable significance. For example, if someone breaks into a church and damages a statue, have they done it out of hostility to the church or have they simply done it as an act of wanton vandalism with no particular purpose or motivation? In the first case it is religiously aggravated criminal damage, in the second case it is 'ordinary' criminal damage.

For there to be an offence of criminal damage the property damaged has to belong to another person. Therefore, if someone buys a religious book or icon and then deliberately defaces or desecrates it in order to provoke or upset members of a particular religion, they would not be guilty of religiously aggravated criminal damage, though they might be guilty of a religiously aggravated public order offence.

Arson is criminal damage by fire but there is no religiously aggravated offence of arson. This is because arson carries a maximum sentence of life imprisonment and it was therefore felt unnecessary to have a religiously aggravated form of it. However, if a person is charged with arson which is motivated by religious hostility, for example an arson attack on a church, then under s 145 of the Criminal Justice Act 2003 the sentence which is given should be heavier than the sentence which would otherwise have been given.

Religiously aggravated Public Order Act offences

The three religiously aggravated offences under the Public Order Act 1986 are the most likely offences to be used in religiously aggravated cases. They are also the offences in which the allegation of religious aggravation is likely to be the most crucial and frequently the most controversial aspect of a prosecution.

Public Order Act 1986, s 4

A religiously aggravated offence under s 4 of the Public Order Act 1986 is punishable with two years' imprisonment, in contrast to the 'ordinary offence', which is punishable only by six months' imprisonment. The offence is not the most clearly drafted of criminal offences and there are a number of factors which have to be proved, as follows:

4—(1) A person is guilty of an offence if he—

(a) uses towards another person threatening, abusive or insulting words or behaviour, or
(b) distributes or displays to another person any writing, sign or other visible representation which is threatening, abusive or insulting,

with intent to cause that person to believe that immediate unlawful violence will be used against him or another by any person, or to provoke the immediate use of unlawful violence by that person or another, or whereby that person is likely to believe that such violence will be used or it is likely that such violence will be provoked.

One of the main elements of the offence is that the words or behaviour or the display of writing or representation must be with the intent of pro-voking 'immediate' unlawful violence or causing another person to believe that 'immediate' unlawful violence will be used against them. In the case of *Valentine v DPP* 1997 COD 339 it was held that the defendant was guilty of an offence under s 4 when his threats caused a women to fear immediate unlawful violence the next time she went to work, but that was only because she might have gone to work the same evening that the threat was made. If a threat is made of some unspecified action in the future then it is an open question whether it falls within the definition of s 4. For example, a phrase such as 'we'll get you the next time you go to church', addressed towards a Muslim convert to Christianity, could be said to cause a fear of immediate unlawful violence, since the person might be going to church shortly after the threat was made. Equally, however, it could be argued that this is not a threat of 'immediate unlawful violence'. In *DPP v Ramos* [2000] Crim LR 768 it was decided that 'it is the victim's state of mind that is crucial rather than the statistical risk of violence actually occurring within a very short space of time'. In that case there was evidence on the basis of which the magistrate could infer the requisite intention as to the belief of the victims, since the letters that were sent contained a very serious threat, of a bombing campaign, and there was nothing to exclude the immediate future from the period when that violence would be used. The High Court in *Horseferry Road Metropolitan Stipendiary Magistrate ex p Siadatan* [1991] 1 QB 260 decided that since there was no evidence that 'immediate unlawful violence' would be provoked as a result of the publication of *The Satanic Verses*, the publication of it was not an offence under s 4.

Whether behaviour is 'threatening, abusive or insulting' is a question of fact. The House of Lords in *Brutus v Cozens* [1973] AC 854 decided that 'insulting' is to be given its ordinary meaning and the question whether words or behaviour are insulting is a question of fact, and the same approach was adopted by the Court of Appeal with regard to the words 'threatening' and 'abusive' in *DPP v Clarke* [1991] 94 Cr App R 359. However, in *R v Ambrose* [1973] 57 Cr App R 538, the Court of Appeal noted that merely because words were rude or offensive did not necessarily mean that they were also insulting. For example, if someone were to stand outside a mosque with a placard displaying the notorious 'Danish cartoons', then he would undoubtedly be displaying something that was 'insulting' and, because he was outside a mosque, he would clearly be engaging in behaviour whereby it would be likely that 'violence would be provoked' and he would be 'displaying it towards another person', i.e. persons entering or leaving the mosque. However, if he had the cartoons on a poster and was taking part in a demonstration to defend free speech, then he would not be guilty of an offence under s 4 because he would not be displaying the poster 'towards another person'.

Public Order Act 1986, s 4A

Section 4A of the Public Order Act 1986 is an offence which is very likely to have particular relevance in religiously aggravated cases:

> (1) A person is guilty of an offence if, with intent to cause a person harassment, alarm or distress, he—

> (a) uses threatening, abusive or insulting words or behaviour, or disorderly behaviour, or
>
> (b) displays any writing, sign or other visible representation which is threatening, abusive or insulting,
>
> thereby causing that or another person harassment, alarm or distress.

It is worthy of note that the wording of s 4A is not dissimilar to the wording of s 295-A of the Indian Penal Code, set out above, and it is therefore possible that s 4A could in many respects serve as a replacement for the existing blasphemy law.

For someone to be convicted of a charge under s 4A they must be proved to have 'intended' to cause 'harassment, alarm or distress'. In law, 'intention' is a word that is usually used in relation to consequences and a person clearly intends a consequence if he wants that consequence to follow from his actions. In *R v Hancock* [1986] AC 455 the House of Lords emphasised that proving 'intent' was ultimately a question of fact and all evidence should be taken into account. If it is likely that a particular result will follow from particular behaviour then it is likely that the result was foreseen, the more likely it is that the result was foreseen, the more likely it is that the result was also intended, it is all a matter of fact and a jury can draw conclusions from the evidence as to what a defendant intended. For example, if somebody displays towards a practising Muslim a copy of the Koran and then deliberately defaces it, he would undoubtedly cause that Muslim distress. If it is the defendant's own copy of the Koran then he cannot be charged with criminal damage because he has not caused criminal damage to the property of another person, but he could be charged with an offence contrary to s 4A because he will have been using 'insulting behaviour' with the intention of causing 'harassment, alarm or distress' to the Muslim believer. In the case of *Percy v DPP* [2001] EWHC Admin 1125 the High Court agreed with the proposition that 'there is a pressing social need in a multi-cultural society to prevent the denigration of objects of veneration and symbolic importance for one cultural group'. However, if a bookshop was displaying copies of *The Satanic Verses* or *The Da Vinci Code* then, even though the display might cause distress to believing Muslims or Christians, the bookseller would not be guilty of an offence under s 4A because there would be no evidence that the display was created with the 'intention' of causing distress.

One of the distinctive points about religiously aggravated harassment offences under s 4A is that actions which on the surface may appear to be innocuous and acceptable can nevertheless constitute harassment because of personal information known to the harasser. If the defendant is aware that a particular individual is a believer in a particular religious cult and is aware that certain symbols or signs carry particular meanings to members of that cult, then either a desecration of such symbols or a showing of them to that person could be done with the intention of causing harassment. In such a case the fact that the defendant knew of the significance of the symbols or signs would be admissible as evidence of his intent.

Public Order Act 1986, s 5

The most commonly used Public Order Act offence is s 5, which says:

(1) A person is guilty of an offence if he—

(a) uses threatening, abusive or insulting words or behaviour, or disorderly behaviour, or

(b) displays any writing, sign or other visible representation which is threatening, abusive or insulting,

within the hearing or sight of a person likely to be caused harassment, alarm or distress thereby.

Section 5 is very similar to s 4A but there is no need to prove that the defendant intended to cause 'harassment, alarm or distress', nor is it necessary to prove that anyone has actually been harassed etc. In the case of *Norwood v DPP* [2003] EWHC 1564 (Admin), it was decided that displaying a poster in a window showing a photograph of one of the twin towers at the World Trade Center in flames, accompanied by the words 'Islam out of Britain', was a religiously aggravated offence contrary to s 5 even though no Muslim had complained about the poster and the only evidence came from a non-Muslim police officer who had seen the poster in the window.

Defences

There are two defences under both s 4A and s 5:

that [the defendant] was inside a dwelling and had no reason to believe that the words or behaviour used, or the writing, sign or other visible representation displayed, would be heard or seen by a person outside that or any other dwelling, or

that [the defendant's] conduct was reasonable.

In religiously aggravated cases under s 4A or s 5 the defence that the behaviour complained of was 'reasonable' is likely to be used frequently in order to claim that the words or behaviour complained of were used as part of an exercise in free speech so as to express disagreement with the actions or belief of a religious group. In the case of *Hammond v DPP* [2004] EWHC 69 (Admin) the High Court accepted that, in deciding on the issue of reasonableness in prosecutions under s 5, a court should have regard to both

Arts 9 and 10 of the European Convention when considering questions relating to freedom of religion or freedom of expression (Chapter 2), and a similar approach will be taken in respect of prosecutions under s 4A. In the case of *Hammond*, which involved an elderly preacher holding up a banner saying 'Stop Immorality, Stop homosexuality, Stop lesbianism', the High Court held that a prosecution under s 5 for displaying the poster could be justified, since the interference with Arts 9 and 10 rights was necessary to 'protect the rights and freedoms of others', i.e. practising homosexuals. It should, however, be noted that the judge did not state that this poster *was* insulting, he merely decided that it was open to the magistrates to *decide* that it was. Even then, he stated that he reached that decision 'not without hesitation' (para 32 of the judgment).

In *Dehal v CPS* [2005] EWHC 2154 (Admin) a member of a gurdwara in Birmingham put up a notice which described the President of the gurdwara and members of its committee as:

> a hypocrite; a liar; a maker of false statements to police in order to have the appellant arrested; a maker of false statements to the press in order to discredit the appellant; a proud, mad dog; a man who has joined with others in assaulting the appellant and who exploits the congregation of the Temple in order to satisfy his own greed.

Following this he was convicted under s 4A. This conviction was overturned by the High Court and Moses J emphasised, in para 12 of his judgment, that prosecutions should not be brought under s 4A or s 5 unless there was a real fear of public disorder:

> I repeat, the important factor upon which the Crown Court should have focused and upon which on its face it appears not to have focused is the justification for bringing any criminal prosecution at all. However insulting, however unjustified what the appellant said about the President of the Temple, a criminal prosecution was unlawful as a result of section 3 of the Human Rights Act and Article 10 unless and until it could be established that such a prosecution was necessary in order to prevent public disorder. There is no such finding or any justification whatever given in the case stated. In those circumstances, whether this case be meritorious or not, I am bound to allow the appeal. There was, in short, no basis found by the Crown Court for concluding that this prosecution was a proportionate response to his conduct.

An unfortunate consequence of this judgment may be that the more violent a religion is and the quicker its adherents are to take offence, the greater the protection they will be given by the law.

Religiously aggravated harassment under s 32

Section 32 offences are the religiously aggravated versions of offences created by ss 2 and 4 of the Protection from Harassment Act 1997, which is discussed in detail in Chapter 6.

Old offences

There remain on the statute book a small number of nineteenth-century offences dealing with disorder in churches and cemeteries which are widely regarded as obsolete today. They are also probably unnecessary because the behaviour they deal with can be dealt with by the normal criminal law either as 'ordinary' or as 'religiously aggravated' public order or violence offences.

Section 59 of the Cemeteries Clauses Act 1847 makes it an offence to 'play at any game or sport, or discharge firearms, save at a military funeral' in a cemetery or to 'wilfully and unlawfully disturb any persons assembled in the cemetery for the purpose of burying any body' or to 'commit any nuisance within' a cemetery. This provision, however, now applies only to privately run cemeteries. Cemeteries run by local authorities are governed by the Local Authorities' Cemeteries Order 1977, s 18 of which contains a similar offence to s 59.

Section 7 of the Burial Laws Amendment Act 1880 applies to burials both 'with or without a religious service' and falls into two parts. First, it makes it an offence to indulge in 'riotous, violent, or indecent behaviour' at any burial under the Act, or to obstruct a burial. The second part of the section makes it an offence to 'bring into contempt or obloquy the Christian religion, or the belief or worship of any church or denomination of Christians, or the members or any minister of any such church or denomination, or any other person'. Who, or what, 'any other person', means is not clear. Therefore, like the blasphemy law, this part of the section creates an offence that provides specific protection for Christians as opposed to members of other faiths. However, unlike the blasphemy law, there seems no reason in principle why the protection of s 7 should not be extended to all religions. No issue of free speech arises, since the interruption to or disturbance of a funeral service, of any religion or none, is indefensible and very likely to provoke violence. The offence under s 7 is only triable in the Crown Court and can be punished with up to two years' imprisonment.

Section 2 of the Ecclesiastical Courts Jurisdiction Act 1860 (ECJA) forbids 'riotous, violent or indecent behaviour in any Cathedral Church, Parish or District Church or Chapel of the Church of England . . . or in any Chapel of any Religious Denomination or . . . in any Place of Religious Worship duly certified' under the Registered Places of Worship Act 1855, 'whether during the celebration of divine service or at any other time'. Section 2 also makes it an offence to 'molest, let, disturb, vex, or trouble, or by any other unlawful means disquiet or misuse any Preacher duly authorised to preach therein, or any Clergyman in Holy Orders ministering or celebrating any Sacrament, or any Divine Service, Rite, or Office, in any Cathedral, Church, or Chapel, or in any Churchyard or Burial Ground'. According to figures given to the House of Lords by the Home Office, there were 60 prosecutions under this Act in the six years 1997–2002, with 21 convictions. These figures need to be seen in the perspective of the totality of crimes against places of worship. According to 'National Churchwatch' there were 6,829 such incidents in 12 (of 42) police areas in the year ending April 2002, 186 of them violent crimes (including two murders) and 2,866 incidents of criminal damage (most of the remainder were thefts or burglaries). It is clear from the figures provided above that, as a proportion of the totality of crimes against places of worship, those prosecuted under the ECJA form a very small minority and the remainder are prosecuted under more general public order legislation. One well-publicised example of a prosecution under the ECJA was the prosecution of Mr Peter Tatchell in 1998, following a demonstration by him in Canterbury Cathedral when the Archbishop of Canterbury was delivering his Easter Sunday sermon. It is, however, difficult to visualise any behaviour contrary to s 2 which could not be prosecuted under ordinary public order legislation.

Section 36 of the Offences Against the Persons Act 1861 makes it an offence to, amongst other things, use 'threats or force, obstruct or prevent or endeavour to obstruct or prevent, any clergyman or other minister in or from celebrating divine service or otherwise officiating in any church, chapel, meeting house, or other place of divine worship'. This offence would seem to protect clergymen of any religion even, for example, an imam or a granthi, even if they would not use the term 'clergyman' to describe themselves. However, most behaviour covered by this section could also be prosecuted as an ordinary, or a religiously aggravated, public order offence or assault.

In 2002 the private member's Religious Offences Bill was introduced in the House of Lords which, amongst other things, unsuccessfully attempted to repeal all of these offences on the basis that the behaviour they cover could be, and should be, dealt with by the existing offences in the Public Order Act.

Anti-social Behaviour Orders

Anti-social behaviour orders (ASBOs) were created by s 1 of the Crime and Disorder Act 1998 and are civil orders similar to injunctions except that breach of an ASBO is a criminal offence punishable with up to five years' imprisonment. Whilst not specifically relevant to religious crimes, ASBOs do have the potential to be used, and misused, in religious situations. For example, in 2005 an ASBO was made against a publican because of a sign in his car park marked 'The Porking Yard', which was regarded as offensive by local Muslims attending a nearby mosque; and in 2006 an ASBO was obtained against Philip Howard, a street preacher in Oxford Street, to stop him using a loudspeaker or other amplification device as part of his street preaching.

ASBOs can be applied for by both police and local authorities and the criteria for making them is relatively low, namely that a person has acted in a manner that 'causes or is likely to cause harassment, alarm or distress to one or more persons not of the same household as himself, and that such an order is necessary to protect persons from further anti-social acts by him'. It is therefore possible that, in the future, ASBOs could be used to stop persons displaying religious, or anti-religious, signs or engaging in proselytising behaviour in particular areas. In any such application the rights of the individual to freedom of religion under Art 9 as well as their right to freedom of expression under Art 10 will have to be seriously considered (Chapter 2). One of the biggest dangers is that courts will make sloppily or loosely worded orders, for example 'the defendant shall not use any Islamaphobic remarks'. Any such sloppily worded ASBOs would, however, fall foul of the general requirement of the law that all court orders should be 'clear and unambiguous': *B v Chief Constable of Avon and Somerset* [2001] 1 WLR 340, para 33.

Chapter 8

Religious hatred

Background

Criminal offences relating to stirring up religious hatred were created by the Racial and Religious Hatred Act 2006. This Act has a complex and controversial history. The government's first attempt to create an offence of stirring up religious hatred was in Pt 5 of the Anti-terrorism, Crime and Security Bill 2001, but that proposal was defeated in the House of Lords. Another attempt was made in 2002 in the private member's Religious Offences Bill and the proposal was reintroduced by the government in the Serious Organised Crime and Police Bill 2004. All of these attempts ran into serious opposition, particularly in the House of Lords, and each time the proposals were withdrawn by the government in order to get the rest of the Bill passed.

In the 2005 general election, the Labour Party included the following in its Manifesto for England and its Manifesto for Wales (though not the Manifesto for Scotland):

> It remains our firm and clear intention to give people of all faiths the same protection against incitement to hatred on the basis of their religion. We will legislate to outlaw it and will continue the dialogue we have started with faith groups from all backgrounds about how best to balance protection, tolerance and free speech.

On 9 June 2005 the government introduced the Racial and Religious Hatred Bill into Parliament and made it clear that it was willing to use the Parliament Act to force the Bill through, even if the House of Lords voted against it. However, once again, the proposals aroused strong opposition from an unusual coalition of comedians, Evangelical Christians and atheists. The comedian Rowan Atkinson was a particularly high-profile opponent, who feared that the proposals would make it impossible safely to satirise religion; the National Secular Society feared that the proposals would make it impossible to criticise any religion; whilst many Christians feared that it would restrict their ability to preach the uniqueness of Christianity in comparison to other religions. Opposition was also stimulated by the way in which 'religious vilification' legislation in Victoria, Australia, had been used by one religious group in order to mount a legal case against another *Islamic Council of Victoria v Catch the Fire Ministries Inc* [2004] VCAT 2510. In effect, all the organisations agreed that they wanted to retain their right to disagree with each other and the freedom to criticise other religions or all religions.

The proposals for a religious hatred law were, however, very strongly supported by the Muslim Council of Britain, which considered that it was unfair that the existing race hatred legislation protected Jews and Sikhs but not Muslims. The government agreed that this was indeed an anomaly and for that reason its attempts to create an offence of religious hatred were based on the idea of modifying the existing offences of stirring up racial hatred found in Pt 3 of the Public Order Act 1986. Jews and Sikhs are protected by this legislation, since they are defined by the courts as races, albeit they also have their own religion. The idea of simply adding religious hatred to the existing race hatred legislation had already been adopted in Northern Ireland in the Public Order (Northern Ireland) Order 1987, which made it an offence to stir up either racial or religious hatred. It is, however, important to bear in mind that this legislation was introduced because of the unique political situation in Northern Ireland, in which religious identity (Catholic/Protestant) is also regarded as an indicator of national identity (Irish/British) and political leanings (Republican/Unionist).

The opponents of the government's proposals argued strongly that race and religion were fundamentally different concepts and therefore the government's basic approach was flawed. On 25 October 2005 the House of Lords defeated the government and modified the Bill so as to make the new offence significantly different from what was originally proposed in the Bill. In particular, the House of Lords' wording separated the offence of religious hatred from racial hatred and made the offence apply only to 'threatening' words or behaviour rather than 'threatening, abusive or insulting' words or behaviour. In addition, the government's original proposals would have applied to a situation where it was 'likely' that religious hatred would be stirred up, but the House of Lords amendments meant that the offence would apply only where the defendant 'intended' to stir up religious hatred. Finally, a comprehensive clause was added to ensure protection for freedom of speech. Rather than trying to negotiate a compromise on these changes, the government, in effect, tried to get the Bill back to its original extent but, on 31 January 2006, the government proposals lost by one vote in the House of Commons when Prime Minister Tony Blair left early rather than staying to cast his vote. The almost unprecedented nature of this close vote led one prominent atheist to admit that it was the closest he had ever come to believing in divine intervention!

One particular consequence of the chequered history of this legislation is that if a court considers that the wording is ambiguous it will be unable to refer to Hansard for clarification. In the case of *Pepper v Hart* [1993] AC 593 the House of Lords decided that in certain circumstances courts could refer to Hansard to find out the purpose and meaning of a Bill by reference to the speeches of the minister who introduced a Bill. When, as in this case, the Bill passed is not the Bill that was introduced and is not the Bill the government wanted, *Pepper v Hart* does not apply and courts will have to rely entirely on the wording of the Act without reference to Hansard.

The Racial and Religious Hatred Act 2006

Schedule 1 to the Racial and Religious Hatred Act 2006 adds a new Pt 3A to the Public Order Act 1986, following Pt 3, which deals with racial hatred. There are a number of offences created by ss 29B–29G of Pt 3A but all of them share certain common characteristics. They deal with words, behaviour or material which are 'threatening'; the offender has to 'intend' to stir up religious hatred and all words and behaviour have to be considered in the light of s 29J, which deals with 'Protection of Freedom of Expression'.

Religious hatred

'Religious hatred' is defined in s 29A as 'hatred against a group of persons defined by reference to religious belief or lack of religious belief'. Hatred itself is not defined in the Act but is defined in the *Oxford English Dictionary* as: 'the emotion or feeling of hate, active dislike, detestation, enmity, ill will, malevolence'. Hate is defined as: 'to hold in very strong dislike, to detest, to bear malice to, the opposite of "to love"'.

The reference in s 29A to lack of religious belief is often described as referring to atheists, i.e. those who have no religious belief, but its meaning is in fact more subtle. Lack of religious belief can cover any person other than believers in a particular religion so that, for example, an exhortation to 'slay the unbelievers wherever you find them' would be an exhortation to hatred and violence directed at absolutely everyone who could be considered to be an 'unbeliever'. Furthermore, the words 'lack of religious belief' can mean those who do not share the specific interpretation of religious belief held by a particular person or group. This means that there could be situations where a group of believers in a particular religion were inciting hatred of other members of the same religion whom they regarded as deficient in religious observance, or compromisers with enemies of the religion; for example, a Muslim group inciting hatred against Muslim women who chose not to wear the jilbab could be accused of stirring up religious hatred even though their hatred was directed at fellow Muslims. This makes the offence of religious hatred distinctly different from the offence of racial hatred. It would be very difficult for a person to incite racial hatred against their own race because they would of course be inciting hatred against themselves, but with religious hatred it is quite possible for someone to be inciting hatred against their co-religionists and this makes the offence of religious hatred relevant to disputes within religions, as well as to disputes between religions.

The wording of s 29A is specific that the group must be defined by 'religious' belief or lack of belief, which means that groups defined by non-religious beliefs or philosophies are not protected. It is therefore a much narrower definition than the definition 'religion or belief' used in Pt 2 of the Equality Act 2006 (Chapter 3) and Art 9 of the European Convention on Human Rights (Chapter 2). Even though Buddhism is more of a philosophy than a religion, Buddhists would be regarded as a group defined by 'religious belief': *Barralet v Attorney General* [1980] 3 All ER 925, but Secularists and Scientologists would not: *Bowman v Secular Society* [1917] AC 406 and *R v Registrar General ex p Segerdal* [1970] 3 All ER 886 (Chapter 1). This means that in a religious hatred case a criminal court may have to make an independent decision as to whether a group's beliefs constitute religious beliefs; it cannot necessarily rely on decisions under the Equality Act 2006 or Art 9.

'Threatening'

The word 'threatening' is not defined in the legislation but is defined in the *Oxford English Dictionary* as follows: 'to try to influence by menaces, to declare (usually conditionally) one's intention of inflicting injury upon, to menace. To declare one's intention of injuring or punishing in order to influence.' However, whether particular words or behaviour are in fact threatening is regarded by the courts as a question of fact to be decided by juries on the basis of the facts of the specific case rather than being a question of law to be decided by a judge: *R v Cakmak* [2002] EWCA Crim 500.

Examples of threatening words or behaviour could include such things as the placards held up in London on 3 February 2006 during a demonstration against cartoons relating to the Muslim prophet Mohammed, with such phrases as 'Behead those who insult Islam'. Such placards could be threatening towards all those who are contemptuous of the Muslim religion, even though they are not threats directed at a specific person or group. However, a banner saying 'God will punish those who watch *Gerry Springer the Opera*' would probably not be regarded as threatening, since it is not a threat or an exhortation to anyone to do anything but, in essence, merely expresses a personal religious belief as to what God will do. Context is also important and words that may not appear to be threatening may be when put into context. For example, if a Muslim family were to convert to Christianity, a statement that they should be 'treated as apostates to Islam' could be described as 'threatening' because under Islamic Shariah law, apostasy from Islam is a crime punishable with death.

One of the peculiar aspects of the legislation is that threatening behaviour has to be directed at a group and not at an individual so that, for example, if the legislation had been in force during the Salman Rushdie affair it would not have applied to those who were inciting hatred of Salman Rushdie because, even though they were clearly inciting hatred on a monumental scale, the hatred they were inciting was against an individual and not against a group. Paradoxically, however, those who defended Salman Rushdie and criticised those aspects of Islamic belief which were being used to justify the campaign against him could have found themselves threatened with prosecution for stirring up religious hatred against Muslims! However, incitement to violence or murder against an individual, such as the threats made against Salman Rushdie, could, and should, have been dealt with under the ordinary criminal law.

'Intends thereby'

When the Racial and Religious Hatred Bill was amended in the House of Lords, so as to ensure that a person could only be convicted of the offence when they 'intended' to stir up religious hatred, both government and police spokesmen were quoted as saying that this would make the offence impossible to enforce. This was a somewhat surprising attitude, since many offences require evidence of intent and the courts deal with the issue of intent or *mens rea* (guilty mind) on a daily basis.

In law, 'intention' is a word that is usually used in relation to consequences. A person clearly intends a consequence if he wants that consequence to follow from his actions and this is so whether the consequence is very likely or very unlikely to result. Thus, a person who shouts 'all Hindus are evil and deserve to die' would, on the face of it, be intending to stir up religious hatred and it would not matter whether he shouts this out during a rowdy demonstration against the building of a Hindu temple or during a meeting of fans of *The Simpsons* debating the character cartoon character Apu. In both situations the defendant could still be guilty of 'intending' to stir up religious hatred even though in the second situation it is highly unlikely that any religious hatred would actually have been stirred up.

Intention is not, however, restricted to consequences which are as obvious as this, nor is it necessary for a defendant to admit that they intended that religious hatred would be stirred up. In *R v Hancock* [1986] AC 455 the House of Lords emphasised that proving 'intent' was ultimately a question of fact and all evidence should be taken into account, if it is likely that a particular result will follow from particular behaviour then it is likely that the result was foreseen and the more likely it is that the result was foreseen the more likely it is that the result was also intended. Lord Scarman said in *Hancock* (p 474):

> . . . the probability, however high, of a consequence is only a factor, though it may in some cases be a very significant factor, to be considered

with all the other evidence in determining whether the accused intended to bring it about.

Therefore, deciding on 'intent' is a question of fact and a jury can look at a variety of evidence and draw logical conclusions as to what a defendant intended. Thus, in a case involving an allegation of intent to stir up religious hatred, the prosecution will probably be allowed to adduce evidence of membership of 'extremist' political parties or religious groups as well as possession of particular types of literature etc. in order to prove that a defendant 'intended' to stir up religious hatred.

Section 29J: protection of freedom of expression

Section 29J provides that:

> Nothing in this Part shall be read or given effect in a way which pro-
> hibits or restricts discussion, criticism or expressions of antipathy,
> dislike, ridicule, insult or abuse of particular religions or the beliefs or
> practices of their adherents, or of any other belief system or the beliefs
> or practices of its adherents, or proselytising or urging adherents of a
> different religion or belief system to cease practising their religion or
> belief system.

This is an overarching 'protection of freedom of expression' clause applying throughout Pt 3A and is designed to act as a gateway to prevent the Act being misused so as to prevent critical debate about specific religions or religious beliefs. This danger was one of the main concerns of the opponents of the legislation.

When it originally introduced the Bill, the government had taken the view that Art 9 (freedom of religion) and Art 10 (freedom of expression) in the European Convention on Human Rights (Chapter 2) would provide adequate protection for religious debate. However, because Arts 9 and 10 are 'qualified' rights, opponents argued that speakers, preachers, etc. could not be sure where the line would be drawn in any particular case and for that reason the House of Lords added s 29J to the legislation in order to provide a comprehensive and specific set of defences to allegations of religious hatred. Whilst s 29J does not override Art 9 or Art 10 it will, in practice, be more important because if a defendant cannot defend their words or behaviour by reference to s 29J then they are unlikely to find any protection under Arts 9 or 10.

What is noticeable about s 29J is that it does not require discussion, criticism, expressions of antipathy, etc., to be 'reasonable'. However, it is quite clear that the clause is to be read as expressing criticism, antipathy, etc. to 'religions', not to the believers in the religion, so that, for example, the phrase 'Islam is a wicked evil faith' would be defended by s 29J, but the phrase 'Muslims are wicked and evil' would not be. There is, however, an extremely fine line between 'stirring up hatred against a group of persons defined by reference to religious belief' and 'expressions of antipathy, dislike, ridicule insult or abuse [of] . . . the beliefs or practices of (a religions) adherents' because it is the beliefs and practices of a religion's adherents which ultimately defines a religious group. Certainly defence lawyers, whether in court or in police stations, are likely to argue that any words or behaviour used by their clients were mere expressions of antipathy etc. and as such protected by s 29J. However, the wording of s 29J is such that it will not protect those who are expressing antipathy etc. towards everyone who does not hold a particular religious belief. For example, an Evangelical Christian expressing antipathy etc. towards Mormonism could rely on s 29J but a Mormon expressing antipathy towards 'Gentiles' (i.e. all people who are not Mormons) could not. In the first case the antipathy would be towards the 'beliefs and practices of a religion's adherents', i.e. Mormons, but in the second case the antipathy would not be at the beliefs and practices of Gentiles but rather at their lack of belief in Mormonism. Judges considering defences raised under s 29J may well be inclined to lay emphasis on the words 'discussion, criticism'; this would enable s 29J to protect legitimate debate and expressions of opinion whilst preventing it from protecting mere vulgar abuse.

One of the most important aspects of s 29J is that it explicitly defends 'proselytising or urging adherents of a different religion or belief system to cease practising their religion or belief system'. This provision therefore reinforces Art 9, which defends an individual's right to 'change his religion or belief'. The right to change religion is, after all, only meaningful if a person is able to hear and discuss alternative religious, or non-religious, views. In general, the way in which s 29J will work in practice is difficult to predict and it may well be that it makes the entire religious hatred law completely unworkable; if this does prove to be the case, then the responsibility is that of the government which, instead of proposing amendments designed to improve s 29J, proposed amendments designed to emasculate it completely and failed in that attempt.

Section 29B: use of words or behaviour or display of written material

This is the workhorse section within Pt 3A, on which the majority of prosecutions and investigations are likely to be based. To commit this offence a defendant must use threatening words or behaviour or display threatening written material and must intend thereby to stir up religious hatred. It does not matter whether the threatening words or behaviour, or display of written material, is done in a public or a private place unless the private place is a dwelling house and the defendant is inside it or another dwelling house. The reason for this exemption is simply to avoid criminalising ordinary conversation taking place in a house. However, the exemption only applies if the defendant is actually within the living area of the house so that, for example, it would not provide any protection to a defendant making a political speech in the upstairs room of a pub, even if the pub landlord actually lives in the pub.

It is also a defence that the person did not know or believe that their words would be heard by anyone outside that dwelling, which means, for example, that if a defendant is speaking inside a dwelling which is bugged he would not be guilty of the offence. Similarly, if a person has a threatening picture or poster on the wall of their house they would not be guilty of an offence even if the picture or poster was seen by a person peering in through their window. The position might be different if the picture or poster could easily be seen by anyone passing the house and a jury decides that the defendant 'intended' the picture or poster to be seen.

Sections 29C, 29E and 29G

These three sections cover possessing, distributing or showing written material or recordings with the intention thereby of stirring up religious hatred. Sections 29C and 29G are similar offences. Under s 29C someone is guilty of the offence if they publish or distribute written material which is threatening, with the intention of stirring up religious hatred. Under s 29G a person is guilty if they have in their possession threatening written material, threatening recordings, visual images or sounds, etc., with a view to their being displayed, published or distributed if they intend to thereby stir up religious hatred. Section 29E refers to distributing or showing a recording and similar principles apply to it as apply to s 29C.

The fact that the offence is restricted to threatening words can be quite significant in this situation, since every religion has its critics and those critics can be vociferous in their opposition. Books written by ex-members of a religion can be especially vituperative. This was one of the main objections to the government's original proposals, which would have criminalised books or other material which were 'insulting', as many books about a religion undoubtedly are. However, these particular sections require that any books or other material have to be 'threatening' before they can be prosecuted under the Act. For example, books or pamphlets which said of the Mormon prophet Joseph Smith, or the Muslim prophet Muhammad, that they were 'evil, dishonest and violent people who established evil, dishonest and violent religions' would clearly be offensive to the believers in these two religions, but they could not be described as threatening. However, if the books or pamphlets added something along the lines of 'and we have to do something to stop them', then that could possibly be described as threatening.

What is also significant with regard to s 29G, 'Possession of inflammatory material', is that any person who has such material in their possession must intend to display, publish or distribute such material *and* must also intend religious hatred to be stirred up thereby. This would seem particularly relevant to organisations and people such as libraries, theologians, charities dealing with oppressed religious minorities, or lawyers writing books on religious hatred, each of whom may well be in possession of material which could be considered to be inflammatory. Provided it is in their possession for personal reading or the purposes of research, then they have a clear defence to a prosecution under s 29G. If they publish the results of their research then s 29C might become involved if part of what they have written or reproduced could be regarded as 'threatening'; however, the mere reproduction of threatening material within the research would not, of itself, be contrary to s 29C if the publication of their research was for the purpose of education and there was no intention to stir up religious hatred.

Sections 29D and 29F

These sections relate to plays and broadcasts and so are particularly relevant to the media. For any prosecution to be brought, the play or broadcast must include threatening words or behaviour and there must be an intention to stir up religious hatred. These are particularly important restrictions in the context of plays and broadcasts.

For example, in 2005 there was considerable controversy in the Sikh community over the play *Bhezti* (Punjabi for 'dishonour'), which involved a rape being committed by a Sikh elder within a Sikh gurdwara. Even though Sikhs are regarded as a race and therefore are protected by existing race hatred law, the producers and writers could not be prosecuted for race hatred because the author of the play was a Sikh, as were actors and actresses, who could hardly be accused of inciting hatred of themselves and, in addition, the race hatred law only protects Sikhs as a race; it does not protect Sikhism as a religion. Though *Bhezti* could have been accused of inciting hatred of Sikhism as a religion and it certainly could be described as 'insulting' towards Sikhism, it was not threatening to Sikhism and therefore it could not have been prosecuted under s 29D.

In any play or broadcast, words may be used which can be regarded as threatening. For example, a play about the Muslim conquest of Constantinople (Istanbul) in 1453 would almost inevitably have Muslim and Christian characters using threatening words and behaviour towards members of the opposing religion. However, unless the intention behind the play was to stir up religious hatred, the use of such words or behaviour would not breach s 29D or s 29F and, in determining intent, it would be necessary to consider the play or broadcast taken as a whole and not merely a specific scene within it.

Police powers and prosecutions

Section 29B(3) gives police officers the power to arrest without warrant anyone who they reasonably suspect of committing an offence under s 29B. The members of Parliament who passed that particular clause seem to have either ignored, or forgotten, that in s 110 of the Serious Organised Crime and Police Act 2005 Parliament had already given police officers the power to arrest anyone for any offence, so making s 29B(3) unnecessary and meaningless.

When the Bill was being considered in Parliament, it was accepted by ministers that there was a danger that over-zealous or over-sensitive people might be tempted to perform 'citizen's arrests' of persons they considered were committing a religious hatred offence and for that reason s 2 of the Act states that a citizen's powers of arrest, as set down in s 24A of the Police and Criminal Evidence Act 1984 (created by s 110 of the Serious Organised Crime and Police Act 2005), do not apply to offences of racial or religious hatred. Therefore, if a private citizen were to arrest or detain anyone for an offence of racial or religious hatred, they could be sued for false arrest even if the offender was subsequently convicted of the offence.

Section 29H gives police officers powers to apply for search warrants where they have reasonable grounds for believing that 'inflammatory material' contrary to s 29G will be found within a particular building. Once again, Parliament seems to have forgotten that in s 113 of the Serious Organised Crime and Police Act 2005 it had already given police officers extensive powers to apply for wide-ranging search warrants relating to any indictable offence. Section 29H is therefore unnecessary and meaningless.

Under s 29L(3) the penalty for breaching any of the provisions of Pt 3A is up to seven years' imprisonment in the Crown Court or up to six months' imprisonment in the magistrates' court. Any prosecution requires the consent of the Attorney General (s 29L(1)) and therefore there can be no private prosecutions. This is an important provision and not a mere technicality because where a prosecution which requires the consent of the Attorney General is brought without his consent first being obtained, any conviction is a nullity: *R v Pearce* 72 Cr App R 295. However, all that needs to be shown is that the Attorney General has given consent to a prosecution being brought; he does not have to give consent to the specific wording of a charge and he does not have to provide any reasons or justification for giving consent: *R v Cain and Schollick* 61 Cr App R 186.

It should be noted, however, that the Attorney General does not have to be involved until the issue of prosecution arises. The police are able to investigate allegations of religious hatred, arrest people and interview them, obtain search warrants and seize property, etc. without any reference whatsoever to either the Attorney General or the Crown Prosecution Service. Defendants may also be charged, put before a court and remanded in custody before the consent of the Attorney General is obtained: *R v Whale and Lockton* [1991] Crim LR 692. However, the case cannot proceed to the taking of a plea or a committal to the Crown Court until the consent has been obtained. In practice, unless there are real fears that a defendant will leave the country, it is likely that police will bail suspects in religious hatred cases and then prepare a file of evidence for the Crown Prosecution Service, who will submit it to the Attorney General.

Religion and international human rights provisions

European Convention on Human Rights
(Schedule 1 Human Rights Act 1998)

Article 9 Freedom of thought, conscience and religion

1. Everyone has the right to freedom of thought, conscience and religion; this right includes freedom to change his religion or belief and freedom, either alone or in community with others and in public or private, to manifest his religion or belief, in worship, teaching, practice and observance.

2. Freedom to manifest one's religion or beliefs shall be subject only to such limitations as are prescribed by law and are necessary in a democratic society in the interests of public safety, for the protection of public order, health or morals, or for the protection of the rights and freedoms of others.

Article 10 Freedom of expression

1. Everyone has the right to freedom of expression. This right shall include freedom to hold opinions and to receive and impart information and ideas without interference by public authority and regardless of frontiers. This Article shall not prevent States from requiring the licensing of broadcasting, television or cinema enterprises.

2. The exercise of these freedoms, since it carries with it duties and responsibilities, may be subject to such formalities, conditions, restrictions or penalties as are prescribed by law and are necessary in a democratic society, in the interests of national security, territorial integrity or public safety, for the prevention of disorder or crime, for the protection of health or morals, for the protection of the reputation or rights of others, for preventing the disclosure of information received in confidence, or for maintaining the authority and impartiality of the judiciary.

Article 11 Freedom of assembly and association

1. Everyone has the right to freedom of peaceful assembly and to freedom of association with others, including the right to form and to join trade unions for the protection of his interests.
2. No restrictions shall be placed on the exercise of these rights other than such as are prescribed by law and are necessary in a democratic society in the interests of national security or public safety, for the prevention of disorder or crime, for the protection of health or morals or for the protection of the rights and freedoms of others. This Article shall not prevent the imposition of lawful restrictions on the exercise of these rights by members of the armed forces, of the police or of the administration of the State.

Article 14 Prohibition of discrimination

The enjoyment of the rights and freedoms set forth in this Convention shall be secured without discrimination on any ground such as sex, race, colour, language, religion, political or other opinion, national or social origin, association with a national minority, property, birth or other status.

Universal Declaration of Human Rights 1948
Article 18

Everyone has the right to freedom of thought, conscience and religion; this right includes freedom to change his religion or belief, and freedom, either alone or in community with others and in public or private, to manifest his religion or belief in teaching, practice, worship and observance.

United Nations Declaration on the Elimination of All Forms of Intolerance and of Discrimination Based on Religion or Belief

(Proclaimed by General Assembly resolution 36/55 of 25 November 1981)

Article 1

1. Everyone shall have the right to freedom of thought, conscience and religion. This right shall include freedom to have a religion or whatever belief of his choice, and freedom, either individually or in community with others and in public or private, to manifest his religion or belief in worship, observance, practice and teaching.
2. No one shall be subject to coercion which would impair his freedom to have a religion or belief of his choice.

3. Freedom to manifest one's religion or belief may be subject only to such limitations as are prescribed by law and are necessary to protect public safety, order, health or morals or the fundamental rights and freedoms of others.

Article 2

1. No one shall be subject to discrimination by any State, institution, group of persons, or person on the grounds of religion or other belief.

2. For the purposes of the present Declaration, the expression 'intolerance and discrimination based on religion or belief' means any distinction, exclusion, restriction or preference based on religion or belief and having as its purpose or as its effect nullification or impairment of the recognition, enjoyment or exercise of human rights and fundamental freedoms on an equal basis.

Article 3

Discrimination between human being on the grounds of religion or belief constitutes an affront to human dignity and a disavowal of the principles of the Charter of the United Nations, and shall be condemned as a violation of the human rights and fundamental freedoms proclaimed in the Universal Declaration of Human Rights and enunciated in detail in the International Covenants on Human Rights, and as an obstacle to friendly and peaceful relations between nations.

Article 4

1. All States shall take effective measures to prevent and eliminate discrimination on the grounds of religion or belief in the recognition, exercise and enjoyment of human rights and fundamental freedoms in all fields of civil, economic, political, social and cultural life.

2. All States shall make all efforts to enact or rescind legislation where necessary to prohibit any such discrimination, and to take all appropriate measures to combat intolerance on the grounds of religion or other beliefs in this matter.

Constitution of the United States of America
1st Amendment

Congress shall make no law respecting an establishment of religion, or prohibiting the free exercise thereof; or abridging the freedom of speech, or of the press; or the right of the people peaceably to assemble, and to petition the Government for a redress of grievances.

Canadian Charter of Rights and Freedoms

Whereas Canada is founded upon principles that recognize the supremacy of God and the rule of law:

1. The Canadian Charter of Rights and Freedoms guarantees the rights and freedoms set out in it subject only to such reasonable limits prescribed by law as can be demonstrably justified in a free and democratic society.

2. Everyone has the following fundamental freedoms:

a) freedom of conscience and religion;
b) freedom of thought, belief, opinion and expression, including freedom of the press and other media of communication;
c) freedom of peaceful assembly; and
d) freedom of association.

Constitution of the Republic of South Africa

Article 15 Freedom of religion, belief and opinion

1. Everyone has the right to freedom of conscience, religion, thought, belief and opinion.

2. Religious observances may be conducted at state or state-aided institutions, provided that—

a. those observances follow rules made by the appropriate public authorities;
b. they are conducted on an equitable basis; and
c. attendance at them is free and voluntary.

3. a. This section does not prevent legislation recognising—

   (i) marriages concluded under any tradition, or a system of religious, personal or family law; or
   (ii) systems of personal and family law under any tradition, or adhered to by persons professing a particular religion.

b. Recognition in terms of paragraph (a) must be consistent with this section and the other provisions of the Constitution.

New Zealand – Bill of Rights Act 1990

Section 13 [Freedom of thought, conscience, and religion]

Everyone has the right to freedom of thought, conscience, religion, and belief, including the right to adopt and hold opinions without interference.

Section 14 [Freedom of expression]

Everyone has the right to freedom of expression, including the freedom to seek, receive, and impart information and opinions of any kind in any form.

Section 15 [Religion and belief]

Every person has the right to manifest that person's religion or belief in worship, observance, practice, or teaching, either individually or in community with others, and either in public or in private.

Constitution of Ireland

In the Name of the Most Holy Trinity, from Whom is all authority and to Whom, as our final end, all actions both of men and States must be referred, We, the people of Éire, Humbly acknowledging all our obligations to our Divine Lord, Jesus Christ, Who sustained our fathers through centuries of trial, . . . Do hereby adopt, enact, and give to ourselves this Constitution.

Article 44

1. The State acknowledges that the homage of public worship is due to Almighty God. It shall hold His Name in reverence, and shall respect and honour religion.

2. 1° Freedom of conscience and the free profession and practice of religion are, subject to public order and morality, guaranteed to every citizen.

   2° The State guarantees not to endow any religion.

   3° The State shall not impose any disabilities or make any discrimination on the ground of religious profession, belief or status.

   4° Legislation providing State aid for schools shall not discriminate between schools under the management of different religious denominations, nor be such as to affect prejudicially the right of any child to attend a school receiving public money without attending religious instruction at that school.

   5° Every religious denomination shall have the right to manage its own affairs, own, acquire and administer property, movable and immovable, and maintain institutions for religious or charitable purposes.

   6° The property of any religious denomination or any educational institution shall not be diverted save for necessary works of public utility and on payment of compensation.

The Constitution of India

15. Prohibition of discrimination on grounds of religion, race, caste, sex or place of birth

(1) The State shall not discriminate against any citizen on grounds only of religion, race, caste, sex, place of birth or any of them.

(2) No citizen shall, on grounds only of religion, race, caste, sex, place of birth or any of them, be subject to any disability, liability, restriction or condition with regard to—

(a) access to shops, public restaurants, hotels and places of public entertainment; or

(b) the use of wells, tanks, bathing ghats, roads and places of public resort
maintained wholly or partly out of State funds or dedicated to the use of
the general public.

(3) Nothing in this article shall prevent the State from making any special
provision for women and children.

(4) Nothing in this article or in clause (2) of article 29 shall prevent the State
from making any special provision for the advancement of any socially
and educationally backward classes of citizens or for the Scheduled Castes
and the Scheduled Tribes.

25. Freedom of conscience and free profession, practice and propagation of religion

(1) Subject to public order, morality and health and to the other provisions
of this Part, all persons are equally entitled to freedom of conscience and the
right freely to profess, practise and propagate religion.

(2) Nothing in this article shall affect the operation of any existing law or
prevent the State from making any law—

(a) regulating or restricting any economic, financial, political or other
secular activity which may be associated with religious practice;

(b) providing for social welfare and reform or the throwing open of Hindu
religious institutions of a public character to all classes and sections of
Hindus.

Explanation I.—The wearing and carrying of kirpans shall be deemed to be
included in the profession of the Sikh religion.

Explanation II.—In sub-clause (b) of clause (2), the reference to Hindus shall
be construed as including a reference to persons professing the Sikh, Jaina or
Buddhist religion, and the reference to Hindu religious institutions shall be
construed accordingly.

26. Freedom to manage religious affairs

Subject to public order, morality and health, every religious denomination or
any section thereof shall have the right—

(a) to establish and maintain institutions for religious and charitable
purposes;

(b) to manage its own affairs in matters of religion;

(c) to own and acquire movable and immovable property; and

(d) to administer such property in accordance with law.

27. Freedom as to payment of taxes for promotion of any particular religion

No person shall be compelled to pay any taxes, the proceeds of which are specifically appropriated in payment of expenses for the promotion or maintenance of any particular religion or religious denomination.

28. Freedom as to attendance at religious instruction or religious worship in certain educational institutions

(1) No religious instruction shall be provided in any educational institution wholly maintained out of State funds.

(2) Nothing in clause (1) shall apply to an educational institution which is administered by the State but has been established under any endowment or trust which requires that religious instruction shall be imparted in such institution.

(3) No person attending any educational institution recognised by the State or receiving aid out of State funds shall be required to take part in any religious instruction that may be imparted in such institution or to attend any religious worship that may be conducted in such institution or in any premises attached thereto unless such person or, if such person is a minor, his guardian has given his consent thereto.

Equality Act 2006, Part 2

DISCRIMINATION ON GROUNDS OF RELIGION OR BELIEF

DISCRIMINATION ON GROUNDS OF RELIGION OR BELIEF

Key concepts

44 Religion and belief

In this Part—

(a) 'religion' means any religion,
(b) 'belief' means any religious or philosophical belief,
(c) a reference to religion includes a reference to lack of religion, and
(d) a reference to belief includes a reference to lack of belief.

45 Discrimination

(1) A person ('A') discriminates against another ('B') for the purposes of this Part if on grounds of the religion or belief of B or of any other person except A (whether or not it is also A's religion or belief) A treats B less favourably than he treats or would treat others (in cases where there is no material difference in the relevant circumstances).

(2) In subsection (1) a reference to a person's religion or belief includes a reference to a religion or belief to which he is thought to belong or subscribe.

(3) A person ('A') discriminates against another ('B') for the purposes of this Part if A applies to B a provision, criterion or practice—

(a) which he applies or would apply equally to persons not of B's religion or belief,

(b) which puts persons of B's religion or belief at a disadvantage compared to some or all others (where there is no material difference in the relevant circumstances),

(c) which puts B at a disadvantage compared to some or all persons who are not of his religion or belief (where there is no material difference in the relevant circumstances), and

(d) which A cannot reasonably justify by reference to matters other than B's religion or belief.

(4) A person ('A') discriminates against another ('B') if A treats B less favourably than he treats or would treat another and does so by reason of the fact that, or by reason of A's knowledge or suspicion that, B—

(a) has brought or intended to bring, or intends to bring, proceedings under this Part,

(b) has given or intended to give, or intends to give, evidence in proceedings under this Part,

(c) has provided or intended to provide, or intends to provide, information in connection with proceedings under this Part,

(d) has done or intended to do, or intends to do, any other thing under or in connection with this Part, or

(e) has alleged or intended to allege, or intends to allege, that a person contravened this Part.

(5) Subsection (4) does not apply where A's treatment of B relates to B's making or intending to make, not in good faith, a false allegation.

Prohibited discrimination

46 Goods, facilities and services

(1) It is unlawful for a person ('A') concerned with the provision to the public or a section of the public of goods, facilities or services to discriminate against a person ('B') who seeks to obtain or use those goods, facilities or services—

(a) by refusing to provide B with goods, facilities or services,

(b) by refusing to provide B with goods, facilities or services of a quality which is the same as or similar to the quality of goods, facilities or services that A normally provides to—

(i) the public, or

(ii) a section of the public to which B belongs,

(c) by refusing to provide B with goods, facilities or services in a manner which is the same as or similar to that in which A normally provides goods, facilities or services to—

(i) the public, or

(ii) a section of the public to which B belongs, or

(d) by refusing to provide B with goods, facilities or services on terms which are the same as or similar to the terms on which A normally provides goods, facilities or services to—

(i) the public, or

(ii) a section of the public to which B belongs.

(2) Subsection (1) applies, in particular, to—

(a) access to and use of a place which the public are permitted to enter,

(b) accommodation in a hotel, boarding house or similar establishment,

(c) facilities by way of banking or insurance or for grants, loans, credit or finance,

(d) facilities for entertainment, recreation or refreshment,

(e) facilities for transport or travel, and

(f) the services of a profession or trade.

(3) Where a skill is commonly exercised in different ways in relation to or for the purposes of different religions or beliefs, a person who normally exercises it in relation to or for the purpose of a religion or belief does not contravene subsection (1) by—

(a) insisting on exercising the skill in the way in which he exercises it in relation to or for the purposes of that religion or belief, or

(b) if he reasonably considers it impracticable to exercise the skill in that way in relation to or for the purposes of another religion or belief, refusing to exercise it in relation to or for the purposes of that other religion or belief.

(4) Subsection (1)—

(a) does not apply in relation to the provision of goods, facilities or services by a person exercising a public function, and

(b) does not apply to discrimination in relation to the provision of goods, facilities or services if discrimination in relation to that provision—

(i) is unlawful by virtue of another provision of this Part or by virtue of a provision of the Employment Equality (Religion or Belief) Regulations 2003 (S.I. 2003/1660), or

(ii) would be unlawful by virtue of another provision of this Part or of those regulations but for an express exception.

(5) For the purposes of subsection (1) it is immaterial whether or not a person charges for the provision of goods, facilities or services.

47 Premises

(1) It is unlawful for a person to discriminate against another—

(a) in the terms on which he offers to dispose of premises to him,

(b) by refusing to dispose of premises to him, or

(c) in connection with a list of persons requiring premises.

(2) It is unlawful for a person managing premises to discriminate against an occupier—

(a) in the manner in which he provides access to a benefit or facility,

(b) by refusing access to a benefit or facility,

(c) by evicting him, or

(d) by subjecting him to another detriment.

(3) It is unlawful for a person to discriminate against another by refusing permission for the disposal of premises to him.

(4) This section applies only to premises in Great Britain.

48 Section 47: exceptions

(1) Section 47 shall not apply to anything done in relation to the disposal or management of part of premises by a person ('the landlord') if—

(a) the landlord or a near relative resides, and intends to continue to reside, in another part of the premises,

(b) the premises include parts (other than storage areas and means of access) shared by residents of the premises, and

(c) the premises are not normally sufficient to accommodate—

    (i) in the case of premises to be occupied by households, more than two households in addition to that of the landlord or his near relative, or

    (ii) in the case of premises to be occupied by individuals, more than six individuals in addition to the landlord or his near relative.

(2) In subsection (1) 'near relative' means—

(a) spouse or civil partner,

(b) parent or grandparent,

(c) child or grandchild (whether or not legitimate),

(d) the spouse or civil partner of a child or grandchild,

(e) brother or sister (whether of full blood or half-blood), and

(f) any of the relationships listed in paragraphs (b) to (e) above that arises through marriage, civil partnership or adoption.

(3) Section 47(1) and (3) shall not apply to the disposal of premises by a person who—

(a) owns an estate or interest in the premises,

(b) occupies the whole of the premises,

(c) does not use the services of an estate agent for the purposes of the disposal, and

(d) does not arrange for the publication of an advertisement for the purposes of the disposal.

49 Educational establishments

(1) It is unlawful for the responsible body of an educational establishment listed in the Table to discriminate against a person—

(a) in the terms on which it offers to admit him as a pupil,
(b) by refusing to accept an application to admit him as a pupil, or
(c) where he is a pupil of the establishment—

    (i) in the way in which it affords him access to any benefit, facility or service,

    (ii) by refusing him access to a benefit, facility or service,

    (iii) by excluding him from the establishment, or

    (iv) by subjecting him to any other detriment.

(2) In the application of this section to England and Wales—

(a) an expression also used in any of the Education Acts (within the meaning of section 578 of the Education Act 1996 (c. 56)) has the same meaning as in that Act, and

(b) 'pupil' in relation to an establishment includes any person who receives education at the establishment.

(3) In the application of this section to Scotland, an expression also used in the Education (Scotland) Act 1980 (c. 44) has the same meaning as in that Act.

Establishment	Responsible body
ENGLAND AND WALES	
School maintained by a local education authority.	Local education authority or governing body.
Independent school (other than a special school).	Proprietor.
Special school (not maintained by local education authority).	Proprietor.
SCOTLAND	
Public school.	Education authority.
Grant-aided school.	Manager.
Independent school.	Proprietor.

50 Section 49: exceptions

(1) Section 49(1)(a), (b) and (c)(i) and (ii) shall not apply in relation to—

(a) a school designated under section 69(3) of the School Standards and Framework Act 1998 (c. 31) (foundation or voluntary school with religious character),

(b) a school listed in the register of independent schools for England or for Wales if the school's entry in the register records that the school has a religious ethos,

(c) a school transferred to an education authority under section 16 of the Education (Scotland) Act 1980 (transfer of certain schools to education authorities) which is conducted in the interest of a church or denominational body,

(d) a school provided by an education authority under section 17(2) of that Act (denominational schools),

(e) a grant-aided school (within the meaning of that Act) which is conducted in the interest of a church or denominational body, or

(f) a school registered in the register of independent schools for Scotland if the school—

(i) admits only pupils who belong, or whose parents belong, to one or more particular denominations, or

(ii) is conducted in the interest of a church or denominational body.

(2) Section 49(1)(c)(i), (ii) or (iv) shall not apply in relation to anything done in connection with—

(a) the content of the curriculum, or

(b) acts of worship or other religious observance organised by or on behalf of an educational establishment (whether or not forming part of the curriculum).

(3) The Secretary of State may by order—

(a) amend or repeal an exception in subsection (1) or (2);

(b) provide for an additional exception to section 49;

(c) make provision about the construction or application of section 45(3)(d) in relation to section 49.

(4) An order under subsection (3)—

(a) may include transitional, incidental or consequential provision (including provision amending an enactment (including an enactment in or under an Act of the Scottish Parliament)),

(b) may make provision generally or only in respect of specified cases or cir-cumstances (which may, in particular, be defined by reference to location),

(c) may make different provision in respect of different cases or circum-stances (which may, in particular, be defined by reference to location),

(d) shall be made by statutory instrument,

(e) may not be made unless the Secretary of State has consulted the Scottish Ministers, the National Assembly for Wales and such other persons as he thinks appropriate, and

(f) may not be made unless a draft has been laid before and approved by resolution of each House of Parliament.

51 Local education authorities and education authorities

(1) It is unlawful for a local education authority (in England and Wales) or an education authority (in Scotland) in the exercise of their functions to discriminate against a person.

(2) In its application to local education authorities the prohibition in subsection (1) shall not apply to—

(a) the exercise of an authority's functions under section 14 of the Education Act 1996 (c. 56) (provision of schools),
(b) the exercise of an authority's functions in relation to transport,
(c) the exercise of an authority's functions under section 13 of that Act (general responsibility for education) in so far as they relate to a matter specified in paragraph (a) or (b) above, or
(d) the exercise of functions as the responsible body for an establishment listed in the Table in section 49.

(3) In its application to education authorities the prohibition in subsection (1) shall not apply to—

(a) the exercise of an authority's functions under section 17 of the Education (Scotland) Act 1980 (c. 44) (provision etc. of schools),
(b) the exercise of an authority's functions in relation to transport,
(c) the exercise of an authority's functions under section 1 of that Act, section 2 of the Standards in Scotland's Schools etc. Act 2000 (asp 6) and sections 4 and 5 of the Education (Additional Support for Learning) (Scotland) Act 2004 (asp 4) (duties in relation to provision of education) in so far as they relate to a matter specified in paragraph (a) or (b) above,
(d) the exercise of an authority's functions under section 50(1) of the Education (Scotland) Act 1980 (education of pupils in exceptional circumstances) in so far as they consist of making arrangements of the kind referred to in subsection (2) of that section, or
(e) the exercise of functions as the responsible body for an establishment listed in the Table in section 49.

52 Public authorities: general

(1) It is unlawful for a public authority exercising a function to do any act which constitutes discrimination.

(2) In subsection (1)—

(a) 'public authority' includes any person who has functions of a public nature (subject to subsections (3) and (4)), and

(b) 'function' means function of a public nature.

(3) The prohibition in subsection (1) shall not apply to—

(a) the House of Commons,

(b) the House of Lords,

(c) the authorities of either House of Parliament,

(d) the Security Service,

(e) the Secret Intelligence Service,

(f) the Government Communications Headquarters, or

(g) a part of the armed forces of the Crown which is, in accordance with a requirement of the Secretary of State, assisting the Government Communications Headquarters.

(4) The prohibition in subsection (1) shall not apply to—

(a) the exercise of a judicial function (whether in connection with a court or a tribunal),

(b) anything done on behalf of or on the instructions of a person exercising a judicial function (whether in connection with a court or a tribunal),

(c) preparing, passing (or making), confirming, approving or considering an enactment (including legislation made by or by virtue of a Measure of the General Synod of the Church of England),

(d) the making of an instrument by a Minister of the Crown under an enactment,

(e) the making of an instrument by the Scottish Ministers or a member of the Scottish Executive under an enactment,

(f) a decision of any of the following kinds taken in accordance with rules under section 3(2) of the Immigration Act 1971 (c. 77) ('immigration rules') or anything done for the purposes of or in pursuance of a decision of any of those kinds—

   (i) a decision to refuse entry clearance or leave to enter the United Kingdom on the grounds that the exclusion of the person from the United Kingdom is conducive to the public good,

   (ii) a decision to cancel leave to enter or remain in the United Kingdom on the grounds that the exclusion of the person from the United Kingdom is conducive to the public good,

   (iii) a decision to refuse an application to vary leave to enter or remain in the United Kingdom on the grounds that it is undesirable to permit the person to remain in the United Kingdom,

   (iv) a decision to vary leave to enter or remain in the United Kingdom on the grounds that it is undesirable to permit the person to remain in the United Kingdom,

(g) a decision in connection with an application for entry clearance or for leave to enter or remain in the United Kingdom or anything done for the purposes of or in pursuance of a decision of that kind (whether or not the decision is taken in pursuance of a provision of immigration rules) if the decision is taken on the grounds—

(i)   that a person holds an office or position in connection with a religion or belief or provides services in connection with a religion or belief,

(ii) that a religion or belief is not to be treated in the same way as certain other religions or beliefs, or

(iii) that the exclusion from the United Kingdom of a person to whom paragraph (i) applies is conducive to the public good,

(h) a decision taken, or guidance given, by the Secretary of State in connection with a decision of a kind specified in paragraph (f) or (g),

(i) a decision taken in accordance with guidance given by the Secretary of State in connection with a decision of a kind specified in paragraph (f) or (g),

(j) a decision not to institute or continue criminal proceedings (and anything done for the purpose of reaching, or in pursuance of, such a decision),

(k) action in relation to—

(i)   the curriculum of an educational institution,

(ii) admission to an educational institution which has a religious ethos,

(iii) acts of worship or other religious observance organised by or on behalf of an educational institution (whether or not forming part of the curriculum),

(iv) the governing body of an educational institution which has a religious ethos,

(v)   transport to or from an educational institution, or

(vi) the establishment, alteration or closure of educational institutions,

(l) the exercise of the power under section 2 of the Local Government Act 2000 (c. 22) (promotion of well-being), or

(m) action which—

(i)   is unlawful by virtue of another provision of this Part or by virtue of a provision of the Employment Equality (Religion or Belief) Regulations 2003 (S.I. 2003/1660), or

(ii) would be unlawful by virtue of another provision of this Part other than section 46, or by virtue of a provision of those regulations, but for an express exception.

(5) In an action under section 66 in respect of a contravention of this section—

(a) the court shall not grant an injunction unless satisfied that it will not prejudice criminal proceedings or a criminal investigation, and

(b) the court shall grant any application to stay the section 66 proceedings on the grounds of prejudice to criminal proceedings or to a criminal investigation, unless satisfied that the proceedings or investigation will not be prejudiced.

(6) Section 70(4) shall not apply in relation to a reply, or a failure to reply, to a question in connection with an alleged contravention of this section—

(a) if the respondent or potential respondent reasonably asserts that to have replied differently or at all might have prejudiced criminal proceedings or a criminal investigation,

(b) if the respondent or potential respondent reasonably asserts that to have replied differently or at all would have revealed the reason for not instituting or not continuing criminal proceedings,

(c) where the reply is of a kind specified for the purposes of this paragraph by order of the Secretary of State,

(d) where the reply is given in circumstances specified for the purposes of this paragraph by order of the Secretary of State, or

(e) where the failure occurs in circumstances specified for the purposes of this paragraph by order of the Secretary of State.

(7) In this section—

'criminal investigation' means—

(a)   an investigation into the commission of an alleged offence, and

(b)   a decision whether to institute criminal proceedings, and

'enactment' includes an enactment in or under an Act of the Scottish Parliament.

(8) An order under subsection (6)(c) to (e)—

(a) may include transitional or incidental provision,

(b) may make provision generally or only for specified cases or circumstances,

(c) may make different provision for different cases or circumstances,

(d) shall be made by statutory instrument, and

(e) shall be subject to annulment in pursuance of a resolution of either House of Parliament.

(9) In the application of this section to proceedings in Scotland—

(a) a reference to the court shall be taken as a reference to the sheriff,

(b) a reference to an injunction shall be taken as a reference to an interdict,

(c) a reference to staying proceedings shall be taken as a reference to sisting proceedings, and

(d) a reference to the respondent or potential respondent shall be taken as a reference to the defender or potential defender.

Other unlawful acts

53 Discriminatory practices

(1) It is unlawful for a person to operate a practice which would be likely to result in unlawful discrimination if applied to persons of any religion or belief.

(2) It is unlawful for a person to adopt or maintain a practice or arrangement in accordance with which in certain circumstances a practice would be operated in contravention of subsection (1).

(3) In this section 'unlawful discrimination' means discrimination which is unlawful by virtue of any of sections 46 to 52.

(4) Proceedings in respect of a contravention of this section may be brought only—

(a) by the Commission for Equality and Human Rights, and
(b) in accordance with sections 20 to 24.

54 Discriminatory advertisements

(1) It is unlawful to publish an advertisement, or to cause an advertisement to be published, if it indicates (expressly or impliedly) an intention by any person to discriminate unlawfully.

(2) In subsection (1) the reference to unlawful discrimination is a reference to discrimination which is unlawful by virtue of any of sections 46 to 52.

(3) Proceedings in respect of a contravention of subsection (1) may be brought only—

(a) by the Commission for Equality and Human Rights, and
(b) in accordance with section 25.

(4) A person who publishes an advertisement shall not be liable in proceedings under that section in respect of the publication of the advertisement if he proves that—

(a) he published in reliance on a statement, made by a person causing the advertisement to be published, that subsection (1) would not apply, and
(b) that it was reasonable to rely on that statement.

(5) A person commits an offence if he knowingly or recklessly makes a false statement of the kind mentioned in subsection (4)(a).

(6) A person guilty of an offence under subsection (5) shall be liable on summary conviction to a fine not exceeding level 5 on the standard scale.

55 Instructing or causing discrimination

(1) It is unlawful for a person to instruct another to unlawfully discriminate.

(2) It is unlawful for a person to cause or attempt to cause another to unlawfully discriminate.

(3) It is unlawful for a person to induce or attempt to induce another to unlawfully discriminate.

(4) For the purposes of subsection (3) inducement may be direct or indirect.

(5) In this section a reference to unlawful discrimination is a reference to discrimination which is unlawful by virtue of any of sections 46 to 52.

(6) Proceedings in respect of a contravention of this section may be brought only—

(a) by the Commission for Equality and Human Rights, and
(b) in accordance with section 25.

General exceptions

56 Statutory requirements

Nothing in this Part shall make it unlawful to do anything which is necessary, or in so far as it is necessary, for the purpose of complying with—

(a) an Act of Parliament,
(b) an Act of the Scottish Parliament,
(c) legislation made or to be made—
    (i)   by a Minister of the Crown,
    (ii) by Order in Council,
    (iii) by the Scottish Ministers or a member of the Scottish Executive,
    (iv) by the National Assembly for Wales, or
    (v) by or by virtue of a Measure of the General Synod of the Church of England, or
(d) a condition or requirement imposed by a Minister of the Crown by virtue of anything listed in paragraphs (a) to (c).

57 Organisations relating to religion or belief

(1) This section applies to an organisation the purpose of which is—

(a) to practice a religion or belief,
(b) to advance a religion or belief,
(c) to teach the practice or principles of a religion or belief,
(d) to enable persons of a religion or belief to receive any benefit, or to engage in any activity, within the framework of that religion or belief, or
(e) to improve relations, or maintain good relations, between persons of different religions or beliefs.

(2) But this section does not apply to an organisation whose sole or main purpose is commercial.

(3) Nothing in this Part shall make it unlawful for an organisation to which this section applies or anyone acting on behalf of or under the auspices of an organisation to which this section applies—

(a) to restrict membership of the organisation,

(b) to restrict participation in activities undertaken by the organisation or on its behalf or under its auspices,

(c) to restrict the provision of goods, facilities or services in the course of activities undertaken by the organisation or on its behalf or under its auspices, or

(d) to restrict the use or disposal of premises owned or controlled by the organisation.

(4) Nothing in this Part shall make it unlawful for a minister—

(a) to restrict participation in activities carried on in the performance of his functions in connection with or in respect of an organisation to which this section relates, or

(b) to restrict the provision of goods, facilities or services in the course of activities carried on in the performance of his functions in connection with or in respect of an organisation to which this section relates.

(5) But subsections (3) and (4) permit a restriction only if imposed—

(a) by reason of or on the grounds of the purpose of the organisation, or

(b) in order to avoid causing offence, on grounds of the religion or belief to which the organisation relates, to persons of that religion or belief.

(6) In subsection (4) the reference to a minister is a reference to a minister of religion, or other person, who—

(a) performs functions in connection with a religion or belief to which an organisation, to which this section applies, relates, and

(b) holds an office or appointment in, or is accredited, approved or recognised for purposes of, an organisation to which this section applies.

58 Charities relating to religion or belief

(1) Nothing in this Part shall make it unlawful for a person to provide benefits only to persons of a particular religion or belief, if—

(a) he acts in pursuance of a charitable instrument, and

(b) the restriction of benefits to persons of that religion or belief is imposed by reason of or on the grounds of the provisions of the charitable instrument.

(2) Nothing in this Part shall make it unlawful for the Charity Commissioners for England and Wales or the holder of the Office of the Scottish Charity Regulator to exercise a function in relation to a charity in a manner which appears to the Commissioners or to the holder to be expedient in the

interests of the charity, having regard to the provisions of the charitable instrument.

(3) In this section 'charitable instrument'—

(a) means an instrument establishing or governing a charity, and

(b) includes a charitable instrument made before the commencement of this section.

59 Faith schools, &c.

(1) Nothing in this Part shall make it unlawful for an educational institution established or conducted for the purpose of providing education relating to, or within the framework of, a specified religion or belief—

(a) to restrict the provision of goods, facilities or services, or

(b) to restrict the use or disposal of premises.

(2) But subsection (1) permits a restriction only if imposed—

(a) by reason of or on the grounds of the purpose of the institution, or

(b) in order to avoid causing offence, on grounds of the religion or belief to which the institution relates, to persons connected with the institution.

(3) In this Part a reference to the provision of facilities or services shall not, in so far as it applies to an educational institution, include a reference to educational facilities or educational services provided to students of the institution.

60 Membership requirement

(1) Nothing in this Part shall make it unlawful for a charity to require members, or persons wishing to become members, to make a statement which asserts or implies membership or acceptance of a religion or belief.

(2) Subsection (1) shall apply to the imposition of a requirement by a charity only if—

(a) the charity, or an organisation of which the charity is part, first imposed a requirement of the kind specified in subsection (1) before 18th May 2005, and

(b) the charity or organisation has not ceased since that date to impose a requirement of that kind.

61 Education, training and welfare

Nothing in this Part shall make it unlawful to do anything by way of—

(a) meeting special needs for education, training or welfare of persons of a religion or belief, or

(b) providing ancillary benefits in connection with meeting the needs mentioned in paragraph (a).

62 Care within family

Nothing in this Part shall make it unlawful for a person to take into his home, and treat in the same manner as a member of his family, a person who requires a special degree of care and attention (whether by reason of being a child or an elderly person or otherwise).

63 National security

Nothing in this Part shall make unlawful anything which is done for, and justified by, the purpose of safeguarding national security.

64 Amendment of exceptions

(1) The Secretary of State may by order amend this Part so as to—

(a) create an exception to the prohibition under section 52(1), or,

(b) vary an exception to a prohibition under this Part.

(2) Before making an order under subsection (1) the Secretary of State shall consult the Commission for Equality and Human Rights.

(3) An order under subsection (1)—

(a) may include transitional, incidental or consequential provision (including provision amending an enactment (including an enactment in or under an Act of the Scottish Parliament)),

(b) may make provision generally or only for specified cases or circumstances,

(c) may make different provision for different cases or circumstances,

(d) shall be made by statutory instrument, and

(e) may not be made unless a draft has been laid before and approved by resolution of each House of Parliament.

Enforcement

65 Restriction of proceedings

(1) Except as provided by this Act, no proceedings, whether criminal or civil, may be brought against a person on the grounds that an act is unlawful by virtue of this Part.

(2) But subsection (1) does not prevent—

(a) an application for judicial review,

(b) proceedings under the Immigration Acts,

(c) proceedings under the Special Immigration Appeals Commission Act 1997 (c. 68), or

(d) in Scotland, the exercise of the jurisdiction of the Court of Session to entertain an application for reduction or suspension of an order or determination or otherwise to consider the validity of an order or determination, or to require reasons for an order or determination to be stated.

66 Claim of unlawful action

(1) A claim that a person has done anything that is unlawful by virtue of this Part may be brought in a county court (in England and Wales) or in the sheriff court (in Scotland) by way of proceedings in tort (or reparation) for breach of statutory duty.

(2) Proceedings in England and Wales alleging that any of the following bodies has acted unlawfully by virtue of section 49 or 51 may not be brought unless the claimant has given written notice to the Secretary of State; and those bodies are—

(a) a local education authority, and

(b) the responsible body of an educational establishment listed in the Table in section 49.

(3) Proceedings in Scotland alleging that any of the following bodies has acted unlawfully by virtue of section 49 or 51 may not be brought unless the pursuer has given written notice to the Scottish Ministers; and those bodies are—

(a) an education authority, and

(b) the responsible body of an educational establishment listed in the Table in section 49.

(4) In subsection (1) the reference to a claim that a person has done an unlawful act includes a reference to a claim that a person is to be treated by virtue of this Part as having done an unlawful act.

(5) In proceedings under this section, if the claimant (or pursuer) proves facts from which the court could conclude, in the absence of a reasonable alternative explanation, that an act which is unlawful by virtue of this Part has been committed, the court shall assume that the act was unlawful unless the respondent (or defender) proves that it was not.

67 Immigration

(1) Proceedings may not be brought under section 66 alleging that a person has acted unlawfully by virtue of section 52 if the question of the lawfulness of the act could be raised (and has not been raised) in immigration pro-ceedings (disregarding the possibility of proceedings brought out of time with permission).

(2) If in immigration proceedings a court or tribunal has found that an act was unlawful by virtue of section 52, a court hearing proceedings under section 66 shall accept that finding.

(3) In this section 'immigration proceedings' means proceedings under or by virtue of—

(a) the Immigration Acts, or

(b) the Special Immigration Appeals Commission Act 1997 (c. 68).

68 Remedies

(1) This section applies to proceedings under section 66.

(2) A court may, in addition to any remedy available to it in proceedings for tort, grant any remedy that the High Court could grant in proceedings for judicial review.

(3) A court may not award damages in proceedings in respect of an act that is unlawful by virtue of section 45(3) if the respondent proves that there was no intention to treat the claimant unfavourably on grounds of religion or belief.

(4) A court may award damages by way of compensation for injury to feelings (whether or not other damages are also awarded).

(5) In the application of this section to proceedings in Scotland—

(a) a reference to the High Court shall be taken as a reference to the Court of Session,

(b) a reference to tort shall be taken as a reference to reparation,

(c) a reference to the respondent shall be taken as a reference to the defender, and

(d) a reference to the claimant shall be taken as a reference to the pursuer.

(6) This section is subject to section 52(5).

69 Timing

(1) Proceedings under section 66 may be brought only—

(a) within the period of six months beginning with the date of the act (or last act) to which the proceedings relate, or

(b) with the permission of the court in which the proceedings are brought.

(2) In relation to immigration proceedings within the meaning of section 67, the period specified in subsection (1)(a) above shall begin with the first date on which proceedings under section 66 may be brought.

70 Information

(1) In this section—

(a) a reference to a claimant is a reference to a person who has brought proceedings under this Part,

(b) a reference to a potential claimant is a reference to a person who—

> (i)   thinks he may have been the subject of an act that is unlawful by virtue of this Part, and
>
> (ii) wishes to consider whether to bring proceedings under this Part, and

(c)   a person questioned by a potential claimant for the purpose of considering whether to bring proceedings is referred to as a potential respondent.

(2)   The Secretary of State shall by order prescribe—

(a)   forms by which a claimant or potential claimant may question the respondent or a potential respondent about the reasons for an action or about any matter that is or may be relevant, and

(b)   forms by which a respondent or potential respondent may reply (if he wishes).

(3)   A claimant's or potential claimant's questions, and a respondent or potential respondent's replies (in each case whether or not put by a prescribed form), shall be admissible as evidence in proceedings in respect of the act to which the questions relate if (and only if) the questions are put—

(a)   within the period of six months beginning with the date of the act (or last act) to which they relate, and

(b)   in such manner as the Secretary of State may prescribe by order.

(4)   A court may draw an inference from—

(a)   a failure to reply to a claimant's or potential claimant's questions (whether or not put by a prescribed form) within the period of eight weeks beginning with the date of receipt, or

(b)   an evasive or equivocal reply to a claimant's or potential claimant's questions (whether or not put by a prescribed form).

(5)   The Secretary of State may by order amend subsection (3)(a) so as to substitute a new period for that specified.

(6)   In the application of this section to Scotland—

(a)   a reference to a claimant or potential claimant shall be taken as a reference to a pursuer or potential pursuer, and

(b)   a reference to a respondent or potential respondent shall be taken as a reference to a defender or potential defender.

(7)   An order under this section—

(a)   shall be made by statutory instrument, and

(b)   shall be subject to annulment in pursuance of a resolution of either House of Parliament.

(8)   This section is subject to section 52(6).

71 National security

(1) Rules of court may make provision for enabling a county court or sheriff court in which a claim is brought under section 66, where the court considers it expedient in the interests of national security—

(a) to exclude from all or part of the proceedings—

    (i)   the claimant;
    (ii) the claimant's representatives;
    (iii) any assessors;

(b) to permit a claimant or representative who has been excluded to make a statement to the court before the commencement of the proceedings, or the part of the proceedings, from which he is excluded;

(c) to take steps to keep secret all or part of the reasons for the court's decision in the proceedings.

(2) The Attorney General or, in Scotland, the Advocate General for Scotland, may appoint a person to represent the interests of a claimant in, or in any part of, proceedings from which the claimant or his representatives are excluded by virtue of subsection (1).

(3) A person may be appointed under subsection (2) only—

(a) in relation to proceedings in England and Wales, if he has a general qualification (within the meaning of section 71 of the Courts and Legal Services Act 1990 (c. 41)), or

(b) in relation to proceedings in Scotland, if he is—

    (i)   an advocate, or
    (ii) qualified to practice as a solicitor in Scotland.

(4) A person appointed under subsection (2) shall not be responsible to the person whose interests he is appointed to represent.

72 Validity and revision of contracts

(1) A term of a contract is void where—

(a) its inclusion renders the making of the contract unlawful by virtue of this Part,

(b) it is included in furtherance of an act which is unlawful by virtue of this Part, or

(c) it provides for the doing of an act which would be unlawful by virtue of this Part.

(2) Subsection (1) does not apply to a term the inclusion of which constitutes, or is in furtherance of, or provides for, unlawful discrimination against a party to the contract; but the term shall be unenforceable against that party.

(3) A term in a contract which purports to exclude or limit a provision of this

Part is unenforceable by a person in whose favour the term would operate apart from this subsection.

(4) Subsection (3) does not apply to a contract settling a claim under section 66.

(5) On the application of a person interested in a contract to which subsection (1) applies, a county court or sheriff court may make an order for removing or modifying a term made unenforceable by that subsection; but an order shall not be made unless all persons affected—

(a) have been given notice of the application (except where notice is dispensed with in accordance with rules of court), and
(b) have been afforded an opportunity to make representations to the court.

(6) An order under subsection (5) may include provision in respect of a period before the making of the order.

General

73 Aiding unlawful acts

(1) It is unlawful knowingly to help another person (whether or not as his employee or agent) to do anything which is unlawful under this Part.

(2) A person commits an offence if he knowingly or recklessly makes a false statement, in connection with assistance sought from another, that a proposed act is not unlawful under this Part.

(3) A person guilty of an offence under subsection (2) shall be liable on summary conviction to a fine not exceeding level 5 on the standard scale.

74 Employers' and principals' liability

(1) Anything done by a person in the course of his employment shall be treated for the purposes of this Part as done by the employer as well as by the person.

(2) Anything done by a person as agent for another shall be treated for the purposes of this Part as done by the principal as well as by the agent.

(3) It is immaterial for the purposes of this section whether an employer or principal knows about or approves of an act.

(4) In proceedings under this Part against a person in respect of an act alleged to have been done by his employee it shall be a defence for the employer to provide that he took such steps as were reasonably practicable to prevent the employee—

(a) from doing the act, or
(b) from doing acts of that kind in the course of his employment.

(5) Subsections (1) and (2) shall not apply to the commission of an offence under section 54.

75 Police, &c.

(1) This section applies to—

(a) a constable who is a member of a police force maintained under the Police Act 1996 (c. 16) or the Police (Scotland) Act 1967 (c. 77),

(b) a special constable appointed for a police area in accordance with either of those Acts, and

(c) a person appointed as a police cadet in accordance with either of those Acts.

(2) A person to whom this section applies shall be treated for the purposes of this Part as the employee of his chief officer of police; and anything done by the person in the performance or purported performance of his functions shall be treated as done in the course of that employment.

(3) There shall be paid out of the police fund—

(a) compensation, costs or expenses awarded against a chief officer of police in proceedings brought against him under this Part;

(b) costs or expenses incurred by a chief officer of police in proceedings brought against him under this Part so far as not recovered in the proceedings;

(c) sums required by a chief officer of police for the settlement of a claim made against him under this Part if the settlement is approved by the police authority.

(4) A police authority may pay out of the police fund—

(a) damages or costs awarded in proceedings under this Part against a person under the direction and control of the chief officer of police;

(b) costs incurred and not recovered by such a person in such proceedings;

(c) sums required in connection with the settlement of a claim that has or might have given rise to such proceedings.

(5) In section 56(4) of the Serious Organised Crime and Police Act 2005 (c. 15) (application of discrimination legislation to seconded staff) after paragraph (f) insert- '; and (g) section 74 of the Equality Act 2006.'

76 Indirect provision of benefit, &c.

A reference in this Part to providing a service, facility or benefit of any kind includes a reference to facilitating access to the service, facility or benefit.

77 Employment Equality Regulations

(1) For regulation 2(1) of the Employment Equality (Religion or Belief) Regulations 2003 (S.I. 2003/1660) (definition of 'religion or belief') substitute—

'(1) In these Regulations—

(a) "religion" means any religion,

(b) "belief" means any religious or philosophical belief,

(c) a reference to religion includes a reference to lack of religion, and

(d) a reference to belief includes a reference to lack of belief.'

(2) For regulation 3(1)(a) of the Regulations substitute—

'(a) on the grounds of the religion or belief of B or of any other person except A (whether or not it is also A's religion or belief) A treats B less favourably than he treats or would treat other persons;'.

(3) Omit regulation 3(2) of the Regulations.

78 Crown application

(1) Section 52 binds the Crown.

(2) The remainder of this Part applies to an act done on behalf of the Crown as it applies to an act done by a private person.

(3) For the purposes of subsection (2) an act is done on behalf of the Crown if (and only if) done—

(a) by or on behalf of a Minister of the Crown,

(b) by or on behalf of the Scottish Ministers,

(c) by a government department,

(d) by a body established by an enactment (including an enactment in or under an Act of the Scottish Parliament) acting on behalf of the Crown,

(e) by or on behalf of the holder of an office established by an enactment (including an enactment in or under an Act of the Scottish Parliament) acting on behalf of the Crown, or

(f) by or on behalf of an office-holder in the Scottish Administration (within the meaning of section 126(7) of the Scotland Act 1998 (c. 46)).

(4) The provisions of Parts II to IV of the Crown Proceedings Act 1947 shall apply to proceedings against the Crown under this Part as they apply to proceedings in England and Wales which by virtue of section 23 of that Act are treated for the purposes of Part II of that Act as civil proceedings by or against the Crown; but section 20 of that Act (removal of proceedings from county court to High Court) shall not apply to proceedings under this Part.

(5) The provisions of Part V of the Crown Proceedings Act 1947 shall apply to proceedings against the Crown under this Part as they apply to pro-ceedings in Scotland which by virtue of the said Part are treated as civil proceedings by or against the Crown; but the proviso to section 44 of that Act (removal of proceedings from the sheriff court to the Court of Session) shall not apply to proceedings under this Part.

79 Interpretation

(1) In this Part 'charity'—

(a) in relation to England and Wales, has the meaning given by the Charities Act 2006, and

(b) in relation to Scotland, means a body entered in the Scottish Charity Register.

(2) In this Part—

(a) a reference to action includes a reference to deliberate omission, and

(b) a reference to refusal includes a reference to deliberate omission.

80 Territorial application

(1) This Part applies in relation to anything done in Great Britain.

(2) This Part also applies to the provision of—

(a) facilities for travel on a British ship, a British hovercraft or a British aircraft, and

(b) benefits, facilities or services provided on a British ship, a British hovercraft or a British aircraft.

(3) Section 52, in so far as it relates to granting entry clearance (within the meaning of the Immigration Acts), applies to anything done whether inside or outside the United Kingdom.

(4) In this section—

'British aircraft' means an aircraft registered in Great Britain,
'British hovercraft' means a hovercraft registered in Great Britain, and
'British ship' means a ship which is—

(a) registered in Great Britain, or

(b) owned by or used for purposes of the Crown.

(5) This section shall not make it unlawful to do anything in or over a country other than the United Kingdom, or in or over the territorial waters of a country other than the United Kingdom, for the purpose of complying with a law of the country.

Employment Equality (Religion or Belief) Regulations 2003

Statutory Instrument 2003 No. 1660

(As amended by The Employment Equality (Religion or Belief) (Amendment) Regulations 2003, The Independent Schools (Employment of Teachers in Schools with a Religious Character) Regulations 2003, The Employment Equality (Religion or Belief) (Amendment) Regulations 2004, The Employment Equality (Religion or Belief) Regulations 2003 (Amendment) (No.2) Regulations 2004, and The Equality Act 2006)

Made	26th June 2003
Coming into force	2nd December 2003

ARRANGEMENT OF REGULATIONS

Whereas a draft of these Regulations was laid before Parliament in accordance with paragraph 2 of Schedule 2 to the European Communities Act 1972, and was approved by resolution of each House of Parliament; Now, therefore, the Secretary of State, being a Minister designated for the purposes of section 2(2) of the European Communities Act 1972 in relation to discrimination, in exercise of the powers conferred by that section, hereby makes the following Regulations:

PART 1 GENERAL

Citation, commencement and extent

1.—(1) These Regulations may be cited as the Employment Equality (Religion or Belief) Regulations 2003, and shall come into force on 2nd December 2003.

(2) These Regulations do not extend to Northern Ireland.

Interpretation

2.—(1) In these Regulations, 'religion or belief' means any religion, religious belief, or similar philosophical belief.

[*Under s77(1) of the Equality Act 2006 the wording of Regulation 2(1) is to be changed to the following*

(1) In these Regulations—

(a) 'religion' means any religion,
(b) 'belief' means any religious or philosophical belief,
(c) a reference to religion includes a reference to lack of religion, and
(d) a reference to belief includes a reference to lack of belief.]

(2) In these Regulations, references to discrimination are to any discrimination falling within regulation 3 (discrimination on grounds of religion or belief) or 4 (discrimination by way of victimisation) and related expressions shall be construed accordingly, and references to harassment shall be construed in accordance with regulation 5 (harassment on grounds of religion or belief).

(3) In these Regulations—

'act' includes a deliberate omission;
'benefits', except in regulation 9A (trustees and managers of occupational pension schemes), includes facilities and services;
'detriment' does not include harassment within the meaning of regulation 5;
references to 'employer', in their application to a person at any time seeking to employ another, include a person who has no employees at that time;
'employment' means employment under a contract of service or of apprenticeship or a contract personally to do any work, and related expressions shall be construed accordingly;
'Great Britain', except where the context otherwise requires in regulation 26 (protection of Sikhs from discrimination in connection with requirements as to wearing of safety helmets), includes such of the territorial waters of the United Kingdom as are adjacent to Great Britain;
'Minister of the Crown' includes the Treasury and the Defence Council; and

'school', in England and Wales, has the meaning given by section 4 of the Education Act 1996, and, in Scotland, has the meaning given by section 135(1) of the Education (Scotland) Act 1980, and references to a school are to an institution in so far as it is engaged in the provision of education under those sections.

Discrimination on grounds of religion or belief

3.—(1) For the purposes of these Regulations, a person ('A') discriminates against another person ('B') if—

(a) on grounds of religion or belief, A treats B less favourably than he treats or would treat other persons; or
(b) A applies to B a provision, criterion or practice which he applies or would apply equally to persons not of the same religion or belief as B, but—

    (i) which puts or would put persons of the same religion or belief as B at a particular disadvantage when compared with other persons,

    (ii) which puts B at that disadvantage, and

    (iii) which A cannot show to be a proportionate means of achieving a legitimate aim.

(2) The reference in paragraph (1)(a) to religion or belief does not include A's religion or belief.

(3) A comparison of B's case with that of another person under paragraph (1) must be such that the relevant circumstances in the one case are the same, or not materially different, in the other.

[*Under s77(2) of the Equality Act 2006 the wording of Regulation 3(1)(a) is to be changed to the following*

(a) on the grounds of the religion or belief of B or of any other person except A (whether or not it is also A's religion or belief) A treats B less favourably than he treats or would treat other persons

and under s77(3) regulation 3(2) will be repealed.]

Discrimination by way of victimisation

4.—(1) For the purposes of these Regulations, a person ('A') discriminates against another person ('B') if he treats B less favourably than he treats or would treat other persons in the same circumstances, and does so by reason that B has—

(a) brought proceedings against A or any other person under these Regulations;
(b) given evidence or information in connection with proceedings brought by any person against A or any other person under these Regulations;

(c) otherwise done anything under or by reference to these Regulations in relation to A or any other person; or

(d) alleged that A or any other person has committed an act which (whether or not the allegation so states) would amount to a contravention of these Regulations, or by reason that A knows that B intends to do any of those things, or suspects that B has done or intends to do any of them.

(2) Paragraph (1) does not apply to treatment of B by reason of any allegation made by him, or evidence or information given by him, if the allegation, evidence or information was false and not made (or, as the case may be, given) in good faith.

Harassment on grounds of religion or belief

5.—(1) For the purposes of these Regulations, a person ('A') subjects another person ('B') to harassment where, on grounds of religion or belief, A engages in unwanted conduct which has the purpose or effect of—

(a) violating B's dignity; or

(b) creating an intimidating, hostile, degrading, humiliating or offensive environment for B.

(2) Conduct shall be regarded as having the effect specified in paragraph (1)(a) or (b) only if, having regard to all the circumstances, including in particular the perception of B, it should reasonably be considered as having that effect.

PART II DISCRIMINATION IN EMPLOYMENT AND VOCATIONAL TRAINING

Applicants and employees

6.—(1) It is unlawful for an employer, in relation to employment by him at an establishment in Great Britain, to discriminate against a person—

(a) in the arrangements he makes for the purpose of determining to whom he should offer employment;

(b) in the terms on which he offers that person employment; or

(c) by refusing to offer, or deliberately not offering, him employment.

(2) It is unlawful for an employer, in relation to a person whom he employs at an establishment in Great Britain, to discriminate against that person—

(a) in the terms of employment which he affords him;

(b) in the opportunities which he affords him for promotion, a transfer, training, or receiving any other benefit;

(c) by refusing to afford him, or deliberately not affording him, any such opportunity; or

(d) by dismissing him, or subjecting him to any other detriment.

(3) It is unlawful for an employer, in relation to employment by him at an establishment in Great Britain, to subject to harassment a person whom he employs or who has applied to him for employment.

(4) Paragraph (2) does not apply to benefits of any description if the employer is concerned with the provision (for payment or not) of benefits of that description to the public, or to a section of the public which includes the employee in question, unless—

(a) that provision differs in a material respect from the provision of the benefits by the employer to his employees; or
(b) the provision of the benefits to the employee in question is regulated by his contract of employment; or
(c) the benefits relate to training.

(5) In paragraph (2)(d) reference to the dismissal of a person from employment includes reference—

(a) to the termination of that person's employment by the expiration of any period (including a period expiring by reference to an event or circumstance), not being a termination immediately after which the employment is renewed on the same terms; and
(b) to the termination of that person's employment by any act of his (including the giving of notice) in circumstances such that he is entitled to terminate it without notice by reason of the conduct of the employer.

Exception for genuine occupational requirement

7.—(1) In relation to discrimination falling within regulation 3 (discrimination on grounds of religion or belief)—

(a) regulation 6(1)(a) or (c) does not apply to any employment;
(b) regulation 6(2)(b) or (c) does not apply to promotion or transfer to, or training for, any employment; and
(c) regulation 6(2)(d) does not apply to dismissal from any employment, where paragraph (2) or (3) applies.

(2) This paragraph applies where, having regard to the nature of the employment or the context in which it is carried out—

(a) being of a particular religion or belief is a genuine and determining occupational requirement;
(b) it is proportionate to apply that requirement in the particular case; and
(c) either—
    (i) the person to whom that requirement is applied does not meet it, or
    (ii) the employer is not satisfied, and in all the circumstances it is reasonable for him not to be satisfied, that that person meets it,

and this paragraph applies whether or not the employer has an ethos based on religion or belief.

(3) This paragraph applies where an employer has an ethos based on religion or belief and, having regard to that ethos and to the nature of the employment or the context in which it is carried out—

(a) being of a particular religion or belief is a genuine occupational requirement for the job;

(b) it is proportionate to apply that requirement in the particular case; and

(c) either—

    (i) the person to whom that requirement is applied does not meet it, or

    (ii) the employer is not satisfied, and in all the circumstances it is reasonable for him not to be satisfied, that that person meets it.

Contract workers

8.—(1) It is unlawful for a principal, in relation to contract work at an establishment in Great Britain, to discriminate against a contract worker—

(a) in the terms on which he allows him to do that work;

(b) by not allowing him to do it or continue to do it;

(c) in the way he affords him access to any benefits or by refusing or deliberately not affording him access to them; or

(d) by subjecting him to any other detriment.

(2) It is unlawful for a principal, in relation to contract work at an establishment in Great Britain, to subject a contract worker to harassment.

(3) A principal does not contravene paragraph (1)(b) by doing any act in relation to a contract worker where, if the work were to be done by a person taken into the principal's employment, that act would be lawful by virtue of regulation 7 (exception for genuine occupational requirement).

(4) Paragraph (1) does not apply to benefits of any description if the principal is concerned with the provision (for payment or not) of benefits of that description to the public, or to a section of the public to which the contract worker in question belongs, unless that provision differs in a material respect from the provision of the benefits by the principal to his contract workers.

(5) In this regulation—

'principal' means a person ('A') who makes work available for doing by individuals who are employed by another person who supplies them under a contract made with A;

'contract work' means work so made available; and

'contract worker' means any individual who is supplied to the principal under such a contract.

Meaning of employment and contract work at establishment in Great Britain

9.—(1) For the purposes of this Part ('the relevant purposes'), employment is to be regarded as being at an establishment in Great Britain if the employee—

(a) does his work wholly or partly in Great Britain; or

(b) does his work wholly outside Great Britain and paragraph (2) applies.

(2) This paragraph applies if—

(a) the employer has a place of business at an establishment in Great Britain;

(b) the work is for the purposes of the business carried on at that establishment; and

(c) the employee is ordinarily resident in Great Britain—

    (i) at the time when he applies for or is offered the employment, or

    (ii) at any time during the course of the employment.

(3) The reference to 'employment' in paragraph (1) includes—

(a) employment on board a ship only if the ship is registered at a port of registry in Great Britain, and

(b) employment on an aircraft or hovercraft only if the aircraft or hovercraft is registered in the United Kingdom and operated by a person who has his principal place of business, or is ordinarily resident, in Great Britain.

(4) Subject to paragraph (5), for the purposes of determining if employment concerned with the exploration of the sea bed or sub-soil or the exploitation of their natural resources is outside Great Britain, this regulation has effect as if references to Great Britain included—

(a) any area designated under section 1(7) of the Continental Shelf Act 1964 except an area or part of an area in which the law of Northern Ireland applies; and

(b) in relation to employment concerned with the exploration or exploitation of the Frigg Gas Field, the part of the Norwegian sector of the Continental Shelf described in Schedule 1.

(5) Paragraph (4) shall not apply to employment which is concerned with the exploration or exploitation of the Frigg Gas Field unless the employer is—

(a) a company registered under the Companies Act 1985;

(b) an oversea company which has established a place of business within Great Britain from which it directs the exploration or exploitation in question; or

(c) any other person who has a place of business within Great Britain from which he directs the exploration or exploitation in question.

(6) In this regulation—

'the Frigg Gas Field' means the naturally occurring gas-bearing sand formations of the lower Eocene age located in the vicinity of the intersection of the line of latitude 59 degrees 53 minutes North and of the dividing line between the sectors of the Continental Shelf of the United Kingdom and the Kingdom of Norway and includes all other gas-bearing strata from which gas at the start of production is capable of flowing into the above-mentioned gas-bearing sand formations;

'oversea company' has the same meaning as in section 744 of the Companies Act 1985.

(7) This regulation applies in relation to contract work within the meaning of regulation 8 as it applies in relation to employment; and, in its application to contract work, references to 'employee', 'employer' and 'employment' are references to (respectively) 'contract worker', 'principal' and 'contract work' within the meaning of regulation 8.

Trustees and managers of occupational pension schemes

9A.—(1) It is unlawful, except in relation to rights accrued or benefits payable in respect of periods of service prior to the coming into force of these Regulations, for the trustees or managers of an occupational pension scheme to discriminate against a member or prospective member of the scheme in carrying out any of their functions in relation to it (including in particular their functions relating to the admission of members to the scheme and the treatment of members of it).

(2) It is unlawful for the trustees or managers of an occupational pension scheme, in relation to the scheme, to subject to harassment a member or prospective member of it.

(3) Schedule 1A (occupational pension schemes) shall have effect for the purposes of—

(a) defining terms used in this regulation and in that Schedule;
(b) treating every occupational pension scheme as including a non-discrimination rule;
(c) giving trustees or managers of an occupational pension scheme power to alter the scheme so as to secure conformity with the non-discrimination rule;
(d) making provision in relation to the procedures, and remedies which may be granted, on certain complaints relating to occupational pension schemes presented to an employment tribunal under regulation 28 (jurisdiction of employment tribunals).

Office-holders etc

10.—(1) It is unlawful for a relevant person, in relation to an appointment to an office or post to which this regulation applies, to discriminate against a person—

(a) in the arrangements which he makes for the purpose of determining to whom the appointment should be offered;
(b) in the terms on which he offers him the appointment; or
(c) by refusing to offer him the appointment.

(2) It is unlawful, in relation to an appointment to an office or post to which this regulation applies and which is an office or post referred to in paragraph (8)(b), for a relevant person on whose recommendation (or subject to whose approval) appointments to the office or post are made, to discriminate against a person—

(a) in the arrangements which he makes for the purpose of determining who should be recommended or approved in relation to the appointment; or

(b) in making or refusing to make a recommendation, or giving or refusing to give an approval, in relation to the appointment.

(3) It is unlawful for a relevant person, in relation to a person who has been appointed to an office or post to which this regulation applies, to discriminate against him—

(a) in the terms of the appointment;
(b) in the opportunities which he affords him for promotion, a transfer, training or receiving any other benefit, or by refusing to afford him any such opportunity;
(c) by terminating the appointment; or
(d) by subjecting him to any other detriment in relation to the appointment.

(4) It is unlawful for a relevant person, in relation to an office or post to which this regulation applies, to subject to harassment a person—

(a) who has been appointed to the office or post;
(b) who is seeking or being considered for appointment to the office or post; or
(c) who is seeking or being considered for a recommendation or approval in relation to an appointment to an office or post referred to in paragraph (8)(b).

(5) Paragraphs (1) and (3) do not apply to any act in relation to an office or post where, if the office or post constituted employment, that act would be lawful by virtue of regulation 7 (exception for genuine occupational requirement); and paragraph (2) does not apply to any act in relation to an office or post where, if the office or post constituted employment, it would be lawful by virtue of regulation 7 to refuse to offer the person such employment.

(6) Paragraph (3) does not apply to benefits of any description if the relevant person is concerned with the provision (for payment or not) of benefits of that description to the public, or a section of the public to which the person appointed belongs, unless—

(a) that provision differs in a material respect from the provision of the benefits by the relevant person to persons appointed to offices or posts which are the same as, or not materially different from, that which the person appointed holds; or

(b) the provision of the benefits to the person appointed is regulated by the terms and conditions of his appointment; or

(c) the benefits relate to training.

(7) In paragraph (3)(c) the reference to the termination of the appointment includes a reference—

(a) to the termination of the appointment by the expiration of any period (including a period expiring by reference to an event or circumstance), not being a termination immediately after which the appointment is renewed on the same terms and conditions; and

(b) to the termination of the appointment by any act of the person appointed (including the giving of notice) in circumstances such that he is entitled to terminate the appointment without notice by reason of the conduct of the relevant person.

(8) This regulation applies to—

(a) any office or post to which persons are appointed to discharge functions personally under the direction of another person, and in respect of which they are entitled to remuneration; and

(b) any office or post to which appointments are made by (or on the recommendation of or subject to the approval of) a Minister of the Crown, a government department, the National Assembly for Wales or any part of the Scottish Administration, but not to a political office or a case where regulation 6 (applicants and employees), 8 (contract workers), 12 (barristers), 13 (advocates) or 14 (partnerships) applies, or would apply but for the operation of any other provision of these Regulations.

(9) For the purposes of paragraph (8)(a) the holder of an office or post—

(a) is to be regarded as discharging his functions under the direction of another person if that other person is entitled to direct him as to when and where he discharges those functions;

(b) is not to be regarded as entitled to remuneration merely because he is entitled to payments—

   (i) in respect of expenses incurred by him in carrying out the functions of the office or post, or

   (ii) by way of compensation for the loss of income or benefits he would or might have received from any person had he not been carrying out the functions of the office or post.

(10) In this regulation—

(a) appointment to an office or post does not include election to an office or post;

(b) 'political office' means—

   (i) any office of the House of Commons held by a member of it,

    (ii)   a life peerage within the meaning of the Life Peerages Act 1958, or any office of the House of Lords held by a member of it,

    (iii) any office mentioned in Schedule 2 (Ministerial offices) to the House of Commons Disqualification Act 1975,

    (iv) the offices of Leader of the Opposition, Chief Opposition Whip or Assistant Opposition Whip within the meaning of the Ministerial and other Salaries Act 1975,

    (v)   any office of the Scottish Parliament held by a member of it,

    (vi) a member of the Scottish Executive within the meaning of section 44 of the Scotland Act 1998, or a junior Scottish Minister within the meaning of section 49 of that Act,

    (vii) any office of the National Assembly for Wales held by a member of it,

    (viii) in England, any office of a county council, a London borough council, a district council, or a parish council held by a member of it,

    (ix) in Wales, any office of a county council, a county borough council, or a community council held by a member of it,

    (x)   in relation to a council constituted under section 2 of the Local Government etc (Scotland) Act 1994 or a community council established under section 51 of the Local Government (Scotland) Act 1973, any office of such a council held by a member of it,

    (xi) any office of the Greater London Authority held by a member of it,

    (xii) any office of the Common Council of the City of London held by a member of it,

    (xiii) any office of the Council of the Isles of Scilly held by a member of it,

    (xiv) any office of a political party;

(c) 'relevant person', in relation to an office or post, means—

    (i)   any person with power to make or terminate appointments to the office or post, or to determine the terms of appointment,

    (ii) any person with power to determine the working conditions of a person appointed to the office or post in relation to opportunities for promotion, a transfer, training or for receiving any other benefit, and

    (iii) any person or body referred to in paragraph (8)(b) on whose recommendation or subject to whose approval appointments are made to the office or post;

(d) references to making a recommendation include references to making a negative recommendation; and

(e) references to refusal include references to deliberate omission.

Police

11.—(1) For the purposes of this Part, the holding of the office of constable shall be treated as employment—

(a) by the chief officer of police as respects any act done by him in relation to a constable or that office;

(b) by the police authority as respects any act done by it in relation to a constable or that office.

(2) For the purposes of regulation 22 (liability of employers and principals)—

(a) the holding of the office of constable shall be treated as employment by the chief officer of police (and as not being employment by any other person); and

(b) anything done by a person holding such an office in the performance, or purported performance, of his functions shall be treated as done in the course of that employment.

(3) There shall be paid out of the police fund—

(a) any compensation, costs or expenses awarded against a chief officer of police in any proceedings brought against him under these Regulations, and any costs or expenses incurred by him in any such proceedings so far as not recovered by him in the proceedings; and

(b) any sum required by a chief officer of police for the settlement of any claim made against him under these Regulations if the settlement is approved by the police authority.

(4) Any proceedings under these Regulations which, by virtue of paragraph (1), would lie against a chief officer of police shall be brought against the chief officer of police for the time being or, in the case of a vacancy in that office, against the person for the time being performing the functions of that office; and references in paragraph (3) to the chief officer of police shall be construed accordingly.

(5) A police authority may, in such cases and to such extent as appear to it to be appropriate, pay out of the police fund—

(a) any compensation, costs or expenses awarded in proceedings under these Regulations against a person under the direction and control of the chief officer of police;

(b) any costs or expenses incurred and not recovered by such a person in such proceedings; and

(c) any sum required in connection with the settlement of a claim that has or might have given rise to such proceedings.

(6) Paragraphs (1) and (2) apply to a police cadet and appointment as a police cadet as they apply to a constable and the office of constable.

(7) Subject to paragraph (8), in this regulation—

'chief officer of police'—

    (a) in relation to a person appointed, or an appointment falling to be made, under a specified Act, has the same meaning as in the Police Act 1996,

    (b) in relation to a person appointed, or an appointment falling to be made, under section 9(1)(b) or 55(1)(b) of the Police Act 1997 (police members of the National Criminal Intelligence Service and the National Crime Squad) means the Director General of the National Criminal Intelligence Service or, as the case may be, the Director General of the National Crime Squad,

    (c) in relation to a person appointed, or an appointment falling to be made, under the Police (Scotland) Act 1967, means the chief constable of the relevant police force,

    (d) in relation to any other person or appointment means the officer or other person who has the direction and control of the body of constables or cadets in question;

'police authority'—

    (a) in relation to a person appointed, or an appointment falling to be made, under a specified Act, has the same meaning as in the Police Act 1996,

    (b) in relation to a person appointed, or an appointment falling to be made, under section 9(1)(b) or 55(1)(b) of the Police Act 1997, means the Service Authority for the National Criminal Intelligence Service or, as the case may be, the Service Authority for the National Crime Squad,

    (c) in relation to a person appointed, or an appointment falling to be made, under the Police (Scotland) Act 1967, has the meaning given in that Act,

    (d) in relation to any other person or appointment, means the authority by whom the person in question is or on appointment would be paid;

'police cadet' means any person appointed to undergo training with a view to becoming a constable;

'police fund'—

    (a) in relation to a chief officer of police within sub-paragraph (a) of the above definition of that term, has the same meaning as in the Police Act 1996,

    (b) in relation to a chief officer of police within sub-paragraph (b) of that definition, means the service fund established under section 16 or (as the case may be) section 61 of the Police Act 1997,

    (c) in any other case means money provided by the police authority;

and 'specified Act' means the Metropolitan Police Act 1829, the City of London Police Act 1839 or the Police Act 1996.

(8) In relation to a constable of a force who is not under the direction and control of the chief officer of police for that force, references in this regulation to the chief officer of police are references to the chief officer of the force under whose direction and control he is, and references in this regulation to the police authority are references to the relevant police authority for that force.

Barristers

12.—(1) It is unlawful for a barrister or barrister's clerk, in relation to any offer of a pupillage or tenancy, to discriminate against a person—

(a) in the arrangements which are made for the purpose of determining to whom the pupillage or tenancy should be offered;
(b) in respect of any terms on which it is offered; or
(c) by refusing, or deliberately not offering, it to him.

(2) It is unlawful for a barrister or barrister's clerk, in relation to a pupil or tenant in the set of chambers in question, to discriminate against him—

(a) in respect of any terms applicable to him as a pupil or tenant;
(b) in the opportunities for training, or gaining experience, which are afforded or denied to him;
(c) in the benefits which are afforded or denied to him; or
(d) by terminating his pupillage, or by subjecting him to any pressure to leave the chambers or other detriment.

(3) It is unlawful for a barrister or barrister's clerk, in relation to a pupillage or tenancy in the set of chambers in question, to subject to harassment a person who is, or has applied to be, a pupil or tenant.

(4) It is unlawful for any person, in relation to the giving, withholding or acceptance of instructions to a barrister, to discriminate against any person by subjecting him to a detriment, or to subject him to harassment.

(5) In this regulation—

'barrister's clerk' includes any person carrying out any of the functions of a barrister's clerk;
'pupil', 'pupillage' and 'set of chambers' have the meanings commonly associated with their use in the context of barristers practising in independent practice; and
'tenancy' and 'tenant' have the meanings commonly associated with their use in the context of barristers practising in independent practice, but also include reference to any barrister permitted to work in a set of chambers who is not a tenant.

(6) This regulation extends to England and Wales only.

Advocates

13.—(1) It is unlawful for an advocate, in relation to taking any person as his pupil, to discriminate against a person—

(a) in the arrangements which he makes for the purpose of determining whom he will take as his pupil;

(b) in respect of any terms on which he offers to take any person as his pupil; or

(c) by refusing to take, or deliberately not taking, a person as his pupil.

(2) It is unlawful for an advocate, in relation to a person who is his pupil, to discriminate against him—

(a) in respect of any terms applicable to him as a pupil;

(b) in the opportunities for training, or gaining experience, which are afforded or denied to him;

(c) in the benefits which are afforded or denied to him; or

(d) by terminating the relationship, or by subjecting him to any pressure to terminate the relationship or other detriment.

(3) It is unlawful for an advocate, in relation to a person who is his pupil or taking any person as his pupil, to subject such a person to harassment.

(4) It is unlawful for any person, in relation to the giving, withholding or acceptance of instructions to an advocate, to discriminate against any person by subjecting him to a detriment, or to subject him to harassment.

(5) In this regulation—

'advocate' means a member of the Faculty of Advocates practising as such; and

'pupil' has the meaning commonly associated with its use in the context of a person training to be an advocate.

(6) This regulation extends to Scotland only.

Partnerships

14.—(1) It is unlawful for a firm, in relation to a position as partner in the firm, to discriminate against a person—

(a) in the arrangements they make for the purpose of determining to whom they should offer that position;

(b) in the terms on which they offer him that position;

(c) by refusing to offer, or deliberately not offering, him that position; or

(d) in a case where the person already holds that position—

(i) in the way they afford him access to any benefits or by refusing to afford, or deliberately not affording, him access to them, or

(ii) by expelling him from that position, or subjecting him to any other detriment.

(2) It is unlawful for a firm, in relation to a position as partner in the firm, to subject to harassment a person who holds or has applied for that position.

(3) Paragraphs (1)(a) to (c) and (2) apply in relation to persons proposing to form themselves into a partnership as they apply in relation to a firm.

(4) Paragraph (1) does not apply to any act in relation to a position as partner where, if the position were employment, that act would be lawful by virtue of regulation 7 (exception for genuine occupational requirement).

(5) In the case of a limited partnership references in this regulation to a partner shall be construed as references to a general partner as defined in section 3 of the Limited Partnerships Act 1907.

(6) This regulation applies to a limited liability partnership as it applies to a firm; and, in its application to a limited liability partnership, references to a partner in a firm are references to a member of the limited liability partnership.

(7) In this regulation, 'firm' has the meaning given by section 4 of the Partnership Act 1890.

(8) In paragraph (1)(d) reference to the expulsion of a person from a position as partner includes reference—

(a) to the termination of that person's partnership by the expiration of any period (including a period expiring by reference to an event or circumstance), not being a termination immediately after which the partnership is renewed on the same terms; and
(b) to the termination of that person's partnership by any act of his (including the giving of notice) in circumstances such that he is entitled to terminate it without notice by reason of the conduct of the other partners.

Trade organisations

15.—(1) It is unlawful for a trade organisation to discriminate against a person—

(a) in the terms on which it is prepared to admit him to membership of the organisation; or
(b) by refusing to accept, or deliberately not accepting, his application for membership.

(2) It is unlawful for a trade organisation, in relation to a member of the organisation, to discriminate against him—

(a) in the way it affords him access to any benefits or by refusing or deliberately omitting to afford him access to them;
(b) by depriving him of membership, or varying the terms on which he is a member; or

(c) by subjecting him to any other detriment.

(3) It is unlawful for a trade organisation, in relation to a person's membership or application for membership of that organisation, to subject that person to harassment.

(4) In this regulation—

'trade organisation' means an organisation of workers, an organisation of employers, or any other organisation whose members carry on a particular profession or trade for the purposes of which the organisation exists; 'profession' includes any vocation or occupation; and 'trade' includes any business.

Qualifications bodies

16.—(1) It is unlawful for a qualifications body to discriminate against a person—

(a) in the terms on which it is prepared to confer a professional or trade qualification on him;
(b) by refusing or deliberately not granting any application by him for such a qualification; or
(c) by withdrawing such a qualification from him or varying the terms on which he holds it.

(2) It is unlawful for a qualifications body, in relation to a professional or trade qualification conferred by it, to subject to harassment a person who holds or applies for such a qualification.

(3) In this regulation—

'qualifications body' means any authority or body which can confer a professional or trade qualification, but it does not include—

(a) an educational establishment to which regulation 20 (institutions of further and higher education) applies, or would apply but for the operation of any other provision of these Regulations, or
(b) a school;

'confer' includes renew or extend; 'professional or trade qualification' means any authorisation, qualification, recognition, registration, enrolment, approval or certification which is needed for, or facilitates engagement in, a particular profession or trade; 'profession' and 'trade' have the same meaning as in regulation 15.

Providers of vocational training

17.—(1) It is unlawful, in relation to a person seeking or undergoing training which would help fit him for any employment, for any training provider to discriminate against him—

(a) in the terms on which the training provider affords him access to any training;

(b) by refusing or deliberately not affording him such access;

(c) by terminating his training; or

(d) by subjecting him to any other detriment during his training.

(2) It is unlawful for a training provider, in relation to a person seeking or undergoing training which would help fit him for any employment, to subject him to harassment.

(3) Paragraph (1) does not apply if the discrimination only concerns training for employment which, by virtue of regulation 7 (exception for genuine occupational requirement), the employer could lawfully refuse to offer the person seeking training.

(4) In this regulation—

'training' includes—

(a) facilities for training; and

(b) practical work experience provided by an employer to a person whom he does not employ;

'training provider' means any person who provides, or makes arrangements for the provision of, training which would help fit another person for any employment, but it does not include—

(a) an employer in relation to training for persons employed by him;

(b) an educational establishment to which regulation 20 (institutions of further and higher education) applies, or would apply but for the operation of any other provision of these Regulations; or

(c) a school.

Employment agencies, careers guidance etc

18.—(1) It is unlawful for an employment agency to discriminate against a person—

(a) in the terms on which the agency offers to provide any of its services;

(b) by refusing or deliberately not providing any of its services; or

(c) in the way it provides any of its services.

(2) It is unlawful for an employment agency, in relation to a person to whom it provides its services, or who has requested it to provide its services, to subject that person to harassment.

(3) Paragraph (1) does not apply to discrimination if it only concerns employment which, by virtue of regulation 7 (exception for genuine occupational requirement), the employer could lawfully refuse to offer the person in question.

(4) An employment agency shall not be subject to any liability under this regulation if it proves that—

(a) it acted in reliance on a statement made to it by the employer to the effect that, by reason of the operation of paragraph (3), its action would not be unlawful, and

(b) it was reasonable for it to rely on the statement.

(5) A person who knowingly or recklessly makes a statement such as is referred to in paragraph (4)(a) which in a material respect is false or misleading commits an offence, and shall be liable on summary conviction to a fine not exceeding level 5 on the standard scale.

(6) For the purposes of this regulation—

(a) 'employment agency' means a person who, for profit or not, provides services for the purpose of finding employment for workers or supplying employers with workers, but it does not include—

(i) an educational establishment to which regulation 20 (institutions of further and higher education) applies, or would apply but for the operation of any other provision of these Regulations, or

(ii) a school; and

(b) references to the services of an employment agency include guidance on careers and any other services related to employment.

Assisting persons to obtain employment etc

19.—(1) It is unlawful for the Secretary of State to discriminate against any person by subjecting him to a detriment, or to subject a person to harassment, in the provision of facilities or services under section 2 of the Employment and Training Act 1973 (arrangements for assisting persons to obtain employment).

(2) It is unlawful for Scottish Enterprise or Highlands and Islands Enterprise to discriminate against any person by subjecting him to a detriment, or to subject a person to harassment, in the provision of facilities or services under such arrangements as are mentioned in section 2(3) of the Enterprise and New Towns (Scotland) Act 1990 (arrangements analogous to arrangements in pursuance of the said Act of 1973).

(3) This regulation does not apply in a case where—

(a) regulation 17 (providers of vocational training) applies, or would apply but for the operation of any other provision of these Regulations, or

(b) the Secretary of State is acting as an employment agency within the meaning of regulation 18.

Institutions of further and higher education

20.—(1) It is unlawful, in relation to an educational establishment to which this regulation applies, for the governing body of that establishment to discriminate against a person—

(a) in the terms on which it offers to admit him to the establishment as a student;

(b) by refusing or deliberately not accepting an application for his admission to the establishment as a student; or

(c) where he is a student of the establishment—

    (i) in the way it affords him access to any benefits,

    (ii) by refusing or deliberately not affording him access to them, or

    (iii) by excluding him from the establishment or subjecting him to any other detriment.

(2) It is unlawful, in relation to an educational establishment to which this regulation applies, for the governing body of that establishment to subject to harassment a person who is a student at the establishment, or who has applied for admission to the establishment as a student.

(3) Paragraph (1) does not apply if the discrimination only concerns training which would help fit a person for employment which, by virtue of regulation 7 (exception for genuine occupational requirement), the employer could lawfully refuse to offer the person in question.

(4) Subject to paragraph (4A) this regulation applies to the following educational establishments in England and Wales, namely—

(a) an institution within the further education sector (within the meaning of section 91(3) of the Further and Higher Education Act 1992);

(b) a university;

(c) an institution, other than a university, within the higher education sector (within the meaning of section 91(5) of the Further and Higher Education Act 1992).

(4A) In relation to an institution specified in Schedule 1B, this regulation applies with the modification set out in that Schedule.

(5) This regulation applies to the following educational establishments in Scotland, namely—

(a) a college of further education within the meaning of section 36(1) of the Further and Higher Education (Scotland) Act 1992 under the management of a board of management within the meaning of Part I of that Act;

(b) a college of further education maintained by an education authority in the exercise of its further education functions in providing courses of further education within the meaning of section 1(5)(b)(ii) of the Education (Scotland) Act 1980;

(c) any other educational establishment (not being a school) which provides further education within the meaning of section 1 of the Further and Higher Education (Scotland) Act 1992;

(d) an institution within the higher education sector (within the meaning of Part II of the Further and Higher Education (Scotland) Act 1992);

(e) a central institution (within the meaning of section 135 of the Education (Scotland) Act 1980).

(6) In this regulation—

'education authority' has the meaning given by section 135(1) of the Education (Scotland) Act 1980;

'governing body' includes—

(a)   the board of management of a college referred to in paragraph (5)(a), and

(b)   the managers of a college or institution referred to in paragraph (5)(b) or (e);

'student' means any person who receives education at an educational establishment to which this regulation applies; and

'university' includes a university college and the college, school or hall of a university.

Relationships which have come to an end

21.—(1) In this regulation a 'relevant relationship' is a relationship during the course of which an act of discrimination against, or harassment of, one party to the relationship ('B') by the other party to it ('A') is unlawful by virtue of any preceding provision of this Part.

(2) Where a relevant relationship has come to an end, it is unlawful for A—

(a) to discriminate against B by subjecting him to a detriment; or

(b) to subject B to harassment,
     where the discrimination or harassment arises out of and is closely connected to that relationship.

(3) In paragraph (1), reference to an act of discrimination or harassment which is unlawful includes, in the case of a relationship which has come to an end before the coming into force of these Regulations, reference to an act of discrimination or harassment which would, after the coming into force of these Regulations, be unlawful.

PART III OTHER UNLAWFUL ACTS

Liability of employers and principals

22.—(1) Anything done by a person in the course of his employment shall be treated for the purposes of these Regulations as done by his employer as well as by him, whether or not it was done with the employer's knowledge or approval.

(2) Anything done by a person as agent for another person with the authority (whether express or implied, and whether precedent or subsequent) of that other person shall be treated for the purposes of these Regulations as done by that other person as well as by him.

(3) In proceedings brought under these Regulations against any person in respect of an act alleged to have been done by an employee of his it shall be a defence for that person to prove that he took such steps as were reasonably practicable to prevent the employee from doing that act, or from doing in the course of his employment acts of that description.

Aiding unlawful acts

23.—(1) A person who knowingly aids another person to do an act made unlawful by these Regulations shall be treated for the purpose of these Regulations as himself doing an unlawful act of the like description.

(2) For the purposes of paragraph (1) an employee or agent for whose act the employer or principal is liable under regulation 22 (or would be so liable but for regulation 22(3)) shall be deemed to aid the doing of the act by the employer or principal.

(3) A person does not under this regulation knowingly aid another to do an unlawful act if—

(a) he acts in reliance on a statement made to him by that other person that, by reason of any provision of these Regulations, the act which he aids would not be unlawful; and

(b) it is reasonable for him to rely on the statement.

(4) A person who knowingly or recklessly makes a statement such as is referred to in paragraph (3)(a) which in a material respect is false or misleading commits an offence, and shall be liable on summary conviction to a fine not exceeding level 5 on the standard scale.

PART IV GENERAL EXCEPTIONS FROM PARTS II AND III

Exception for national security

24. Nothing in Part II or III shall render unlawful an act done for the purpose of safeguarding national security, if the doing of the act was justified by that purpose.

Exceptions for positive action

25.—(1) Nothing in Part II or III shall render unlawful any act done in or in connection with—

(a) affording persons of a particular religion or belief access to facilities for training which would help fit them for particular work; or

(b) encouraging persons of a particular religion or belief to take advantage of opportunities for doing particular work,

where it reasonably appears to the person doing the act that it prevents or compensates for disadvantages linked to religion or belief suffered by persons of that religion or belief doing that work or likely to take up that work.

(2) Nothing in Part II or III shall render unlawful any act done by a trade organisation within the meaning of regulation 15 in or in connection with—

(a) affording only members of the organisation who are of a particular religion or belief access to facilities for training which would help fit them for holding a post of any kind in the organisation; or

(b) encouraging only members of the organisation who are of a particular religion or belief to take advantage of opportunities for holding such posts in the organisation, where it reasonably appears to the organisation that the act prevents or compensates for disadvantages linked to religion or belief suffered by those of that religion or belief holding such posts or likely to hold such posts.

(3) Nothing in Part II or III shall render unlawful any act done by a trade organisation within the meaning of regulation 15 in or in connection with encouraging only persons of a particular religion or belief to become members of the organisation where it reasonably appears to the organisation that the act prevents or compensates for disadvantages linked to religion or belief suffered by persons of that religion or belief who are, or are eligible to become, members.

Protection of Sikhs from discrimination in connection with requirements as to wearing of safety helmets

26.—(1) Where—

(a) any person applies to a Sikh any provision, criterion or practice relating to the wearing by him of a safety helmet while he is on a construction site; and

(b) at the time when he so applies the provision, criterion or practice that person has no reasonable grounds for believing that the Sikh would not wear a turban at all times when on such a site,

then, for the purposes of regulation 3(1)(b)(iii), the provision, criterion or practice shall be taken to be one which cannot be shown to be a proportionate means of achieving a legitimate aim.

(2) Any special treatment afforded to a Sikh in consequence of section 11(1) or (2) of the Employment Act 1989 (exemption of Sikhs from requirements

as to wearing of safety helmets on construction sites) shall not be regarded as giving rise, in relation to any other person, to any discrimination falling within regulation 3.

(3) In this regulation—

'construction site' means any place in Great Britain where any building operations or works of engineering construction are being undertaken, but does not include any site within the territorial sea adjacent to Great Britain unless there are being undertaken on that site such operations or works as are activities falling within Article 8(a) of the Health and Safety at Work etc Act 1974 (Application outside Great Britain) Order 2001; and

'safety helmet' means any form of protective headgear.

(4) In this regulation—

(a) any reference to a Sikh is a reference to a follower of the Sikh religion; and

(b) any reference to a Sikh being on a construction site is a reference to his being there whether while at work or otherwise.

PART V ENFORCEMENT

Restriction of proceedings for breach of Regulations

27.—(1) Except as provided by these Regulations no proceedings, whether civil or criminal, shall lie against any person in respect of an act by reason that the act is unlawful by virtue of a provision of these Regulations.

(2) Paragraph (1) does not prevent the making of an application for judicial review or the investigation or determination of any matter in accordance with Part X (investigations: the Pensions Ombudsman) of the Pension Schemes Act 1993 by the Pensions Ombudsman.

Jurisdiction of employment tribunals

28.—(1) A complaint by any person ('the complainant') that another person ('the respondent')—

(a) has committed against the complainant an act to which this regulation applies; or

(b) is by virtue of regulation 22 (liability of employers and principals) or 23 (aiding unlawful acts) to be treated as having committed against the complainant such an act,

may be presented to an employment tribunal.

(2) This regulation applies to any act of discrimination or harassment which is unlawful by virtue of any provision of Part II other than—

(a) where the act is one in respect of which an appeal or proceedings in the nature of an appeal may be brought under any enactment, regulation 16 (qualifications bodies);

(b) regulation 20 (institutions of further and higher education); or

(c) where the act arises out of and is closely connected to a relationship between the complainant and the respondent which has come to an end but during the course of which an act of discrimination against, or harassment of, the complainant by the respondent would have been unlawful by virtue of regulation 20, regulation 21 (relationships which have come to an end).

(3) In paragraph (2)(c), reference to an act of discrimination or harassment which would have been unlawful includes, in the case of a relationship which has come to an end before the coming into force of these Regulations, reference to an act of discrimination or harassment which would, after the coming into force of these Regulations, have been unlawful.

(4) In this regulation, 'enactment' includes an enactment comprised in, or in an instrument made under, an Act of the Scottish Parliament.

Burden of proof: employment tribunals

29.—(1) This regulation applies to any complaint presented under regulation 28 to an employment tribunal.

(2) Where, on the hearing of the complaint, the complainant proves facts from which the tribunal could, apart from this regulation, conclude in the absence of an adequate explanation that the respondent—

(a) has committed against the complainant an act to which regulation 28 applies; or

(b) is by virtue of regulation 22 (liability of employers and principals) or 23 (aiding unlawful acts) to be treated as having committed against the complainant such an act

the tribunal shall uphold the complaint unless the respondent proves that he did not commit, or as the case may be, is not to be treated as having committed, that act.

Remedies on complaints in employment tribunals

30.—(1) Where an employment tribunal finds that a complaint presented to it under regulation 28 is well founded, the tribunal shall make such of the following as it considers just and equitable—

(a) an order declaring the rights of the complainant and the respondent in relation to the act to which the complaint relates;

(b) an order requiring the respondent to pay to the complainant compensation of an amount corresponding to any damages he could have been ordered by a county court or by a sheriff court to pay to the complainant if the complaint had fallen to be dealt with under regulation 31 (jurisdiction of county and sheriff courts);

(c) a recommendation that the respondent take within a specified period action appearing to the tribunal to be practicable for the purpose of obviating or reducing the adverse effect on the complainant of any act of discrimination or harassment to which the complaint relates.

(2) As respects an unlawful act of discrimination falling within regulation 3(1)(b), if the respondent proves that the provision, criterion or practice was not applied with the intention of treating the complainant unfavourably on grounds of religion or belief, an order may be made under paragraph (1)(b) only if the employment tribunal—

(a) makes such order under paragraph (1)(a) (if any) and such recommendation under paragraph (1)(c) (if any) as it would have made if it had no power to make an order under paragraph (1)(b); and

(b) (where it makes an order under paragraph (1)(a) or a recommendation under paragraph (1)(c) or both) considers that it is just and equitable to make an order under paragraph (1)(b) as well.

(3) If without reasonable justification the respondent to a complaint fails to comply with a recommendation made by an employment tribunal under paragraph (1)(c), then, if it thinks it just and equitable to do so—

(a) the tribunal may increase the amount of compensation required to be paid to the complainant in respect of the complaint by an order made under paragraph (1)(b); or

(b) if an order under paragraph (1)(b) was not made, the tribunal may make such an order.

(4) Where an amount of compensation falls to be awarded under paragraph (1)(b), the tribunal may include in the award interest on that amount subject to, and in accordance with, the provisions of the Employment Tribunals (Interest on Awards in Discrimination Cases) Regulations 1996.

(5) This regulation has effect subject to paragraph 7 of Schedule 1A (occupational pension schemes).

Jurisdiction of county and sheriff courts

31.—(1) A claim by any person ('the claimant') that another person ('the respondent')—

(a) has committed against the claimant an act to which this regulation applies; or

(b) is by virtue of regulation 22 (liability of employers and principals) or 23 (aiding unlawful acts) to be treated as having committed against the claimant such an act, may be made the subject of civil proceedings in like manner as any other claim in tort or (in Scotland) in reparation for breach of statutory duty.

(2) Proceedings brought under paragraph (1) shall—

(a) in England and Wales, be brought only in a county court; and
(b) in Scotland, be brought only in a sheriff court.

(3) For the avoidance of doubt it is hereby declared that damages in respect of an unlawful act to which this regulation applies may include compensation for injury to feelings whether or not they include compensation under any other head.

(4) This regulation applies to any act of discrimination or harassment which is unlawful by virtue of—

(a) regulation 20 (institutions of further and higher education); or
(b) where the act arises out of and is closely connected to a relationship between the claimant and the respondent which has come to an end but during the course of which an act of discrimination against, or harassment of, the claimant by the respondent would have been unlawful by virtue of regulation 20, regulation 21 (relationships which have come to an end).

(5) In paragraph (4)(b), reference to an act of discrimination or harassment which would have been unlawful includes, in the case of a relationship which has come to an end before the coming into force of these Regulations, reference to an act of discrimination or harassment which would, after the coming into force of these Regulations, have been unlawful.

Burden of proof: county and sheriff courts

32.—(1) This regulation applies to any claim brought under regulation 31 in a county court in England and Wales or a sheriff court in Scotland.

(2) Where, on the hearing of the claim, the claimant proves facts from which the court could, apart from this regulation, conclude in the absence of an adequate explanation that the respondent—

(a) has committed against the claimant an act to which regulation 31 applies; or
(b) is by virtue of regulation 22 (liability of employers and principals) or 23 (aiding unlawful acts) to be treated as having committed against the claimant such an act, the court shall uphold the claim unless the respondent proves that he did not commit, or as the case may be, is not to be treated as having committed, that act.

Help for persons in obtaining information etc

33.—(1) In accordance with this regulation, a person ('the person aggrieved') who considers he may have been discriminated against, or subjected to harassment, in contravention of these Regulations may serve on the respondent to a complaint presented under regulation 28 (jurisdiction of employment tribunals) or a claim brought under regulation 31 (jurisdiction of county and sheriff courts) questions in the form set out in Schedule 2 or forms to the like effect with such variation as the circumstances require; and the respondent may if he so wishes reply to such questions by way of the form set out in Schedule 3 or forms to the like effect with such variation as the circumstances require.

(2) Where the person aggrieved questions the respondent (whether in accordance with paragraph (1) or not)—

(a) the questions, and any reply by the respondent (whether in accordance with paragraph (1) or not) shall, subject to the following provisions of this regulation, be admissible as evidence in the proceedings;

(b) if it appears to the court or tribunal that the respondent deliberately, and without reasonable excuse, omitted to reply within eight weeks of service of the questions or that his reply is evasive or equivocal, the court or tribunal may draw any inference from that fact that it considers it just and equitable to draw, including an inference that he committed an unlawful act.

(3) In proceedings before a county court in England or Wales or a sheriff court in Scotland, a question shall only be admissible as evidence in pursuance of paragraph (2)(a)—

(a) where it was served before those proceedings had been instituted, if it was so served within the period of six months beginning when the act complained of was done;

(b) where it was served when those proceedings had been instituted, if it was served with the leave of, and within a period specified by, the court in question.

(4) In proceedings before an employment tribunal, a question shall only be admissible as evidence in pursuance of paragraph (2)(a)—

(a) where it was served before a complaint had been presented to the tribunal, if it was so served within the period of three months beginning when the act complained of was done;

(b) where it was served when a complaint had been presented to the tribunal, either—

   (i) if it was so served within the period of twenty-one days beginning with the day on which the complaint was presented, or

   (ii) if it was so served later with leave given, and within a period specified, by a direction of the tribunal.

(5) A question and any reply thereto may be served on the respondent or, as the case may be, on the person aggrieved—

(a) by delivering it to him;

(b) by sending it by post to him at his usual or last-known residence or place of business;

(c) where the person to be served is a body corporate or is a trade union or employers' association within the meaning of the Trade Union and Labour Relations (Consolidation) Act 1992, by delivering it to the secretary or clerk of the body, union or association at its registered or principal office or by sending it by post to the secretary or clerk at that office;

(d) where the person to be served is acting by a solicitor, by delivering it at, or by sending it by post to, the solicitor's address for service; or

(e) where the person to be served is the person aggrieved, by delivering the reply, or sending it by post, to him at his address for reply as stated by him in the document containing the questions.

(6) This regulation is without prejudice to any other enactment or rule of law regulating interlocutory and preliminary matters in proceedings before a county court, sheriff court or employment tribunal, and has effect subject to any enactment or rule of law regulating the admissibility of evidence in such proceedings.

(7) In this regulation 'respondent' includes a prospective respondent.

Period within which proceedings to be brought

34.—(1) An employment tribunal shall not consider a complaint under regulation 28 unless it is presented to the tribunal before the end of—

(a) the period of three months beginning when the act complained of was done; or

(b) in a case to which regulation 36(7) (armed forces) applies, the period of six months so beginning.

(2) A county court or a sheriff court shall not consider a claim brought under regulation 31 unless proceedings in respect of the claim are instituted before the end of the period of six months beginning when the act complained of was done.

(3) A court or tribunal may nevertheless consider any such complaint or claim which is out of time if, in all the circumstances of the case, it considers that it is just and equitable to do so.

(4) For the purposes of this regulation and regulation 33 (help for persons in obtaining information etc)—

(a) when the making of a contract is, by reason of the inclusion of any term, an unlawful act, that act shall be treated as extending throughout the duration of the contract; and

(b) any act extending over a period shall be treated as done at the end of that period; and

(c) a deliberate omission shall be treated as done when the person in question decided upon it,

and in the absence of evidence establishing the contrary a person shall be taken for the purposes of this regulation to decide upon an omission when he does an act inconsistent with doing the omitted act or, if he has done no such inconsistent act, when the period expires within which he might reasonably have been expected to do the omitted act if it was to be done.

PART VI SUPPLEMENTAL

Validity of contracts, collective agreements and rules of undertakings

35. Schedule 4 (validity of contracts, collective agreements and rules of undertakings) shall have effect.

Application to the Crown etc

36.—(1) These Regulations apply—

(a) to an act done by or for purposes of a Minister of the Crown or government department; or
(b) to an act done on behalf of the Crown by a statutory body, or a person holding a statutory office,

as they apply to an act done by a private person.

(2) These Regulations apply to—

(a) service for purposes of a Minister of the Crown or government department, other than service of a person holding a statutory office;
(b) service on behalf of the Crown for purposes of a person holding a statutory office or purposes of a statutory body; or
(c) service in the armed forces,
    as they apply to employment by a private person, and shall so apply as if references to a contract of employment included references to the terms of service.

(3) Paragraphs (1) and (2) have effect subject to regulation 11 (police).

(4) Regulation 9(3) (meaning of employment and contract work at establishment in Great Britain) shall have effect in relation to any ship, aircraft or hovercraft belonging to or possessed by Her Majesty in right of the government of the United Kingdom as it has effect in relation to a ship, aircraft or hovercraft specified in regulation 9(3)(a) or (b).

(5) The provisions of Parts II to IV of the Crown Proceedings Act 1947 shall apply to proceedings against the Crown under these Regulations as they apply to proceedings in England and Wales which by virtue of section 23 of that Act are treated for the purposes of Part II of that Act as civil proceedings by or against the Crown, except that in their application to proceedings under

these Regulations section 20 of that Act (removal of proceedings from county court to High Court) shall not apply.

(6) The provisions of Part V of the Crown Proceedings Act 1947 shall apply to proceedings against the Crown under these Regulations as they apply to proceedings in Scotland which by virtue of the said Part are treated as civil proceedings by or against the Crown, except that in their application to proceedings under these Regulations the proviso to section 44 of that Act (removal of proceedings from the sheriff court to the Court of Session) shall not apply.

(7) This paragraph applies to any complaint by a person ('the complainant') that another person—

(a) has committed an act of discrimination or harassment against the complainant which is unlawful by virtue of regulation 6 (applicants and employees); or

(b) is by virtue of regulation 22 (liability of employers and principals) or 23 (aiding unlawful acts) to be treated as having committed such an act of discrimination or harassment against the complainant,

if at the time when the act complained of was done the complainant was serving in the armed forces and the discrimination or harassment in question relates to his service in those forces.

(8) A complainant may present a complaint to which paragraph (7) applies to an employment tribunal under regulation 28 only if—

(a) he has made a complaint in respect of the same matter to an officer under the service redress procedures applicable to him; and

(b) that complaint has not been withdrawn.

(9) For the purpose of paragraph (8)(b), a complainant shall be treated as having withdrawn his complaint if, having made a complaint to an officer under the service redress procedures applicable to him, he fails to submit that complaint to the Defence Council under those procedures.

(10) Where a complaint is presented to an employment tribunal under regulation 28 by virtue of paragraph (8), the service redress procedures may continue after the complaint is so presented.

(11) In this regulation—

'armed forces' means any of the naval, military or air forces of the Crown;

'service for purposes of a Minister of the Crown or government department' does not include service in any office mentioned in Schedule 2 (Ministerial offices) to the House of Commons Disqualification Act 1975;

'the service redress procedures' means the procedures, excluding those which relate to the making of a report on a complaint to Her Majesty, referred to in section 180 of the Army Act 1955, section 180 of the Air Force Act 1955 and section 130 of the Naval Discipline Act 1957; and

'statutory body' means a body set up by or in pursuance of an enactment, and 'statutory office' means an office so set up.

Application to House of Commons staff

37.—(1) These Regulations apply to an act done by an employer of a relevant member of the House of Commons staff, and to service as such a member, as they apply to an act done by and to service for purposes of a Minister of the Crown or government department, and accordingly apply as if references to a contract of employment included references to the terms of service of such a member.

(2) In this regulation 'relevant member of the House of Commons staff' means any person—

(a) who was appointed by the House of Commons Commission; or
(b) who is a member of the Speaker's personal staff,
    and subsections (6) to (12) of section 195 of the Employment Rights Act 1996 (person to be treated as employer of House of Commons staff) apply, with any necessary modifications, for the purposes of these Regulations.

Application to House of Lords staff

38.—(1) These Regulations apply in relation to employment as a relevant member of the House of Lords staff as they apply in relation to other employment.

(2) In this regulation 'relevant member of the House of Lords staff' means any person who is employed under a contract of employment with the Corporate Officer of the House of Lords, and section 194(7) of the Employment Rights Act 1996 (continuity of employment) applies for the purposes of this regulation.

Savings of, and amendments to, legislation

39.—(1) These Regulations are without prejudice to—

(a) sections 58 to 60 and 124A of the School Standards and Framework Act 1998 (appointment and dismissal of teachers in schools with a religious character etc); and
(b) section 21 of the Education (Scotland) Act 1980 (management of denominational schools).

(2) Schedule 5 (amendments to legislation) shall have effect.

Jacqui Smith
Minister of State, for Industry and the Regions and Deputy Minister for Women and Equality, Department of Trade and Industry

26th June 2003

SCHEDULES

SCHEDULE 1   Regulation 9(4)

Norwegian part of the Frigg Gas Field

1. The part of the Norwegian sector of the Continental Shelf described in this Schedule is the area defined by—

(a) the sets of lines of latitude and longitude joining the following surface co-ordinates—

Longitude	Latitude
02 degrees 05 minutes 30 seconds E	60 degrees 00 minutes 45 seconds N
02 degrees 05 minutes 30 seconds E	59 degrees 58 minutes 45 seconds N
02 degrees 06 minutes 00 seconds E	59 degrees 58 minutes 45 seconds N
02 degrees 06 minutes 00 seconds E	59 degrees 57 minutes 45 seconds N
02 degrees 07 minutes 00 seconds E	59 degrees 57 minutes 45 seconds N
02 degrees 07 minutes 00 seconds E	59 degrees 57 minutes 30 seconds N
02 degrees 07 minutes 30 seconds E	59 degrees 57 minutes 30 seconds N
02 degrees 07 minutes 30 seconds E	59 degrees 55 minutes 30 seconds N
02 degrees 10 minutes 30 seconds E	59 degrees 55 minutes 30 seconds N
02 degrees 10 minutes 30 seconds E	59 degrees 54 minutes 45 seconds N
02 degrees 11 minutes 00 seconds E	59 degrees 54 minutes 45 seconds N
02 degrees 11 minutes 00 seconds E	59 degrees 54 minutes 15 seconds N
02 degrees 12 minutes 30 seconds E	59 degrees 54 minutes 15 seconds N
02 degrees 12 minutes 30 seconds E	59 degrees 54 minutes 00 seconds N
02 degrees 13 minutes 30 seconds E	59 degrees 54 minutes 00 seconds N
02 degrees 13 minutes 30 seconds E	59 degrees 54 minutes 30 seconds N
02 degrees 15 minutes 30 seconds E	59 degrees 54 minutes 30 seconds N
02 degrees 15 minutes 30 seconds E	59 degrees 53 minutes 15 seconds N
02 degrees 10 minutes 30 seconds E	59 degrees 53 minutes 15 seconds N
02 degrees 10 minutes 30 seconds E	59 degrees 52 minutes 45 seconds N
02 degrees 09 minutes 30 seconds E	59 degrees 52 minutes 45 seconds N
02 degrees 09 minutes 30 seconds E	59 degrees 52 minutes 15 seconds N
02 degrees 08 minutes 30 seconds E	59 degrees 52 minutes 15 seconds N
02 degrees 08 minutes 30 seconds E	59 degrees 52 minutes 00 seconds N
02 degrees 07 minutes 30 seconds E	59 degrees 52 minutes 00 seconds N
02 degrees 07 minutes 30 seconds E	59 degrees 51 minutes 30 seconds N
02 degrees 05 minutes 30 seconds E	59 degrees 51 minutes 30 seconds N
02 degrees 05 minutes 30 seconds E	59 degrees 51 minutes 00 seconds N
02 degrees 04 minutes 00 seconds E	59 degrees 51 minutes 00 seconds N
02 degrees 04 minutes 00 seconds E	59 degrees 50 minutes 30 seconds N
02 degrees 03 minutes 00 seconds E	59 degrees 50 minutes 30 seconds N
02 degrees 03 minutes 00 seconds E	59 degrees 50 minutes 00 seconds N

(b) a line from the point 02 degrees 03 minutes 00 seconds E 59 degrees 50 minutes 00 seconds N west along the parallel of latitude 59 degrees 50 minutes 00 seconds N until its intersection with the Dividing Line;

(c) a line from the point of intersection specified in sub-paragraph (b) along the Dividing Line until its intersection with the parallel of latitude 60 degrees 00 minutes 45 seconds N;

(d) a line from the point of intersection specified in sub-paragraph (c) east along the parallel of latitude 60 degrees 00 minutes 45 degrees N until its intersection with the meridian 02 degrees 05 minutes 30 seconds E.

2. In this Schedule, the 'Dividing Line' means the dividing line as defined in an Agreement dated 10th March 1965 and made between the government of the United Kingdom of Great Britain and Northern Ireland and the government of the Kingdom of Norway as supplemented by a Protocol dated 22nd December 1978.

SCHEDULE 1A
Regulation 9A(3)

Occupational pension schemes

Interpretation

1.   (1) In this Schedule—

'active member', 'deferred member', 'managers', 'pensioner member' and 'trustees or managers', in relation to an occupational pension scheme, have the meanings given by section 124(1) of the Pensions Act 1995 as at the date of the coming into force of these Regulations;

'member', in relation to an occupational pension scheme, means any active member, deferred member or pensioner member;

'non-discrimination rule' means the rule in paragraph 2;

'occupational pension scheme' has the same meaning as in the Pension Schemes Act 1993 as at the date of the coming into force of these Regulations;

'prospective member', in relation to an occupational pension scheme, means any person who, under the terms of his employment or the rules of the scheme or both—

(a) is able, at his own option, to become a member of the scheme,

(b) shall become so able if he continues in the same employment for a sufficient period of time,

(c) shall be admitted to it automatically unless he makes an election not to become a member, or

(d) may be admitted to it subject to the consent of his employer.

(2) In paragraph 6 (procedure in employment tribunals), 'employer', in relation to an occupational pension scheme, has the meaning given by section

124(1) of the Pensions Act 1995 as at the date of the coming into force of these Regulations.

(3) Any term used in regulation 9A (trustees and managers of occupational pension schemes) and in this Schedule shall have the same meaning in that regulation as it has in this Schedule.

Non-discrimination rule

2. Every occupational pension scheme shall be treated as including a provision ('the non-discrimination rule') containing a requirement that the trustees or managers of the scheme refrain from doing any act which is unlawful by virtue of regulation 9A.

3. The other provisions of the scheme are to have effect subject to the non-discrimination rule.

4. The trustees or managers of an occupational pension scheme may—

(a) if they do not (apart from this paragraph) have power to make such alterations to the scheme as may be required to secure conformity with the non-discrimination rule, or

(b) if they have such power but the procedure for doing so—

   (i) is liable to be unduly complex or protracted, or
   (ii) involves the obtaining of consents which cannot be obtained, or can only be obtained with undue delay or difficulty,

by resolution make such alterations to the scheme.

5. Alterations made by a resolution such as is referred to in paragraph 4 may have effect in relation to a period before the alterations are made (but may not have effect in relation to any time before the coming into force of these Regulations).

Procedure in employment tribunals

6. Where under regulation 28 (jurisdiction of employment tribunals) a member or prospective member of an occupational pension scheme presents to an employment tribunal a complaint that the trustees or managers of the scheme—

(a) have committed against him an act which is unlawful by virtue of regulation 9A (trustees and managers of occupational pension schemes) or 21 (relationships which have come to an end); or

(b) are by virtue of regulation 22 (liability of employers and principals) or 23 (aiding unlawful acts) to be treated as having committed against him such an act,

the employer in relation to the scheme shall, for the purposes of the rules governing procedure, be treated as a party and be entitled to appear and be heard in accordance with those rules.

Remedies in employment tribunals

7.   (1) This paragraph applies where—

(a) under regulation 28 (jurisdiction of employment tribunals) a member or prospective member of an occupational pension scheme ('the complainant') presents to an employment tribunal a complaint against the trustees or managers of the scheme or an employer;

(b) the complainant is not a pensioner member of the scheme;

(c) the complaint relates to the terms on which persons become members of the scheme, or the terms on which members of the scheme are treated; and

(d) the tribunal finds the complaint to be well founded.

(2) Where this paragraph applies, the employment tribunal may, without prejudice to the generality of its power under regulation 30(1)(a) (power to make order declaring rights of complainant and respondent), make an order declaring that the complainant has a right—

(a) where the complaint relates to the terms on which persons become members of the scheme, to be admitted to the scheme;

(b) where the complaint relates to the terms on which members of the scheme are treated, to membership of the scheme without discrimination.

(3) An order under sub-paragraph (2)—

(a) may be made in respect of such period as is specified in the order (but may not be made in respect of any time before the coming into force of these Regulations);

(b) may make such provision as the employment tribunal considers appropriate as to the terms on which, or the capacity in which, the complainant is to enjoy such admission or membership.

(4) Where this paragraph applies, the employment tribunal may not make an order for compensation under regulation 30(1)(b), whether in relation to arrears of benefits or otherwise, except—

(a) for injury to feelings;

(b) by virtue of regulation 30(3).

SCHEDULE 1B

Regulation 20(4A)

Institutions in relation to which regulation 20 (Institutions of further and higher education) is modified

1. This Schedule applies to the following institutions:—

Aquinas Sixth Form College,	Stockport
Cardinal Newman College,	Preston
Carmel College,	St Helens
Christ The King Sixth Form College,	Lewisham
Holy Cross Sixth Form College,	Bury
Loreto College,	Manchester
Notre Dame Catholic Sixth Form College,	Leeds
St Brendan's Sixth Form College,	Bristol
St Charles Catholic Sixth Form College,	London W10
St David's Catholic College,	Cardiff
St Dominic's Sixth Form College,	Harrow on the Hill
St Francis Xavier Sixth Form College,	Clapham
Saint John Rigby Catholic Sixth Form College,	Wigan
St Mary's College,	Blackburn
St Mary's Sixth Form College,	Middlesbrough
Xaverian Sixth Form College,	Manchester

2. Subject to paragraph 3, regulation 20(1)(b) shall not apply to the institutions specified in paragraph 1 in so far as it is necessary for an institution to give preference in its admissions to persons of a particular religion or belief in order to preserve that institution's religious ethos.

3. Paragraph 2 does not apply in relation to any admission to a course of vocational training.

SCHEDULE 2
Regulation 33(1)

Questionnaire of person aggrieved

To

....

(*name of person to be questioned*) of

....

(*address*)

   1.—(1) I

....

(*name of questioner*) of

....

....

(*address*)

consider that you may have discriminated against me [subjected me to harassment] contrary to the Employment Equality (Religion or Belief) Regulations 2003.

(2) (*Give date, approximate time and a factual description of the treatment received and of the circumstances leading up to the treatment.*)

(3) I consider that this treatment may have been unlawful because

....

(*complete if you wish to give reasons, otherwise delete*).

2. Do you agree that the statement in paragraph 1(2) above is an accurate description of what happened? If not, in what respect do you disagree or what is your version of what happened?

3. Do you accept that your treatment of me was unlawful discrimination [harassment]?

If not—

(a) why not,
(b) for what reason did I receive the treatment accorded to me, and
(c) how far did considerations of religion or belief affect your treatment of me?

4. (*Any other questions you wish to ask.*)

5. My address for any reply you may wish to give to the questions raised above is [that set out in paragraph 1(1) above] [the following address

....

....].

(*signature of questioner*)

....

(*date*)

N.B. – By virtue of regulation 33 of the Employment Equality (Religion or Belief) Regulations 2003 this questionnaire and any reply are (subject to the provisions of that regulation) admissible in proceedings under the Regulations. A court or tribunal may draw any such inference as is just and equitable from a failure without reasonable excuse to reply within eight weeks of service of this questionnaire, or from an evasive or equivocal reply, including an inference that the person questioned has committed an unlawful act.

SCHEDULE 3

Regulation 33(1)

Reply by respondent

To

....

(*name of questioner*) of

....

(*address*)

1. I

....

(*name of person questioned*) of

....

(address)

hereby acknowledge receipt of the questionnaire signed by you and dated

....

which was served on me on (*date*).

....

2. [I agree that the statement in paragraph 1(2) of the questionnaire is an accurate description of what happened.]

I disagree with the statement in paragraph 1(2) of the questionnaire in that

....

....

3. I accept/dispute that my treatment of you was unlawful discrimination [harassment].

My reasons for so disputing are

....

The reason why you received the treatment accorded to you and the answers to the other questions in paragraph 3 of the questionnaire are

....

4. (*Replies to questions in paragraph 4 of the questionnaire.*)

[5. I have deleted (in whole or in part) the paragraph(s) numbered

....

above, since I am unable/unwilling to reply to the relevant questions in the correspondingly numbered paragraph(s) of the questionnaire for the following reasons

....

....].

(*signature of person questioned*)

....

(*date*)

SCHEDULE 4
Regulation 35

Validity of contracts, collective agreement and rules of undertakings

Part 1
Validity and revision of contracts

1.   (1) A term of a contract is void where—

(a) the making of the contract is, by reason of the inclusion of the term, unlawful by virtue of these Regulations;

(b) it is included in furtherance of an act which is unlawful by virtue of these Regulations; or

(c) it provides for the doing of an act which is unlawful by virtue of these Regulations.

(2) Sub-paragraph (1) does not apply to a term the inclusion of which constitutes, or is in furtherance of, or provides for, unlawful discrimination against, or harassment of, a party to the contract, but the term shall be unenforceable against that party.

(3) A term in a contract which purports to exclude or limit any provision of these Regulations is unenforceable by any person in whose favour the term would operate apart from this paragraph.

(4) Sub-paragraphs (1), (2) and (3) shall apply whether the contract was entered into before or after the date on which these Regulations come into force; but in the case of a contract made before that date, those sub-paragraphs do not apply in relation to any period before that date.

2.   (1) Paragraph 1(3) does not apply—

(a) to a contract settling a complaint to which regulation 28(1) (jurisdiction of employment tribunals) applies where the contract is made with the assistance of a conciliation officer within the meaning of section 211 of the Trade Union and Labour Relations (Consolidation) Act 1992;

(b) to a contract settling a complaint to which regulation 28(1) applies if the conditions regulating compromise contracts under this Schedule are satisfied in relation to the contract; or

(c) to a contract settling a claim to which regulation 31 (jurisdiction of county or sheriff courts) applies.

(2) The conditions regulating compromise contracts under this Schedule are that—

(a) the contract must be in writing;

(b) the contract must relate to the particular complaint;

(c) the complainant must have received advice from a relevant independent adviser as to the terms and effect of the proposed contract and in particular its effect on his ability to pursue a complaint before an employment tribunal;

(d) there must be in force, when the adviser gives the advice, a contract of insurance, or an indemnity provided for members of a profession or professional body, covering the risk of a claim by the complainant in respect of loss arising in consequence of the advice;

(e) the contract must identify the adviser; and

(f) the contract must state that the conditions regulating compromise contracts under this Schedule are satisfied.

(3) A person is a relevant independent adviser for the purposes of subparagraph (2)(c)—

(a) if he is a qualified lawyer;

(b) if he is an officer, official, employee or member of an independent trade union who has been certified in writing by the trade union as competent to give advice and as authorised to do so on behalf of the trade union; or

(c) if he works at an advice centre (whether as an employee or a volunteer) and has been certified in writing by the centre as competent to give advice and as authorised to do so on behalf of the centre.

(4) But a person is not a relevant independent adviser for the purposes of sub-paragraph (2)(c) in relation to the complainant—

(a) if he is, is employed by or is acting in the matter for the other party or a person who is connected with the other party;

(b) in the case of a person within sub-paragraph (3)(b) or (c), if the trade union or advice centre is the other party or a person who is connected with the other party; or

(c) in the case of a person within sub-paragraph (3)(c), if the complainant makes a payment for the advice received from him.

(5) In sub-paragraph (3)(a) 'qualified lawyer' means—

(a) as respects England and Wales, a barrister (whether in practice as such or employed to give legal advice), a solicitor who holds a practising certificate, or a person other than a barrister or solicitor who is an authorised advocate or authorised litigator (within the meaning of the Courts and Legal Services Act 1990); and

(b) as respects Scotland, an advocate (whether in practice as such or employed to give legal advice), or a solicitor who holds a practising certificate.

(5A) A person shall be treated as being a qualified lawyer within sub-paragraph (5)(a) if he is a Fellow of the Institute of Legal Executives employed by a solicitors' practice.

(6) In sub-paragraph (3)(b) 'independent trade union' has the same meaning as in the Trade Union and Labour Relations (Consolidation) Act 1992.

(7) For the purposes of sub-paragraph (4)(a) any two persons are to be treated as connected—

(a) if one is a company of which the other (directly or indirectly) has control; or

(b) if both are companies of which a third person (directly or indirectly) has control.

(8) An agreement under which the parties agree to submit a dispute to arbitration—

(a) shall be regarded for the purposes of sub-paragraph (1)(a) and (b) as being a contract settling a complaint if—

(i)   the dispute is covered by a scheme having effect by virtue of an order under section 212A of the Trade Union and Labour Relations (Consolidation) Act 1992, and

(ii) the agreement is to submit it to arbitration in accordance with the scheme, but

(b) shall be regarded as neither being nor including such a contract in any other case.

3. (1) On the application of a person interested in a contract to which paragraph 1(1) or (2) applies, a county court or a sheriff court may make such order as it thinks fit for—

(a) removing or modifying any term rendered void by paragraph 1(1); or

(b) removing or modifying any term made unenforceable by paragraph 1(2);

but such an order shall not be made unless all persons affected have been given notice in writing of the application (except where under rules of court notice may be dispensed with) and have been afforded an opportunity to make representations to the court.

(2) An order under sub-paragraph (1) may include provision as respects any period before the making of the order (but after the coming into force of these Regulations).

Part 2
Collective agreements and rules of undertakings

4. (1) This Part of this Schedule applies to—

(a) any term of a collective agreement, including an agreement which was not intended, or is presumed not to have been intended, to be a legally enforceable contract;
(b) any rule made by an employer for application to all or any of the persons who are employed by him or who apply to be, or are, considered by him for employment;
(c) any rule made by a trade organisation (within the meaning of regulation 15) or a qualifications body (within the meaning of regulation 16) for application to—
    (i) all or any of its members or prospective members; or
    (ii) all or any of the persons on whom it has conferred professional or trade qualifications (within the meaning of regulation 16) or who are seeking the professional or trade qualifications which it has power to confer.

(2) Any term or rule to which this Part of this Schedule applies is void where—

(a) the making of the collective agreement is, by reason of the inclusion of the term, unlawful by virtue of these Regulations;
(b) the term or rule is included or made in furtherance of an act which is unlawful by virtue of these Regulations; or
(c) the term or rule provides for the doing of an act which is unlawful by virtue of these Regulations.

(3) Sub-paragraph (2) shall apply whether the agreement was entered into, or the rule made, before or after the date on which these Regulations come into force; but in the case of an agreement entered into, or a rule made, before the date on which these Regulations come into force, that sub-paragraph does not apply in relation to any period before that date.

5. A person to whom this paragraph applies may present a complaint to an employment tribunal that a term or rule is void by virtue of paragraph 4 if he has reason to believe—

(a) that the term or rule may at some future time have effect in relation to him; and

(b) where he alleges that it is void by virtue of paragraph 4(2)(c), that—

   (i) an act for the doing of which it provides, may at some such time be done in relation to him, and
   (ii) the act would be unlawful by virtue of these Regulations if done in relation to him in present circumstances.

6. In the case of a complaint about—

(a) a term of a collective agreement made by or on behalf of—

   (i) an employer,
   (ii) an organisation of employers of which an employer is a member, or
   (iii) an association of such organisations of one of which an employer is a member, or

(b) a rule made by an employer within the meaning of paragraph 4(1)(b),

paragraph 5 applies to any person who is, or is genuinely and actively seeking to become, one of his employees.

7. In the case of a complaint about a rule made by an organisation or body to which paragraph 4(1)(c) applies, paragraph 5 applies to any person—

(a) who is, or is genuinely and actively seeking to become, a member of the organisation or body;
(b) on whom the organisation or body has conferred a professional or trade qualification (within the meaning of regulation 16); or
(c) who is genuinely and actively seeking such a professional or trade qualification which the organisation or body has power to confer.

8. (1) When an employment tribunal finds that a complaint presented to it under paragraph 5 is well founded the tribunal shall make an order declaring that the term or rule is void.

(2) An order under sub-paragraph (1) may include provision as respects any period before the making of the order (but after the coming into force of these Regulations).

9. The avoidance by virtue of paragraph 4(2) of any term or rule which provides for any person to be discriminated against shall be without prejudice to the following rights (except in so far as they enable any person to require another person to be treated less favourably than himself), namely—

(a) such of the rights of the person to be discriminated against; and
(b) such of the rights of any person who will be treated more favourably in direct or indirect consequence of the discrimination,

as are conferred by or in respect of a contract made or modified wholly or partly in pursuance of, or by reference to, that term or rule.

10. In this Schedule 'collective agreement' means any agreement relating to one or more of the matters mentioned in section 178(2) of the Trade Union and Labour Relations (Consolidation) Act 1992 (meaning of trade dispute), being an agreement made by or on behalf of one or more employers or one or more organisations of employers or associations of such organisations with one or more organisations of workers or associations of such organisations.

SCHEDULE 5

Regulation 39(2)

Amendments to legislation

1. The Employment Tribunals Act 1996 is amended as follows—

(a) in section 18(1) (cases where conciliation provisions apply)—

    (i) at the end of paragraph (j), there is omitted 'or', and

    (ii) after paragraph (k) there is inserted—

> 'or
>
> (1) under regulation 28 of the Employment Equality (Religion or Belief) Regulations 2003';

(b) in section 21 (jurisdiction of the Employment Appeal Tribunal), in subsection (1) (which specifies the proceedings and claims to which the section applies)—

    (i) at the end of paragraph (k), there is omitted 'or', and

    (ii) after paragraph (l) there is inserted—

> 'or (m) the Employment Equality (Religion or Belief) Regulations 2003'.

2. Section 126(1)(b) (compensation for acts which are both unfair dismissal and discrimination) of the Employment Rights Act 1996 is amended as follows—

(a) after 'Disability Discrimination Act 1995' there is omitted 'and'; and

(b) after 'the Employment Equality (Sexual Orientation) Regulations 2003' there is inserted—

> 'and the Employment Equality (Religion or Belief) Regulations 2003'.

3. Sub-paragraph (b) of the definition of 'an award under the relevant legislation' in regulation 1(2) (interpretation) of the Employment Tribunals (Interest on Awards in Discrimination Cases) Regulations 1996 is amended as follows—

(a) after 'section 8(2)(b) of the 1995 Act' there is omitted 'or'; and

(b) after 'the Employment Equality (Sexual Orientation) Regulations 2003' there is inserted—

'or regulation 30(1)(b) of the Employment Equality (Religion or Belief) Regulations 2003'.

4. In the Employment Act 2002 at the end of each of the following schedules—

(a) Schedule 3 (tribunal jurisdictions to which section 31 applies for adjustment of awards for non-completion of statutory procedure);

(b) Schedule 4 (tribunal jurisdictions to which section 32 applies for complaints where the employee must first submit a statement of grievance to employer); and

(c) Schedule 5 (tribunal jurisdictions to which section 38 applies in relation to proceedings where the employer has failed to give a statement of employment particulars),

there is inserted—

'Regulation 28 of the Employment Equality (Religion or Belief) Regulations 2003 (discrimination in the employment field)'.

ACAS Guidance on religion or belief in the workplace

Putting the Employment Equality (Religion or Belief) Regulations 2003 into practice For Employers and Their Staff

INDEX

Introduction

From 2nd December 2003, when the Employment Equality (Religion or Belief) Regulations come into force, it will be unlawful to discriminate against workers because of religion or similar belief. The regulations also cover providers of vocational training. This booklet describes the regulations and gives guidance on associated good employment practice.

Fairness at work and good job performance go hand in hand. Tackling discrimination helps to attract, motivate and retain staff and enhances an organisation's reputation as an employer. Eliminating discrimination helps everyone to have an equal opportunity to work and to develop their skills.

There is already legislation to protect people against discrimination on the grounds of sex, race, disability and gender reassignment. From 1st December 2003 separate regulations to protect people from discrimination on the grounds of sexual orientation also come into force.

A lot of the good practice in this booklet will be familiar from existing advice on avoiding sex, race and disability discrimination. The new regulations should pose few difficulties in organisations where people are treated fairly and with consideration.

WHAT THE REGULATIONS SAY – *in summary*

These Regulations apply to vocational training and all facets of employment – including recruitment, terms and conditions, promotions, transfers, dismissals and training. They make it unlawful on the grounds of religion or belief to

- discriminate directly against anyone. That is, to treat them less favourably than others because of their religion or belief;
- discriminate indirectly against anyone. That is, to apply a criterion, provision or practice which disadvantages people of a particular religion or belief unless it can be objectively justified;
- subject someone to harassment. Harassment is unwanted conduct that violates a person's dignity or creates an intimidating, hostile, degrading, humiliating or offensive environment having regard to all the circumstances and the perception of the victim;
- victimise someone because they have made or intend to make a complaint or allegation or have given or intend to give evidence in relation to a complaint of discrimination on the grounds of religion or belief;
- discriminate or harass someone in certain circumstances after the working relationship has ended.

Exceptions may be made in very limited circumstances if there is a genuine occupational requirement for the worker to be of a particular religion or belief in order to do the job or to comply with the religious or belief ethos of the organisation.

Religion or belief is defined as being any religion, religious belief or similar philosophical belief. This does not include any philosophical or political belief unless it is similar to religious belief. It will be for the Employment Tribunals and other Courts to decide whether particular circumstances are covered by the regulations.

---

1. What do the Regulations mean?

A brief explanation of the Regulations

1.1 **Religion or belief** is not explicitly defined in the Regulations. In most applications to a tribunal it will be clear what is or is not a religion or a similar belief. It will be for the tribunals and higher courts to decide where the issue is disputed. They may consider a number of factors when deciding what is a religion or similar belief. It is likely that they will consider things such as collective worship, a clear belief system, a profound belief affecting the way of life or view of the world. Employers should be aware that these Regulations extend beyond the more well known religions and faiths to include beliefs such as Paganism and Humanism. The Regulations also cover those without religious or similar beliefs.

1.2 **Direct discrimination** means that workers or job applicants must not be treated less favourably than others because they follow, are perceived to follow, or do not follow a particular (or any) religion or belief. For example it is unlawful to

- decide not to employ someone
- dismiss them
- refuse to provide them with training
- deny them promotion
- give them adverse terms and conditions

because they follow, or do not follow, a particular religion or belief.

> *Example: At interview it becomes apparent that a job applicant is Hindu. Although the applicant has all the skills and competences required of the job, the organisation decides not to offer him the job because he is a Hindu. This is direct discrimination.*
>
> *NB A job applicant can make a claim to an Employment Tribunal. It is not necessary for them to have been employed by the organisation to make a claim of discrimination.*

Direct discrimination may only be justified in the *very* limited circumstances where a genuine occupational requirement can be shown to apply.

1.3 **Indirect discrimination** means that an organisation must not have selection criteria, policies, employment rules or any other practices which, although they are applied to all employees, have the effect of disadvantaging people of a particular religion or belief unless the practice can be justified. Indirect discrimination is unlawful whether it is intentional or not.

> *Example: Disliking the baseball caps his delivery drivers like to wear, a Chief Executive applies a 'no headwear' policy to all his staff. The policy, although applied to all employees, disadvantages his Sikh staff who wear turbans for religious reasons. This policy is indirect discrimination.*

The example above is already well recognised. However, there are less well documented examples which are equally important to the followers of particular religions.

> *Example: An organisation has a dress code which states that men may not wear ponytails. This may indirectly disadvantage Hindu men some of whom wear a Shika, (a small knotted tuft of hair worn at the back of the head, as a symbol of their belief). Such a policy could be discriminatory if it cannot be justified.*

In contrast to direct discrimination, indirect discrimination will not be unlawful if it can be justified. To justify it, an employer must show that there is a legitimate aim, (ie a real business need) and that the practice is proportionate to that aim (ie necessary and there is no alternative means available).

> *Example: A small finance company needs its staff to work late on a Friday afternoon to analyse stock prices in the American finance market. The figures arrive late on Friday because of the global time differences. During the winter months some staff would like to be released early on Friday afternoon in order to be home before nightfall – a requirement of their religion. They propose to make the time up later during the remainder of the week.*
>
> *The company is not able to agree to this request because the American figures are necessary to the business, they need to be worked on immediately and the company is too small to have anyone else able to do the work.*
>
> *The requirement to work on Friday afternoon is not unlawful discrimination as it meets a legitimate business aim and there is no alternative means available.*

1.4 **Harassment** includes behaviour that is offensive, frightening or in any way distressing. It may be intentional bullying which is obvious or violent, but it can also be unintentional or subtle and insidious. It may involve nicknames, teasing, name calling or other behaviour which may not be intended to be malicious but nevertheless is upsetting. It may be about the individual's religion or belief or it may be about the religion or belief of those with whom the individual associates. It may not be targeted at an individual(s) but consist of a general culture which, for instance, appears to tolerate the telling of religious jokes.

Organisations may be held responsible for the actions of their staff as well as the staff being individually responsible for their own actions. If harassment takes place in the workplace or at a time and/or place associated with the workplace, for example a work related social gathering, the organisation may be liable and may be ordered to pay compensation unless it can show that it took reasonable steps to prevent harassment. Individuals who harass may also be ordered to pay compensation. Employers should, where possible, also protect their workers from harassment by third parties such as service users and customers.

Employers investigating claims of harassment should consider all the circumstances before reaching a conclusion, and particularly the views of the person making the complaint; harassment is often subjective. Having gathered all the evidence, employers should ask themselves 'could what has taken place be reasonably considered to have caused offence?'

> *Example: A member of staff is devout in her belief. She continually refers to her colleagues as 'heathens' and warns them of the consequences they may suffer as a result of their lack of belief. Distressed by her intimidating behaviour, her colleagues complain to their manager that they are being harassed.*
>
> *NB The harassment is unlawful because it is directed at work colleagues because they have different beliefs or no beliefs.*

> *Example: Mr 'A' is continually teased about his partner's religious convictions. He finds being subjected to such teasing offensive and distressing and complains to his manager. His manager tells him not to be silly, that the teasing is only harmless workplace banter and is nothing to do with the organisation. This is harassment on the grounds of religion or belief even though it is not the victim's own religion or belief that is the subject of the teasing. Mr 'A' is able to complain through an Employment Tribunal. His colleagues may have to pay compensation. The organisation may have to pay compensation because it has liability for the actions of its staff.*

1.5 **Victimisation** is when an individual is treated detrimentally because they have made a complaint or intend to make a complaint about discrimination or harassment or have given evidence or intend to give evidence relating to a complaint about discrimination or harassment. They may become labelled 'troublemaker', denied promotion or training, or be 'sent to Coventry' by their colleagues. If this happens or if organisations fail to take reasonable steps to prevent it from happening, they will be liable and may be ordered to pay compensation. Individuals who victimise may also be ordered to pay compensation.

> *Example: After giving evidence for a colleague who had brought an Employment Tribunal claim against the organisation on the grounds of religion or belief, a worker applies for promotion. Her application is rejected even though she shows that she has all the necessary skills and experience. Her manager says she is a 'troublemaker' because she has given evidence at the Tribunal and as a result should not be promoted. This would be victimisation.*

Discrimination, harassment or victimisation following the end of a working relationship covers issues such as references either written or verbal.

> *Example: A manager is approached by someone from another organisation saying that Mr 'Z' has applied for a job and asks for a reference. The manager says that he cannot recommend the worker on the grounds that he did not 'fit in' because he refused to socialise in the pub with his colleagues (his religion forbade alcohol). This worker may have been discriminated against on the grounds of his religion after his working relationship with the organisation has ended.*

> *Example: Some time after resigning from employment with an organisation, a Muslim man meets his ex-colleagues at a football match. They are hostile towards him, alluding to current world events. He is distressed by their attitude but has no claim against the organisation as the harassment is not connected with nor arises out of his previous working relationship with the company.*
>
> *NB The individual in this example has no recourse through employment law but may be able to make a complaint through other legal avenues.*

1.6 **A genuine occupational requirement.** In very limited circumstances it will be lawful for an employer to treat people differently if it is a genuine occupational requirement that the job holder must be of a particular religion or belief. When deciding if this applies it is necessary to consider the nature of the work and the context in which it is carried out. Jobs may change over time and organisations should periodically consider whether the requirement continues to apply, particularly when recruiting. Further guidance is given in Appendix 1.

> *Example: A hospital which is not a religious foundation wishes to appoint a chaplain to minister to the spiritual needs of patients and staff who are mainly Christian. The hospital may be able to show that in the context in which the job is carried out it is a genuine occupational requirement that the appointee be a minister of the Christian faith.*

An occupational requirement on the grounds of religion or belief, as in the example above, must not be used as a basis for discrimination on other grounds such as race or disability.

Some organisations have an ethos based on a religion or belief, for instance a care home managed by a religious charity. Where organisations can show that they are founded on such an ethos they may be able to apply a genuine occupational requirement to jobs where in other circumstances such a requirement would not apply. In these cases the need for a particular religion or belief may not be a 'decisive' factor for the job but organisations must still be able to show that it is a requirement of the job in order to adhere to the ethos of the organisation and that it is proportionate to apply the requirement. Such an organisation should not assume that it is able to apply a 'blanket' GOR to all posts as they may be required to show that each GOR is reasonable when considering the nature of the job and the context within which it is carried out.

> *Example: A faith based care home may be able to show that being of a particular faith is a genuine requirement of its carers because they are required to carry out their duties in a manner that fulfils both the physical and spiritual needs of its patients.*
>
> *However, they may not be able to justify a similar requirement for their maintenance or reception staff whose jobs do not require them to provide spiritual leadership or support to the patients.*

1.7 **Positive action.** Selection for recruitment or promotion must be on merit, irrespective of religion or belief. However, it is possible to take certain steps to redress the effects of previous inequality of opportunity. This is called positive action. Employers may give special encouragement to, or provide specific training for people from religions or beliefs who are in a minority in the workplace. Employers may wish to consider positive measures such as:

– training their existing employees for work which has historically been the preserve of individuals from a particular religion or belief:

– advertisements which encourage applications from a minority religion but making it clear that selection will be on merit without reference to religion or belief.

There is a sound business case for eliminating discrimination in the workplace. Staff who are subjected to discrimination, harassment or victimisation may

• be unhappy, less productive and demotivated
• resign
• make a complaint to an Employment Tribunal.

If staff are subjected to discrimination, harassment or victimisation this may affect an organisation in terms of,

• damage to reputation both as a business and as an employer
• increased costs of staff leaving and consequent recruitment and training
• cost of compensation if they take a claim to an Employment Tribunal – there is no upper limit to the amount of compensation you may be ordered to pay.

2. Recruitment:

2.1 It makes sound business sense for an organisation to attract a wide field of job applicants – it is not a good idea to rely on the friends or family of current staff as this may limit the diversity of the organisation.

2.2   Advertising is best undertaken in a form accessible to a diverse audience. For instance, use of a wide interest publication or agency rather than one focussed on a niche or specialist culture or interest area which will limit the diversity of applicants and may constitute indirect discrimination.

> *Example: An advertisement placed only in a particular religious magazine may constitute indirect discrimination as it is unlikely to be seen by people of other religions or beliefs. Although the magazine may be available to all potential applicants, it effectively disadvantages groups of people who for religious or belief reasons may not subscribe to that particular publication.*

2.3   Organisations should be clear about what skills they actually need for the post, differentiating them from those which are merely desirable or reflect the personal preferences of the selector. They should recruit and/or promote for those skills and aptitudes – there is nothing to prevent an employer from deciding not to recruit or promote someone if they do not have the necessary skills or abilities.

2.4   Organisations should ensure they do not set unnecessary selection criteria or standards which might prevent people from applying because of their religion or belief.

2.5   Organisations should make sure that job applicants are clear about what the post actually entails. This should give applicants the opportunity to consider fully whether there is any chance the job might conflict with their religious or belief convictions enabling them to make an informed decision about whether to apply.

2.6   Where it is reasonable to do so, organisations should adapt their methods of recruitment so that anyone who is suitably qualified can apply and attend for selection. Some flexibility around interview/selection times allowing avoidance of significant religious times (for example Friday afternoons) is good practice.

> *Example: Where the recruitment process includes a social gathering care should be taken to avoid disadvantaging anyone for whom alcohol is prohibited on the grounds of religion or belief. For instance, holding the gathering in a hotel bar may pose particular difficulties for those whose religion forbids association with alcohol. Invitations should make it clear that applicants with specific dietary requirements (which may be associated with their religion or belief) will not be disadvantaged by the process or the venue. Employers do not have to provide specific food such as Halal or Kosher if it is not proportionate for them to do so but they should ensure that there is some appropriate food available (eg vegetarian).*

2.7 Where employers believe a genuine religious occupational requirement applies to a post, this should be made clear in the advertisement. The reasoning should also be explained in any application pack and during the selection process. More guidance is given in Appendix 1.

2.8 Whilst organisations should be sensitive to the religious or belief needs of job applicants, individuals invited to attend a selection process should ensure that they make their needs known to the organisation in good time so that employers have an opportunity to take them into account when arranging the selection process. It is a good idea for organisations to specifically invite applicants to make any special needs known.

2.9 At the interview or selection process questions should be asked, or tests set, to check for the skills and competences needed for the post. Interviewers should not be tempted to ask personal questions which may be perceived to be intrusive and imply potential discrimination. Where applicants volunteer personal information, those selecting should take particular care not to be influenced by such information. An organisation only needs to know if the person can do the job and if they are willing to do the job. Assumptions should not be made about who will and who will not fit in.

Where personal information is required for purposes such as security clearance, it should be sought in confidence and retained separately. It should not be available to those conducting the selection process.

> *Good Practice: The perception of the interviewee is important. Questions not obviously related to the post may be perceived as providing a basis for discrimination. It is accepted good practice to avoid irrelevant questions relating to marital status, or child care arrangements from which the applicant could infer an intention to discriminate on grounds of sex. To the category of questions best avoided should be added unnecessary questions about religion or belief such as ones about place or frequency of worship, communal involvement, or the religious ethos of educational establishments attended.*

2.10 At recruitment and beyond, staff welcome an organisation having a robust Equality Policy which includes religion or belief as well as other forms of discrimination and which takes the matter seriously if the policy is contravened. Although not a legal necessity, such a policy makes applicants feel confident and serves to discourage those whose attitudes and behaviours do not embrace equality of opportunity. ACAS can help organisations to draw up and implement such a policy and with their training needs.

2.11 Sunday working: The Employment Rights Act 1996 provides for those working in the retail or betting trades to opt out of Sunday working by giving their employer three months notice of their intention to stop working on Sundays. This does not apply to those working only on Sundays. This provision remains unchanged. This provision is currently applicable only in England and Wales and will become applicable in Scotland on 6 April 2004.

Where other employees request cessation of Sunday working on the grounds of their religion or belief, employers should consider whether Sunday working can be justified as a legitimate business need and whether it is proportionate to apply that justification to the individual. Refusal to adjust the individual's working patterns may be indirect discrimination if adequate justification cannot be shown.

3. Retaining good staff

3.1 Opportunities for promotion and training should be made known to all staff and be available to everyone on a fair and equal basis.

3.2 Where staff apply for internal transfers it should be remembered that informal references, including verbal references, between departmental heads, supervisors etc. should be fair and non-discriminatory. Such informal references are covered by the Regulations.

3.3 If it is reasonable to do so, organisations should consider adapting their methods of delivering training if current arrangements have the effect of disadvantaging someone because of religion or belief. This may be particularly relevant if training takes place outside normal working hours, workplace or in a residential environment.

Some things to consider:

- *times within work schedules for religious observance*
- *special dietary requirements, for example kosher, halal and vegetarian food*
- *avoid ice breakers and training activities that use language or physical contact that might be inappropriate for some beliefs*
- *avoid exercises which require the exchange of personal information*
- *ensure related social activities do not exclude people by choice of venue avoid significant religious festivals such as Ramadan*

3.4 Whilst organisations should be sensitive to the needs of their staff, staff have a responsibility to ensure that their managers and training departments are aware of their individual needs in good time so that there is an opportunity for them to be met.

3.5 Everyone should understand what harassment is and that it is hurtful, unlawful and totally unacceptable. However large or small an organisation, it is good practice for them to have an Equality Policy, to train all staff on its application and to update everyone on a regular basis. This will help to reduce the likelihood of discrimination, harassment and victimisation taking place and may help to limit liability if a complaint is made.

3.6 Organisations should ensure that their staff understand that if they harass their colleagues, they could be personally liable and may have to pay compensation in addition to anything that the organisation may have to pay. Handouts to workers visiting your premises could include a summary of your Equality Policy as well as the more usual Health & Safety instructions.

> *An Employment Tribunal Case brought under the Sex Discrimination Act. A male public service worker wrote down sexual comments about a woman colleague which, together with the general behaviour of the men towards women in her section, caused her distress. When she complained the management sought to minimise the matter. An Employment Tribunal found that her complaints were justified. She was awarded £15,000 injury to feelings against the employer and £1,000 against the individual concerned. Tribunals may be expected to adopt a similar approach in religion or belief cases as they do in existing discrimination legislation.*

3.7 Staff should be aware of what steps they could take if they feel they have been discriminated against, harassed or victimised. They should feel confident that their complaint will be treated seriously, that management will deal with the cause of the problem and that the process will be undertaken in confidence. If it is practical, it is a good idea to have a named individual who is trained and specifically responsible for dealing with employment equality issues and complaints.

> *Example: A particular religion featured largely in the media due to an international crisis. Stereotypical, pejorative and hurtful comments in the workplace were routinely made about all followers of that religion. A group of distressed workers complained to managers who promptly arranged a training session during which it was explained that not all followers of that religion agreed with what was happening elsewhere and that they were hurt and worried by their colleagues' comments. Better understanding helped to resolve the situation.*

4. Religious observance in the workplace

4.1 The Regulations do not say that employers must provide time and facilities for religious or belief observance in the workplace. However, employers should consider whether their policies, rules and procedures indirectly discriminate against staff of particular religions or beliefs and if so whether reasonable changes might be made.

4.2 Many religions or beliefs have special festival or spiritual observance days. A worker may request holiday in order to celebrate festivals or attend ceremonies. An employer should sympathetically consider such a request where it is reasonable and practical for the employee to be away from work, and they have sufficient holiday entitlement in hand.

While it may be practical for one or a small number to be absent it might be difficult if numerous such requests are made. In these circumstances the employer should discuss the matter with the employees affected, and with any recognised trade union, with the aim of balancing the needs of the business and those of other employees. Employers should carefully consider whether their criteria for deciding who should and who should not be granted leave may indirectly discriminate.

Some things to consider:
Successful equality policies may mean that your longest serving staff are less likely to be from minority groups than your more recently recruited staff. Could seniority of service therefore indirectly discriminate?

Women from some cultural backgrounds may be less assertive than men from the same backgrounds. Would a 'first come/first served' policy disadvantage them?

Example: A small toy shop employing 4 staff may be unable to release an individual for a religious festival in the busy pre-Christmas period. It may be justifiable to refuse a request for such absence.

A large department store employing 250 staff would probably be unable to justify refusing the same absence for one person because it would not substantially impact on the business as other staff would be able to cover for the absence.

4.3 Employers who operate a holiday system whereby the organisation closes for specific periods when all staff must take their annual leave should consider whether such closures are justified as they may prevent individuals taking annual leave at times of specific religious significance to them. Such closures may be justified by the business need to undertake machinery maintenance for instance. However, it would be good practice for such employers to consider how they might balance the needs of the business and those of their staff.

4.4 Organisations should have clear, reasonable procedures for handling requests for leave and ensure that all staff are aware of and adhere to the procedures. Staff should give as much notice as possible when requesting leave and in doing so should also consider that there may be a number of their colleagues who would like leave at the same time. Employers should be aware that some religious or belief festivals are aligned with lunar phases and therefore dates change from year to year; the dates for some festivals do not become clear until quite close to the actual day. Discussion and flexibility between staff and managers will usually result in a mutually acceptable compromise. Organisations should take care not to disadvantage those workers who do not hold any specific religion or belief.

4.5 Some religions or beliefs have specific dietary requirements. If staff bring food into the workplace they may need to store and heat food separately from other food, for example Muslims will wish to ensure their food is not in contact with pork (or anything that may have been in contact with pork, such as cloths or sponges). It is good practice to consult your employees on such issues and find a mutually acceptable solution to any dietary problems.

> *Example: A worker who for religious reasons is vegetarian felt unable to store her lunch in a refrigerator next to the meat sandwiches belonging to a co-worker. Following consultation with the staff and their representatives, the organisation introduced a policy by which all food must be stored in sealed containers and shelves were separately designated 'meat' and 'vegetarian'. This arrangement met the needs of all staff and at no cost to the employer.*

4.6 Some religions require their followers to pray at specific times during the day. Staff may therefore request access to an appropriate quiet place (or prayer room) to undertake their religious observance. Employers are not required to provide a prayer room. However, if a quiet place is available and allowing its use for prayer does not cause problems for other workers or the business, organisations should agree to the request.

Where possible, it is good employee relations practice for organisations to set aside a quiet room or area for prayer or private contemplation. In consultation with staff, it may be possible to designate an area for all staff for the specific purpose of prayer or contemplation rather than just a general rest room. Such a room might also be welcomed by those for whom prayer is a religious obligation and also by those who, for example, have suffered a recent bereavement. Organisations should consider providing separate storage facilities for ceremonial objects.

4.7 Employers are not required to enter into significant expenditure and/or building alterations to meet religious needs. In any event many needs will involve little or no change. For instance some religions or beliefs require a person to wash before prayer. This is often done symbolically or by using the existing facilities. However, it is good practice to consult with staff and to consider whether there is anything reasonable and practical which can be done to help staff meet the ritual requirements of their religion. It may help, for example, if all workers understand the religious observances of their colleagues thus avoiding embarrassment or difficulties for those practising their religious obligations.

4.8 Some religions or beliefs do not allow individuals to undress or shower in the company of others. If an organisation requires its staff, for reasons of health and safety, to change their clothing and/or shower, it is good employee relations practice to explore how such needs can be met. Insistence upon same-sex communal shower and changing facilities could constitute indirect discrimination (or harassment) as it may disadvantage or offend staff of a particular religion or belief whose requirement for modesty extend to changing their clothing in the presence of others, even of the same sex.

4.9   Some religions require extended periods of fasting. Employers may wish to consider how they can support staff through such a period. However, employers should take care to ensure that they do not place unreasonable extra burdens on other workers which may cause conflict between workers or claims of discrimination.

4.10   If it is practical and safe to do so, staff may welcome the opportunity to wear clothing consistent with their religion. Where organisations adopt a specific dress code careful consideration should be given to the proposed code to ensure it does not conflict with the dress requirements of some religions. General dress codes which have the effect of conflicting with religious requirements may constitute indirect discrimination unless they can be justified for example, on the grounds of Health & Safety.

> *Example: Some religions require their female followers to dress particularly modestly. A dress code which requires a blouse to be tucked inside a skirt may conflict with that requirement as it accentuates body shape. However, if the individual is allowed to wear the blouse over the outside of the skirt it may be quite acceptable.*

4.11   If organisations have a policy on the wearing of jewellery, having tattoos or other markings, they should try and be flexible and reasonable concerning items of jewellery and markings which are traditional within some religions or beliefs. Unjustifiable policies and rules may constitute indirect discrimination.

> *Example: In addition to a wedding ring, many Hindu women wear a necklace (Mangal Sutra) which is placed around their neck during the wedding ceremony and is therefore highly symbolic. Some may find it distressing if they are not allowed to wear it in their place of work, unless the rule was for Health & Safety or other justifiable reasons.*

5. Know your staff

5.1   There is no legal requirement to keep information on how staff groups are made up (gender, ethnic groups, and age, those with disabilities) other than in the public sector where racial monitoring is a statutory requirement. However, such monitoring is considered good practice. Information helps organisations to make sure their equality policy is working to the benefit of all concerned and to test whether recruitment or training policies are reaching a wide audience reflecting the local community. It can also help organisations understand their employees' needs (eg when they may want to request leave for festivals), and monitor recourse to grievance procedures and ensure that staff turnover does not reflect a disproportionate number of people from specific religions or beliefs.

5.2 If organisations decide to include religion or belief in their equality monitoring processes, staff should be told why such information is being collected and how it will be used. Staff should be assured of confidentiality and anonymity. It should be explained that they are under no obligation to give such information. Employers are reminded that such information is sensitive under the Data Protection Act.

5.3 If organisations decide not to include religion or belief in their equality monitoring processes, they may consider including a question on their staff attitude surveys to ascertain whether workers have ever felt harassed on a range of issues which should include religion or belief. Employers should take these issues seriously and make it known that discrimination is a disciplinary issue and give support to the victims.

5.4 Managers/supervisors should be as flexible and open minded as the operating environment allows. This will encourage staff to be equally flexible and open minded, and is the best way of making sure that both the needs of the organisation and those of individuals can be met.

6. What to do if you think you have suffered discrimination or harassment

6.1 If you think you are being harassed or discriminated against it is a good idea to make it clear to the person who is harassing you that their behaviour is unwelcome and that you want it to stop. However, you do not have to do this, particularly if you are feeling bullied or intimidated. If you do choose to address your concerns to the person be clear and assertive but take care that you are not perceived to be bullying the individual. Individuals may find it helpful to ask a friend, colleague, welfare officer or trade union representative to be with them in a support role.

6.2 If speaking to the person in question has failed to stop the problem, you should talk to your manager or your trade union representative. If it is your manager or supervisor who is harassing you, speak to someone higher up. Employers should deal with such complaints quickly, thoroughly and sympathetically.

6.3 It is usually best to try and sort things out quickly and as close to the problem as possible. If your organisation has a personnel or human resources department or an equality adviser you might find it helpful to talk to them. Discrimination can happen accidentally or through thoughtlessness.

Harassment can be unintentional. Often, once a manager understands the problem, he or she will be willing to try and put things right.

6.4 If your manager is unable to help you, or refuses to help you, you should use your organisation's grievance procedure. Organisations with 20 or more employees should have a grievance procedure and this requirement will be extended to all employers once Section 36 of the Employment Act 2002 is commenced (probably in late 2004). You have a legal right to be accompanied by a trade union representative or a work colleague at any hearing into your grievance.

6.5 If you are not satisfied with the result of a grievance procedure, you have a right of appeal which should be heard, if the organisation's size allows it, by someone different from the person who conducted the original grievance hearing. You have a right to be accompanied by a trade union representative or a work colleague during the appeal hearing.

6.6 If you have tried all these things, or if your employer does not have a grievance procedure, you may be able to bring a complaint to an Employment Tribunal under the Employment Equality (Religion or Belief) Regulations 2003. You do not have to hand in your notice to bring such a complaint.

6.7 You and any witnesses have a right not to be victimised for following up a grievance or complaining to an Employment Tribunal under these Regulations provided the complaint was made in good faith.

6.8 If you have been dismissed because you objected to conduct towards you, you may be able to bring a complaint of unfair dismissal to an Employment Tribunal.

6.9 Complaints to an Employment Tribunal must normally be brought within three months of the act you are complaining about. Care should be taken to ensure that the three month point is not exceeded during any internal grievance/appeals process.

7. Some frequently asked questions

Q Do organisations have to do anything new or different when the legislation comes in?

A They should ensure that religion and belief are included in their Equality Policy. It is good idea to revisit the Equality Policy from time to time to ensure it has not become outdated, to test any new employment policies and procedures for discrimination and to ensure the policy itself meets current legislation requirements.

Staff need to be made aware (through training, notice boards, circulars, contracts of employment etc.) that it is not only unacceptable to discriminate, harass or victimise someone on the grounds of religion or belief, it is also unlawful. Organisations should also make it clear that they will not tolerate such behaviour. Staff should know what to do if they believe they have been discriminated against or harassed, or if they believe someone else is being discriminated against or harassed, and this should be included in the grievance procedure. Organisations should also consider adding all forms of discrimination and harassment (religion or belief, sex, race, disability, gender reassignment and sexual orientation) to their disciplinary rules which should also include bullying. It is good practice to include age in your policies ahead of age discrimination becoming unlawful in October 2006.

> Reminder: The Employment Act 2002 requires all employers, however large or small, to have both a disciplinary procedure and a grievance procedure. The requirement is expected to take effect in late 2004.

Q Must organisations have an Equality Policy?

A Whilst organisations do not have to have an Equality Policy, implementing and observing such a policy is a commonplace means of demonstrating that an employer has taken reasonably practicable steps to prevent employees discriminating against or harassing other employees. The policy should set out minimum standards of behaviour expected of all staff through recruitment and onwards and what staff can expect of the organisation. It acts as a reminder, gives staff confidence that they will be treated with dignity and respect, and may be used as an integral part of a grievance or disciplinary process if necessary.

If organisations do not have an Equality Policy and would like help in putting in place an effective policy ACAS can help.

Q Do the Regulations cover all religions and beliefs?

A It is unlawful to discriminate against a person on the grounds of religion, religious belief, perceived religion or religious belief, or similar philosophical belief. Political beliefs are specifically excluded from these Regulations (see 1.7). It is as unlawful to discriminate against a person for not holding a specific religion or belief as it is to discriminate against someone for actually holding to or subscribing to a particular religion or belief.

Q Do these Regulations cover all workers?

A The Regulations apply to all workers, including office holders, police, barristers, partners in a business and members of the armed forces. They also cover related areas such as membership of trade organisations, the award of qualifications, the services of careers guidance organisations, employment agencies and vocational training providers, including further and higher education institutions.

The Regulations cover anyone who applies to an organisation for work, or who already works for an organisation whether they are directly employed or work under some other kind of contract or are an agency worker. Organisations are also responsible for the behaviour of their staff towards an individual working for someone else but on their premises, for example someone from another organisation repairing a piece of equipment.

Workers are sometimes harassed by third parties, such as customers or clients. Where possible organisations should protect their staff from such harassment and should take steps to deal with actual or potential situations of this kind. This will enhance the organisation's reputation as a good employer and make the organisation a welcoming and safe place to work.

Many organisations provide visitors and visiting workers with guidance on Health & Safety matters. It may be appropriate to include some comments in any policy your organisation has on harassment.

Q Do organisations have to ask about someone's religion or belief at interview?

A No. Interviews are about finding out whether someone has the right skills for the job. Personal questions about an individual's beliefs should not be asked unless they are relevant to the duties of the job in question. It is good practice not to ask any personal questions at interview unless it is to make sure that appropriate adjustments are made for anyone with a disability.

Organisations do not have to employ people whose beliefs mean they are unable to undertake essential parts of the job. It should be made clear to candidates what type of work the organisation does and what duties the job involves so they can consider whether there is any chance it might conflict with their religion or beliefs.

Example: An individual applying for a job in a large supermarket stacking shelves may not be willing to handle pork products for religious reasons. Such products probably represent only a small proportion of the goods displayed on the shelves. It may not be reasonable to reject such job applicants if it is practicable to allocate work in a way that does not involve handling pork products. However, it may not be practical for the store to adjust the work of a check-out operative in order that they are not required to handle pork products.

Example: A waiter who is a Humanist or Sikh may not be prepared to serve meat which has not been slaughtered in a manner he or she considers to be humane. In this case redistribution of the work may not be possible if the restaurant serves such meat and it may be reasonable to reject the job application on the grounds of religion or belief.

If an organisation changes the type of work it does they should give careful consideration to the effect it may have on their staff for reasons of religion or belief. Early consultation with staff and/or their trade union will usually result in a mutually acceptable arrangement.

Q Do organisations have to collect data on religion or belief?

A The Regulations do not require the collection of such data but it may help organisations to provide appropriate facilities for their staff and to understand employees' needs (eg when they might seek annual leave). It is important that managers talk to people and/or their trades unions to ensure an understanding of individual needs and to avoid making assumptions about them. Not all followers of each religion or belief will necessarily have the same practices or follow their religion in exactly the same way.

If an organisation decides to collect data, it may give staff added confidence if it is made clear why they want the information, how it is going to be used and that giving such information is entirely voluntary. All such information should be confidential and anonymous. It is designated 'sensitive' under the Data Protection Act 1998. Staff permission should be obtained before using such information.

Q How will organisations know if they are discriminating inadvertently?

A Individual staff, or their trade union, will generally tell managers, particularly if managers are able to create a culture whereby staff feel comfortable in sharing such information. It can be helpful for organisations to have a designated individual to whom people can go in confidence. It is a good idea for management teams, staff representatives or a specially convened group of employees to think through and test whether any organisational policies and procedures impact on people's religion or belief, or discriminate on any other grounds such as disability, sexual orientation, sex or race.

It is good practice to include age in your equality policies ahead of age discrimination becoming unlawful in October 2006.

Organisations should consider carefully whether they are inadvertently discriminating indirectly. For example, if team meetings always take place on a Friday afternoon this may discriminate against Jewish and Muslim staff for whom Friday afternoon has a particular religious significance, although not everyone follows their faith in the same way. Employers will not escape liability in an Employment Tribunal by showing that discrimination was inadvertent or accidental.

Q No one in my organisation has ever complained of discrimination or harassment so we don't need to do anything new, do we?

A People do not always feel able or confident enough to complain, particularly if the harasser is a manager or senior executive. Sometimes they will simply resign. One way to find out is to undertake exit interviews when people leave your organisation and as part of that process to ask if they have ever felt harassed, bullied or discriminated against at work. If it is possible, exit interviews should be undertaken by someone out of the individual's line of management, for instance a personnel officer.

Discrimination includes harassment which can take place without management being aware of it. Organisations should make sure all their staff understand that harassment means any unwanted behaviour that makes someone feel either intimidated, humiliated or offended and that includes teasing, tormenting, name calling etc. and applies whoever the perpetrator may be. The victim's perception of the effect of the behaviour is also important. Managers should take all practical steps to make sure staff understand that organisations and their management teams will not tolerate such behaviour and that they will deal with whoever is causing the problem through the disciplinary process.

Q Should we ban discussions about religion and belief in the workplace? We are concerned that someone might complain about harassment.

A If harassment has been explained to staff they should be able to distinguish between reasonable discussion and offensive behaviour. Staff should be aware that if their discussions cause offence then this may be considered to be harassment and therefore unlawful. A ban on discussions about religion or belief may create more bad feeling amongst staff and cause more problems than it solves.

Q Do organisations have to provide a prayer room?

A The Regulations do not say that organisations have to provide a prayer room (see 4.4). However, if employees request access to a quiet place in which to meet their religious obligations and such a place is available without it having any adverse impact on the business or other staff, then employers may be acting in a discriminatory way if they refuse such a request.

Example: It may not be reasonable or practical to provide a prayer room for staff in a small motor garage employing 12 staff, where the only space available is a communal kitchen/rest room.

However, a larger organisation with meeting/conference rooms that are often unused may be considered unreasonable if it is not willing to organise its operations in such a way as to make such a room available for prayer at specific and known times each day.

If employers are able to do so, it is good practice to consider providing a suitable area for religious observance or private contemplation by anyone wishing to use it for that purpose. Be careful when providing such a room not to put staff that do not have need of a prayer room at an unjustifiable disadvantage. For example, if an organisation were to convert their only rest room into a prayer room then staff who do not have need of a prayer room would be disadvantaged and may have a grievance on the grounds of religion or belief.

It is a good idea to consult with staff representatives or individuals about policies for the use of such a room. Amicable agreement can be reached on issues such as the storage and display of religious symbols and the wearing or otherwise of shoes within the room.

Q Do organisations have to release staff for prayer outside normal rest/break periods or religious festivals?

A Organisations do not have to release staff for prayer outside normal rest breaks or holiday periods. Under the Working Time Regulations 1998, (further details available at Appendix 2) staff are, in general, entitled to a rest break of not less than 20 minutes where working time is more than 6 hours. Staff may request that their rest break coincide with their religious obligations to pray at certain times of the day. Employers may be justified in refusing such a request if, for example, it conflicts with legitimate business needs which they are unable to meet in any other way. If they are unable to justify such a refusal this may be discrimination.

The Working Time Regulations also provide that staff are entitled to not less than 4 weeks annual leave each year (see introduction to Appendix 2). Staff may request annual leave to coincide with religious festivals (see 4.1 and 4.2). Refusal to grant such leave may be discriminatory if it cannot be justified by a legitimate business need which cannot be met by any other reasonable means.

Managers should try to be flexible about when rest breaks or annual holidays are taken. It is good practice to ensure that staff know how to request such flexibility and how much reasonable notice is required to meet their needs. There may be a few jobs where it is not possible to be flexible but explanation and discussion may enable a compromise to be achieved. No organisation is expected to accept unreasonable disruption to its activities. Managers may wish to consider that the time taken for prayer is rarely longer than that of a tea or coffee break. Staff need to understand that they have a responsibility to be reasonable to both their employer and their colleagues when asking for time off.

Q My organisation has rules on personal appearance and dress. Are we in breach of the legislation?

A If your company rules are in place for health and safety reasons or to protect your image with customers they may be lawful. It is important to explain the company's policy on dress and appearance, but organisations should try to be flexible where they can to enable staff to dress in accordance with their beliefs but still meet the organisation's requirements.

Some religions require their women to dress modestly and organisations should consider whether this requirement is contravened by their dress code. For example Jewish women may wish to wear a shirt or blouse outside their skirt in order to avoid accentuating their body shape. This may also apply to women from other religions.

There are items of jewellery which are culturally specific to some religions, for instance Hindu men wear neck beads (known as kanthi mala) which are an indication of their faith. Additionally, some religions are designated by body markings such as a red spot on the forehead (bindi dindur) and organisations should consider allowing for these within their policies.

Q I am concerned that, on the grounds of religion, some of my staff may refuse to work with their gay or lesbian colleagues.

A Some religions do have strong views concerning sexual orientation but most do not advocate persecution of people because of their sexual orientation. Everyone has the right to be treated with dignity and respect in the workplace whatever their sex, race, colour, disability, age, religion or sexual orientation. You should include this over-riding premise in your Equality Policy and show that you take a robust view when this principle is not adhered to. Your workers do not have to be friends but you can insist that they treat each other professionally.

Q Our organisation has a religious ethos. How do we determine if a person's religion or belief can be justified as a genuine occupational requirement for a post?

A Staff can be recruited on the basis of their religion or belief where this is a genuine occupational requirement for the job. The Regulations require you to consider the nature of the job and the context within which it is carried out when considering whether the job holder needs to practise a specific religion in order to undertake the role within the ethos of the organisation. Appendix 1 provides some further guidance on this subject.

When considering applying such a requirement look at each post individually both in terms of the duties of the job and the context within which it is carried out. Organisations should not expect to apply a blanket requirement to all its posts even if it has a religious ethos.

Organisations should consider whether there are alternatives to applying an occupational requirement. For instance, if only a small part of the job needs someone from that religion then it may be possible to redistribute work or reorganise roles in such a way as to avoid applying a religious requirement to a particular post. Organisations can reasonably expect their staff to keep to their organisational values and culture and should bear in mind that people may be able to maintain those values and culture, and therefore the ethos of the organisation, without actually belonging to the particular religion or belief.

Organisations should be clear about the link between the requirements of the job and the requirement to be of a particular religion or belief. As, in the event of an Employment Tribunal claim on the grounds of religious or belief discrimination, the burden of proof will be on the employer to show a genuine occupational requirement. Tribunals tend to interpret such requirements *very* narrowly since they effectively go against the principle of equal treatment.

A genuine occupational requirement on the grounds of religion or belief should not be used to discriminate on any other grounds such as sex, race or disability; although in some *very* limited circumstances a religious organisation may lawfully be able to discriminate on the grounds of sexual orientation or sex.

APPENDIX 1

Genuine Occupational Requirements – Guidance

Employers wishing to claim a genuine occupational requirement (GOR) should bear in mind the following points.

1. GORs should be identified at the beginning of the recruitment, training or promotion process, before the vacancy is advertised. Advertisements and material sent to potential applicants should clearly show that the employer considers that a GOR applies and the point should be reiterated during the selection process.

    Reminder: Applicants who do not agree that there is a GOR for the post holder are at liberty to make a claim to an Employment Tribunal because they believe they have been prevented from applying for the post on the grounds of religion or belief. It would be for the employer to show that such a GOR is justified.

2. If an employer wishes to claim a GOR s/he must consider what the duties are for which an exemption is to be claimed; a GOR cannot be claimed unless some or all of those duties, or the totality of the role, are covered by a specific exemption and an assessment has been made showing that it would be unreasonable to require other employees of the appropriate religion or belief to undertake those duties. Also it must be shown that those duties must be carried out to achieve the objectives of the job.

3. In an organisation a GOR exemption cannot be claimed in relation to particular duties if the employer already has sufficient employees who are capable of carrying out the required duties and whom it would be reasonable to employ on those duties without undue inconvenience.

    Where the organisation has a religious ethos, a GOR exemption cannot be claimed if the nature of the role and the context within which it is carried out is not of sufficient profile or impact within the organisation to affect the overall ethos of the organisation.

4. Each job for which a GOR may apply must be considered individually; it should not be assumed that because a GOR exists for one job it also exists for jobs of a similar nature or in a similar location. The nature or extent of the relevant duties may be different or, for instance, there may be other employees who could undertake those duties.

5.   A GOR can be claimed where it is necessary for the relevant duties to be carried out by someone of a specific religion or belief because being of that religion or belief is a 'determining' factor, for example in the Islamic faith a halal butcher must be Muslim.
6.   GOR must be reassessed on each occasion a post becomes vacant to ensure that it can still be validly claimed. Circumstances may have changed, rendering the GOR inapplicable.
7.   A GOR cannot be used to establish or maintain a balance or quota of employees of a particular religion or belief.
8.   GORs are always open to challenge by an individual. The burden of proof lies with the employer to establish the validity of a GOR by providing evidence to substantiate a claim.
9.   Only an Employment Tribunal or a higher court can give an authoritative ruling as to whether or not a GOR is valid.
10. The following legislation remains extant
     The School Standards and Framework Act 1998
     The Amendments to the School Standards and Framework Act 2003
     The Education (Scotland) Act 1980.

APPENDIX 2

The Regulations cover religion, religious belief and similar philosophical beliefs. Until the Courts and Tribunals have had an opportunity to consider which religions or beliefs are covered by these Regulations it is not possible to provide definitive guidance. However, those listed below are some of the most commonly practised religions and beliefs in Britain. They are listed in alphabetical order for ease of reference only. However, there are many more and this list should not be considered to be exhaustive.

The information is intended for guidance only. It may assist employers to plan and implement policies and systems which meet the needs of both the employer and employee. Calendars indicating festivals in world religions are available from a number of sources.

Not all members of each religion follow all the practices and observances. Neither will every member of each religion request time off for each and every festival. In some instances an adjustment to the working day to allow time to attend a prayer meeting before or after work may be all that is requested. In many instances nothing will be requested. Whilst employers are encouraged to be flexible where reasonable and appropriate, employees should recognise that they also have a responsibility to be reasonable and to consider the needs of the business in which they are employed.

Reminder: The Working Time Regulations 1998 provide most workers with an entitlement to 4 weeks annual leave per year; that is 4 weeks x normal working week. If a worker normally works a 6 day week his/her leave annual entitlement is 24 days per year. If a worker works a 2 day week his/her annual leave entitlement is 8 days. The Working Time Regulations do not apply to workers on board sea-going fishing vessels, to certain sea-farers nor to workers on board most ships which operate on inland waterways. In addition, the annual leave entitlement does not apply to the armed forces, police nor to certain specific activities in the civil protection services; to mobile staff in civil aviation; nor, until 1 August 2004, to doctors in training. Under the Regulations this leave entitlement is not additional to bank holidays, unless otherwise stated in the workers Terms & Conditions.

Employers can set the times that staff take their leave, for example, for a Christmas shutdown. However, employers should consider whether setting times for annual leave may be discriminatory because of religion or belief.

Under the Working Time Regulations an employer can require an employee to give twice as many days notice of annual leave as the number of days to be taken as annual leave. Therefore 2 days annual leave may require 4 days notice.

Further information on the Working Time Regulations is available from ACAS or the DTI.

Baha'i

Baha'is should say one of three obligatory prayers during the day. Prayers need to be recited in a quiet place where the Baha'i will wish to face the Qiblih (the Shrine of Baha'u'llah, near Akka, Israel), which is in a south-easterly direction from the UK. Two of the prayers require movement and prostrations.

Baha'is are required to wash their hands and face before prayers but can use a normal washroom facility for this purpose.

Festivals

Baha'i festivals take place from sunset to sunset and followers may wish to leave work early in order to be home for sunset on the day prior to the festival date. Baha'is will wish to refrain from working on the key festival dates.

The Baha'i Fast   2 March–20 March

Baha'is refrain from eating or drinking from sunrise to sunset during this period. Baha'is working evening or night shifts will appreciate the opportunity to prepare food at sundown. There are exemptions from fasting for sickness, pregnancy, travelling and strenuous physical work.

Naw-Ruz (Baha'i New Year)   21 March
Ridvan   21 April–2 May

Ridvan is the most important of the Baha'i festivals and includes 3 holy days on which Baha'is would wish to refrain from working. They are:

1st Day of Ridvan	21 April
9th Day of Ridvan	29 April
12th Day of Ridvan	2 May
Declaration of the Bab	23 May
Ascension of the Baha'u'llah	29 May
Martyrdom of the Bab	9 July
Birth of the Bab	20 October
Birth of Baha'u'llah	12 November

Food As a matter of principle most Baha'is do not take alcohol. Otherwise there are no dietary restrictions.

Bereavement Burial should take place as soon as possible after legal formalities and funeral arrangements can be put in hand. The body should be transported no more than one hour's journey from the place where the person died, so funerals take place relatively close to the place of death. The usual arrangements for compassionate leave should generally suffice. Baha'is have no specific period of mourning.

Buddhism

Festivals There are a number of different traditions in Buddhism arising from different cultural and ethnic backgrounds. Different traditions will celebrate different festivals. Some Buddhist traditions do not celebrate any festivals. Buddhist members of staff should be asked which festivals are important to them. Festivals follow the lunar calendar and will therefore not take place on the same day each year.

Saindran Memorial Day	January
Parinirvana	February
Magha Puja Day	February/March
Honen Memorial Day	March
Buddha Day (Vesak or Visakah Puja)	May
The Ploughing Festival	May
Buddhist New Year	(varies according to tradition)
Asalha Puja Day (Dhamma Day)	July
Ulambana (Ancestor Day)	July
Abhidhamma Day	October
Kathina Day	October
The Elephant Festival	November
Loy Krathorg	December
Bodhi Day	December
Uposatha	(weekly on the lunar quarter day)
Avalokitesvara's Birthday	

Food Most Buddhists are vegetarian reflecting their adherence to the precept of non-harm to self and others. Many would not want to prepare or serve meat for others. Buddhists upholding the precept to avoid intoxication may not wish to drink alcohol, or serve it.

Clothing Many Buddhists would prefer to wear clothing which reflects their adherence to non-harm eg not wearing leather clothing and leather shoes.

Christianity

There are a wide variety of Christian Churches and organisations all of which have their own specific needs, rituals and observations.

Festivals

Christmas Day	25 December
Ash Wednesday	Feb/March (date set by lunar calendar)

This is a day of fasting/abstinence for many Christians.

Maundy Thursday	March/April (date set by lunar calendar)
Good Friday	March/April (date set by lunar calendar)
Easter Sunday	March/April (date set by lunar calendar)
All Saints Day	1 November
Christmas Eve	24 December

In addition there are a number of 'holy days of obligation' when Christians may wish to attend a church service and request a late start to the working day, or early finish in order that they can attend their local church. Many practising Christians will wish to attend their church on Sundays throughout the year.

Food Some Christians avoid alcohol.

Clothing Some Christian churches forbid the use of cosmetics and require their female members to dress particularly modestly.

Bereavement No special requirements beyond normal compassionate leave.

Hinduism

Festivals

Hinduism is a diverse religion and not all Hindus will celebrate the same festivals.

Makar Sakranti	14 January
Maha Shiva Ratri	February
Holi	March
Ramnavami	April
Rakshabandham	August
Janmashtami	August
Ganesh Chaturthi	August/September

Navaratri	September/October
Dushera (aka Vijayadashmi)	September/October
Karava Chauth	October
Diwali	Late October/Early November
New Year	Late October/Early November

There are a number of occasions through the year when some Hindus fast.

Clothing Hindu women will often wear a bindi which is a red spot worn on the forehead and denotes that she is of the Hindu faith. In addition, many married Hindu women wear a necklace (mangal sutra) which is placed around their necks during the marriage ceremony and is in addition to a wedding ring.

A few Orthodox Hindu men wear a small tuft of hair (shikha) similar to a ponytail but this is often hidden beneath the remaining hair. Some Orthodox Hindu men also wear a clay marking on their foreheads known as a tilak.

Food Most Hindus are vegetarian and will not eat meat, fish or eggs. None eat beef.

Bereavement Following cremation, close relatives of the deceased will observe a 13 day mourning period during which they will wish to remain at home. The closest male relatives may take the ashes of the deceased to the Ganges, in India. They may therefore request extended leave. Close male relatives of the deceased may shave their heads as a mark of respect.

Islam (Muslims)

Observant Muslims are required to pray five times a day. Each prayer time takes about 15 minutes and can take place anywhere clean and quiet. Prayer times are:–

At dawn (Fajr)

At mid-day (Zuhr) in Winter sometime between 1200–1300hrs and in Summer between 1300–1600hrs.

Late Afternoon (Asr) in Winter 1430–1530

After Sunset (Maghrib)

Late Evening (Isha)

Friday mid-day prayers are particularly important to Muslims and may take a little longer than other prayer times. Friday prayers must be said in congregation and may require Muslims to travel to the nearest mosque or prayer gathering.

Before prayers, observant Muslims undertake a ritual act of purification. This involves the use of running water to wash hands, face, mouth, nose, arms up to the elbows and feet up to the ankles, although often the washing of the feet will be performed symbolically.

Festivals The dates of festivals are reliant on a sighting of the new moon and will therefore vary from year to year. While approximate dates will be known well in advance, it is not always possible to give a definitive date until much nearer to the time.

Ramadan, which takes place in the 9th month of the Muslim lunar calendar, is a particularly significant time for Muslims. Fasting is required between dawn and sunset. Most Muslims will attend work in the normal way but in the winter they may wish to break fast with other Muslims at sunset. This could be seen as a delayed lunch break. For those working evening or night shifts, the opportunity to heat food at sunset and/or sunrise will be appreciated.

Eid al-Fitr – 3 days to mark the end of Ramadan – most Muslims will only seek annual leave for the first of the three days.

Eid al-Adha takes place 2 months and 10 days after Eid al-Fitr and is a 3 day festival. Again, most Muslims will usually only seek leave for the first of the three days.

All Muslims are required to make a pilgrimage to Mecca once in their lifetime. Muslims may therefore seek one extended leave period in which to make such a pilgrimage.

Clothing Muslims are required to cover the body. Men may therefore be unwilling to wear shorts. Women may wish to cover their whole body, except their face, hands and feet.

Food Muslims are forbidden to eat any food which is derived from the pig, this includes lard which may be present in bread or even ice cream. In addition they are forbidden to eat any food which is derived from a carnivorous animal. Meat that may be consumed must be slaughtered by the halal method. Islam also forbids the consumption of alcohol which includes its presence in dishes such as risotto or fruit salad.

Bereavement Burial must take place as soon as possible following death and may therefore occur at short notice.

Other
1. Any form of gambling is forbidden under Islam.
2. Observant Muslims are required to wash following use of the toilet and will therefore appreciate access to water in the toilet cubicle, often Muslims will carry a small container of water into the cubicle for this purpose. By agreement with other staff and cleaners, these containers could be kept in the cubicle.

3.   Physical contact between the sexes is discouraged and some Muslims may politely refuse to shake hands with the opposite sex. This should not be viewed negatively.

Jainism

Jains are required to worship three times daily, before dawn, at sunset and at night. Jains working evening or night shifts may wish to take time out to worship or take their meals before sunset.

Festivals

Jain festivals are spiritual in nature.

Oli   April and October

8 days semi-fasting twice a year when some take one bland, tasteless meal during day time.

Mahavira Jayanti   April – birth anniversary of Lord Mahavira
Paryusan   August/September

During this sacred period of fasting and forgiveness for 8 days Jains fast, observe spiritual rituals, meditate and live a pious life taking only boiled water during day time.

Samvatsari   September

The last day of Paryushan when Jains ask for forgiveness and forgive one another.

Diwali   October/November

Death anniversary of Lord Mahavira, includes a 2 day fast and listening to the last message of Mahavira.

Food Jains practice avoidance of harm to all life – self and others. They are, therefore, strict vegetarians including the avoidance of eggs; some may take milk products. Many also avoid root vegetables. Jains do not eat between sunset and sunrise. Jains do not drink alcohol.

Bereavement Cremation will take place as soon as practical after death (usually 3–5 days). There is no specified mourning period and normal compassionate leave arrangements will suffice.

Judaism (Jews)

Observant Jews are required to refrain from work on the Sabbath and Festivals, except where life is at risk. This includes travelling (except on foot), writing, carrying, switching on and off electricity, using a telephone and transactions of a commercial nature (that is buying and selling). The Sabbath and all other Festivals begin one hour before dusk and so practising Jews need to be home by then. Sabbath begins one hour before dusk on Friday.

Festivals

Passover	March/April	2 sets of 2 days
Pentecost (Shavuoth)	May/June	2 days
New Year	Sept/Oct	2 days
Day of Atonement	Sept/Oct	1 day fasting
Tabernacles (Sukkot)	Sept/Oct	2 sets of 2 days

Clothing Orthodox Jewish men keep their head covered at all times. Orthodox Jewish women will wish to dress modestly and may not want to wear trousers, short skirts or short sleeves; some may wish to keep their heads covered by a scarf or beret.

Food Jews are required to eat only kosher food (which has been treated and prepared in a particular manner).

Bereavement Funerals must take place as soon as possible following the death – the same day where possible – and therefore take place at short notice. Following a death, the immediate family must stay at home and mourn for 7 days (Shiva). Following the death of a Father or Mother, an observant Jewish man will be required to go to a Synagogue to pray morning, afternoon and evening for 11 months of the Jewish calendar.

Muslim (see Islam)

Other Ancient Religions
These include religions covered by the Council of British Druid Orders and examples are Druidry, Paganism and Wicca.

Some examples of Festivals

Candlemas	2 February
Spring Equinox*	21/22 March
Beltaine	30 April
Summer Solstice*	21/22 June
Lughnasadh	2 August
Autumn Equinox*	21/22 September
Samhain 3	1 October
Winter Solstice*	21/22 December

*Dates movable due to astronomical times set in accordance with GMT.

Food Generally vegetarian or vegan, although not always.

Clothing Some items of jewellery as associated with Pagan faiths such as ankh, pentagram, hammer and crystal.

Bereavement No specific requirements beyond that of normal compassionate leave.

There are also other ancient religions such as Astaru, Odinism and Shamanism.

Parsi (see Zorastrianism)

Rastafarianism

Festivals

Birthday of Haile Selassie	23 July
Ethiopian New Year	11 Sept
Anniversary of the Crowning of	
Haile Selassie 1	2 Nov
Christmas	25 Dec

Food Vegetarian including the avoidance of eggs. Many Rastafarians eat only organic food as close to its raw state as possible.

Clothing Hair is worn uncut and plaited into 'dreadlocks'. It is often covered by a hat which is usually red, green and gold.

Other Whilst the faith supports the smoking of ganga (marijuana) this practice remains unlawful in the UK and is unaffected by the Employment Equality (Religion or Belief) Regulations 2003.

Bereavement No specific requirements beyond that of normal compassionate leave.

Sikhism

Festivals

Birthday of Guru Gobind Singh	5 January
Vaisakhi	14 April
Martyrdom of Guru Arjan Dev	16 June
Sri Guru Granth Sahib Day	1 September
Divali (Diwali)	October/November (date set by lunar calendar)
Martyrdom of Guru Tegh Bahadur	24 November
Birthday of Guru Nanak	November

Food Sikhs do not eat halal meat. Some do not eat beef and many are vegetarian.

Clothes Practising male Sikhs observe the 5 Ks of the faith. These are:

Kesh	Uncut hair. Observant Sikhs do not remove or cut any hair from their body. Sikh men and some women will wear a turban.
Kangha	Wooden comb usually worn in the hair.
Kara	Metal bracelet worn on the wrist.
Kachhahera	Knee length underpants.
Kirpan	Short sword worn under the clothing so that it is not visible.

Bereavement Sikhs are cremated and have a preference for this to take place as soon after the death as possible. There is no specified mourning period and normal compassionate leave arrangements will suffice.

Zoroastrians (Parsi)

Zoroastrians are required to pray 5 times during the day, saying a special prayer for each part of the day.

Hawab	(sunrise to midday)
Rapithwin	(midday to mid-afternoon)
Uzerin	(mid-afternoon to sunset)
Aiwisruthrem	(sunset to midnight)
Ushahin	(midnight to dawn)

Prayers should be said in front of a fire – or a symbolic replica of fire.

In addition, a ritual is performed each time a Zoroastrian washes his/her hands although the ritual is not always strictly performed in all its detail. When it is performed, the individual will stand on the same spot and must speak to no one during the ritual. No special facilities are required. A prayer will also be said before eating.

Festivals Dates follow the lunar calendar and will therefore vary from year to year.

Khordad Sal	The Prophet's Birthday
Fravardigan	Remembrance of departed souls
Tiragan	Water Festival
Mehergan	Harvest Festival
Ave roj nu Parab	Water Festival
Adar roj nu Parab	Fire Festival
Jashn-e-Sadeh	Mid Winter Festival
Zardosht no Disco	Death of the Prophet
Maktad	Festival of All Souls
NoRuz	New Year

In addition there are 6 seasonal festivals

Maidyoizaremaya	Mid Spring
Maidyoishema	Mid Summer
Paitishahya	Early Autumn
Ayathrima	Mid Autumn
Maidhyairya	Mid Winter
Hamaspathmaedaya	Pre-Spring

Clothes Zoroastrians, both male and female, wear two pieces of sacred clothing. The Sudreh (shirt) and the Kusti (cord) which is a string that passes loosely around the waist three times and is tied in a double knot at the back. It is the Kusti which is ritualistically retied each time the hands are washed.

Bereavement Following the death of a close family member there is a mourning period of 10 days followed by a ceremony to mark the 1st month, the 6th month and the 12th month of bereavement.

Legislation relating to religion and education

European Convention on Human Rights

(PART II Schedule I Human Rights Act 1998)

THE FIRST PROTOCOL Article 2 Right to education

No person shall be denied the right to education. In the exercise of any functions which it assumes in relation to education and to teaching, the State shall respect the right of parents to ensure such education and teaching in conformity with their own religious and philosophical convictions.

Education (No 2) Act 1986

Section 43 (Freedom of Speech in Universities, Polytechnics and Colleges)

(1) Every individual and body of persons concerned in the government of any establishment to which this section applies shall take such steps as are reasonably practicable to ensure that freedom of speech within the law is secured for members, students and employees of the establishment and for visiting speakers.

(2) The duty imposed by subsection 1 above includes (in particular) the duty to ensure, so far as is reasonably practicable, that the use of any premises of the establishment is not denied to any individual or body of persons on any ground connected with:

(a) the beliefs or views of that individual or any member of that body; or
(b) the policy or objectives of that body.

(3) The governing body of every such establishment shall, with a view to facilitating the discharge of the duty imposed by subsection 1 above in relation to that establishment, issue and keep up to date a code of practice setting out:

(a) the procedures to be followed by members, students and employees of the establishment in connection with the organisation:

(i) of meetings which are to be held on premises of the establishment and which fall within any class of meeting specified in the code; and

(ii) of other activities which are to take place on those premises and which fall within any class of activity so specified; and

(b) the conduct required of such persons in connection with any such meeting or activity; and dealing with such other matters as the governing body considers appropriate.

(4) Every individual and body of persons concerned in the government of any such establishment shall take such steps as are reasonably practicable (including where appropriate the initiation of disciplinary measures) to secure that the requirements of the code of practice for that establishment, issued under subsection 3 above, are complied with.

(5) The establishments to which this section applies are:

(a) any university;

(b) any establishment which is maintained by a local education authority and for which section 1 of the 1968 (No 2) Act (government and conduct of colleges of education and other institutions providing further education) requires there to be an instrument of government; and

(c) any establishment of further education designated by or under Regulations made under section 27 of the 1980 Act as an establishment substantially dependent for its maintenance on assistance from local education authorities or on grants under section 100(1)(b) of the 1944 Act.

(6) In this section:

'governing body', in relation to any university, means the executive governing body which has responsibility for the management and administration of its revenue and property and the conduct of its affairs (that is to say the body commonly called the council of the university); 'university' includes a university college and any college, or institution in the nature of a college, in a university.

(7) Where any establishment:

(a) falls within subsection 5(b) above; or

(b) falls within subsection 5(c) above by virtue of being substantially dependent for its maintenance on assistance from local education authorities;

the local education authority or authorities maintaining or (as the case may be) assisting with the establishment shall, for the purpose of this section, be taken to be concerned in its government.

(8) Where a students' union occupies premises which are not premises of the establishment in connection with which the union is constituted, any

reference in this section to the premises of the establishment shall be taken to include a reference to the premises occupied by the students' union.

Equality Act 2006 – PART 2

49 Educational establishments

(1) It is unlawful for the responsible body of an educational establishment listed in the Table to discriminate against a person—

(a) in the terms on which it offers to admit him as a pupil,

(b) by refusing to accept an application to admit him as a pupil, or

(c) where he is a pupil of the establishment—

    (i)   in the way in which it affords him access to any benefit, facility or service,

    (ii) by refusing him access to a benefit, facility or service,

    (iii) by excluding him from the establishment, or

    (iv) by subjecting him to any other detriment.

(2) In the application of this section to England and Wales—

(a) an expression also used in any of the Education Acts (within the meaning of section 578 of the Education Act 1996 (c. 56)) has the same meaning as in that Act, and

(b) 'pupil' in relation to an establishment includes any person who receives education at the establishment.

(3) In the application of this section to Scotland, an expression also used in the Education (Scotland) Act 1980 (c. 44) has the same meaning as in that Act.

Establishment	Responsible body
ENGLAND AND WALES	
School maintained by a local education authority.	Local education authority or governing body.
Independent school (other than a special school).	Proprietor.
Special school (not maintained by local education authority).	Proprietor.
SCOTLAND	
Public school.	Education authority.
Grant-aided school.	Manager.
Independent school.	Proprietor.

50 Section 49: exceptions

(1) Section 49(1)(a), (b) and (c)(i) and (ii) shall not apply in relation to—

(a) a school designated under section 69(3) of the School Standards and Framework Act 1998 (c. 31) (foundation or voluntary school with religious character),

['School Standards and Framework Act 1998

69(3) For the purposes of this Part a foundation or voluntary school has a religious character if it is designated as a school having such a character by an order made by the Secretary of State']

(b) a school listed in the register of independent schools for England or for Wales if the school's entry in the register records that the school has a religious ethos,

[Education Act 2002

s 158 The registers

(1) There shall continue to be—

(a) a register of independent schools in England, and
(b) a register of independent schools in Wales.

(2) The register of independent schools in England shall be kept by the Secretary of State.

(3) The register of independent schools in Wales shall be kept by the National Assembly for Wales.

159 Unregistered schools

(1) A person who conducts an independent school which is not a registered school is guilty of an offence.

(2) A person guilty of an offence under subsection (1) is liable on summary conviction to—

(a) a fine not exceeding level 5 on the standard scale, or
(b) imprisonment for a term not exceeding six months,

or to both.]

(c) a school transferred to an education authority under section 16 of the Education (Scotland) Act 1980 (transfer of certain schools to education authorities) which is conducted in the interest of a church or denominational body,

(d) a school provided by an education authority under section 17(2) of that Act (denominational schools),

(e) a grant-aided school (within the meaning of that Act) which is conducted in the interest of a church or denominational body, or

(f) a school registered in the register of independent schools for Scotland if the school—

(i) admits only pupils who belong, or whose parents belong, to one or more particular denominations, or

(ii) is conducted in the interest of a church or denominational body.

(2) Section 49(1)(c)(i), (ii) or (iv) shall not apply in relation to anything done in connection with—

(a) the content of the curriculum, or

(b) acts of worship or other religious observance organised by or on behalf of an educational establishment (whether or not forming part of the curriculum).

(3) The Secretary of State may by order—

(a) amend or repeal an exception in subsection (1) or (2);

(b) provide for an additional exception to section 49;

(c) make provision about the construction or application of section 45(3)(d) in relation to section 49.

(4) An order under subsection (3)—

(a) may include transitional, incidental or consequential provision (including provision amending an enactment (including an enactment in or under an Act of the Scottish Parliament)),

(b) may make provision generally or only in respect of specified cases or circumstances (which may, in particular, be defined by reference to location),

(c) may make different provision in respect of different cases or circumstances (which may, in particular, be defined by reference to location),

(d) shall be made by statutory instrument,

(e) may not be made unless the Secretary of State has consulted the Scottish Ministers, the National Assembly for Wales and such other persons as he thinks appropriate, and

(f) may not be made unless a draft has been laid before and approved by resolution of each House of Parliament.

51 Local education authorities and education authorities

(1) It is unlawful for a local education authority (in England and Wales) or an education authority (in Scotland) in the exercise of their functions to discriminate against a person.

(2) In its application to local education authorities the prohibition in subsection (1) shall not apply to—

(a) the exercise of an authority's functions under section 14 of the Education Act 1996 (c. 56) (provision of schools),

(b) the exercise of an authority's functions in relation to transport,

(c) the exercise of an authority's functions under section 13 of that Act (general responsibility for education) in so far as they relate to a matter specified in paragraph (a) or (b) above, or

(d) the exercise of functions as the responsible body for an establishment listed in the Table in section 49.

(3) In its application to education authorities the prohibition in subsection (1) shall not apply to—

(a) the exercise of an authority's functions under section 17 of the Education (Scotland) Act 1980 (c. 44) (provision etc. of schools),
(b) the exercise of an authority's functions in relation to transport,
(c) the exercise of an authority's functions under section 1 of that Act, section 2 of the Standards in Scotland's Schools etc. Act 2000 (asp 6) and sections 4 and 5 of the Education (Additional Support for Learning) (Scotland) Act 2004 (asp 4) (duties in relation to provision of education) in so far as they relate to a matter specified in paragraph (a) or (b) above,
(d) the exercise of an authority's functions under section 50(1) of the Education (Scotland) Act 1980 (education of pupils in exceptional circumstances) in so far as they consist of making arrangements of the kind referred to in subsection (2) of that section, or
(e) the exercise of functions as the responsible body for an establishment listed in the Table in section 49.

59 Faith schools, &c.

(1) Nothing in this Part shall make it unlawful for an educational institution established or conducted for the purpose of providing education relating to, or within the framework of, a specified religion or belief—

(a) to restrict the provision of goods, facilities or services, or
(b) to restrict the use or disposal of premises.

(2) But subsection (1) permits a restriction only if imposed—

(a) by reason of or on the grounds of the purpose of the institution, or
(b) in order to avoid causing offence, on grounds of the religion or belief to which the institution relates, to persons connected with the institution.

(3) In this Part a reference to the provision of facilities or services shall not, in so far as it applies to an educational institution, include a reference to educational facilities or educational services provided to students of the institution.

61 Education, training and welfare

Nothing in this Part shall make it unlawful to do anything by way of—

(a) meeting special needs for education, training or welfare of persons of a religion or belief, or
(b) providing ancillary benefits in connection with meeting the needs mentioned in paragraph (a).

66 Claim of unlawful action

(1) A claim that a person has done anything that is unlawful by virtue of this Part may be brought in a county court (in England and Wales) or in the

sheriff court (in Scotland) by way of proceedings in tort (or reparation) for breach of statutory duty.

(2) Proceedings in England and Wales alleging that any of the following bodies has acted unlawfully by virtue of section 49 or 51 may not be brought unless the claimant has given written notice to the Secretary of State; and those bodies are—

(a) a local education authority, and
(b) the responsible body of an educational establishment listed in the Table in section 49.

(3) Proceedings in Scotland alleging that any of the following bodies has acted unlawfully by virtue of section 49 or 51 may not be brought unless the pursuer has given written notice to the Scottish Ministers; and those bodies are—

(a) an education authority, and
(b) the responsible body of an educational establishment listed in the Table in section 49.

The Employment Equality (Religion or Belief) Regulations 2003

Institutions of further and higher education

20.—(1) It is unlawful, in relation to an educational establishment to which this regulation applies, for the governing body of that establishment to discriminate against a person—

(a) in the terms on which it offers to admit him to the establishment as a student;
(b) by refusing or deliberately not accepting an application for his admission to the establishment as a student; or
(c) where he is a student of the establishment—
    (i) in the way it affords him access to any benefits,
    (ii) by refusing or deliberately not affording him access to them, or
    (iii) by excluding him from the establishment or subjecting him to any other detriment.

(2) It is unlawful, in relation to an educational establishment to which this regulation applies, for the governing body of that establishment to subject to harassment a person who is a student at the establishment, or who has applied for admission to the establishment as a student.

(3) Paragraph (1) does not apply if the discrimination only concerns training which would help fit a person for employment which, by virtue of regulation 7 (exception for genuine occupational requirement), the employer could lawfully refuse to offer the person in question.

(4) Subject to paragraph (4A) this regulation applies to the following educational establishments in England and Wales, namely—

(a) an institution within the further education sector (within the meaning of section 91(3) of the Further and Higher Education Act 1992);

(b) a university;

(c) an institution, other than a university, within the higher education sector (within the meaning of section 91(5) of the Further and Higher Education Act 1992).

(4A) In relation to an institution specified in Schedule 1B, this regulation applies with the modification set out in that Schedule.

[SCHEDULE 1B

Institutions in relation to which regulation 20 (Institutions of further and higher education) is modified.

1. This Schedule applies to the following institutions:—

Aquinas Sixth Form College,	*Stockport*
Cardinal Newman College,	*Preston*
Carmel College,	*St Helens*
Christ The King Sixth Form College,	*Lewisham*
Holy Cross Sixth Form College,	*Bury*
Loreto College,	*Manchester*
Notre Dame Catholic Sixth Form College,	*Leeds*
St. Brendan's Sixth Form College,	*Bristol*
St. Charles Catholic Sixth Form College,	*London W10*
St. David's Catholic College,	*Cardiff*
St. Dominic's Sixth Form College,	*Harrow on the Hill*
St. Francis Xavier Sixth Form College,	*Clapham*
Saint John Rigby Catholic Sixth Form College,	*Wigan*
St. Mary's College,	*Blackburn*
St. Mary's Sixth Form College,	*Middlesbrough*
Xaverian Sixth Form College,	*Manchester*

2. Subject to paragraph 3, regulation 20(1)(b) shall not apply to the institutions specified in paragraph 1 in so far as it is necessary for an institution to give preference in its admissions to persons of a particular religion or belief in order to preserve that institution's religious ethos.

3. Paragraph 2 does not apply in relation to any admission to a course of vocational training.]

(5) This regulation applies to the following educational establishments in Scotland, namely—

(a) a college of further education within the meaning of section 36(1) of the Further and Higher Education (Scotland) Act 1992 under the management of a board of management within the meaning of Part I of that Act;

(b) a college of further education maintained by an education authority in the exercise of its further education functions in providing courses of further education within the meaning of section 1(5)(b)(ii) of the Education (Scotland) Act 1980;

(c) any other educational establishment (not being a school) which provides further education within the meaning of section 1 of the Further and Higher Education (Scotland) Act 1992;

(d) an institution within the higher education sector (within the meaning of Part II of the Further and Higher Education (Scotland) Act 1992);

(e) a central institution (within the meaning of section 135 of the Education (Scotland) Act 1980).

(6) In this regulation—

'education authority' has the meaning given by section 135(1) of the Education (Scotland) Act 1980;
'governing body' includes—

(a) the board of management of a college referred to in paragraph (5)(a), and

(b) the managers of a college or institution referred to in paragraph (5)(b) or (e);

'student' means any person who receives education at an educational establishment to which this regulation applies; and
'university' includes a university college and the college, school or hall of a university.

Savings of, and amendments to, legislation

39.—(1) These Regulations are without prejudice to—

(a) sections 58 to 60 and 124A of the School Standards and Framework Act 1998 (appointment and dismissal of teachers in schools with a religious character etc); and

(b) section 21 of the Education (Scotland) Act 1980 (management of denominational schools).

[School Standards and Framework Act 1998.
Appointment and dismissal of certain teachers at schools with a religious character.

58.—(1) In this section—

(a) subsections (2) to (6) apply to a foundation or voluntary controlled school which has a religious character; and

(b) subsection (7) applies (subject to subsection (8)) to a voluntary aided school which has a religious character,

and references in this Chapter to a school which has (or does not have) a religious character shall be construed in accordance with section 69(3).

(2) Where the number of the teaching staff of a school to which this subsection applies is more than two, the teaching staff shall include persons who—

(a) are selected for their fitness and competence to give such religious education as is required in accordance with arrangements under paragraph 3(3) of Schedule 19 (arrangements for religious education in accordance with the school's trust deed or with the tenets of the school's specified religion or religious denomination), and

(b) are specifically appointed to do so.

(3) The number of reserved teachers in such a school shall not exceed one-fifth of the number of the teaching staff, including the head teacher (and for this purpose, where the number of the teaching staff is not a multiple of five, it shall be treated as if it were the next higher multiple of five).

(4) The head teacher of such a school shall not, while holding the post of head teacher of the school, be a reserved teacher.

(5) Where the appropriate body propose to appoint a person to be a reserved teacher in such a school, that body—

(a) shall consult the foundation governors, and

(b) shall not so appoint that person unless the foundation governors are satisfied as to his fitness and competence to give such religious education as is mentioned in subsection (2)(a).

(6) If the foundation governors of such a school consider that a reserved teacher has failed to give such religious education efficiently and suitably, they may require the appropriate body to dismiss him from employment as a reserved teacher in the school.

(7) If a teacher appointed to give religious education in a school to which this subsection applies fails to give such education efficiently and suitably, he may be dismissed on that ground by the governing body without the consent of the local education authority.

(8) Subsection (7) does not apply—

(a) where the school has a delegated budget, or

(b) to religious education in accordance with an agreed syllabus.

(9) In this section—

'the appropriate body' means—

(a) in relation to a foundation school, the governing body, and

(b) in relation to a voluntary controlled school, the local education authority;

'reserved teacher', in relation to a foundation or voluntary controlled school, means a person employed at the school in pursuance of subsection (2).

Religious opinions etc. of staff
Staff at community, secular foundation or voluntary, or special school

59.—(1) This section applies to—

(a) a community school or a community or foundation special school, or

(b) a foundation or voluntary school which does not have a religious character.

(2) No person shall be disqualified by reason of his religious opinions, or of his attending or omitting to attend religious worship—

(a) from being a teacher at the school, or

(b) from being employed for the purposes of the school otherwise than as a teacher.

(3) No teacher at the school shall be required to give religious education.

(4) No teacher at the school shall receive any less remuneration or be deprived of, or disqualified for, any promotion or other advantage—

(a) by reason of the fact that he does or does not give religious education, or

(b) by reason of his religious opinions or of his attending or omitting to attend religious worship.

Staff at foundation or voluntary school with religious character.

60.—(1) This section applies to a foundation or voluntary school which has a religious character.

(2) If the school is a foundation or voluntary controlled school, then (subject to subsections (3) and (4) below) section 59(2) to (4) shall apply to the school as they apply to a foundation or voluntary controlled school which does not have a religious character.

(3) Section 59(2) to (4) shall not so apply in relation to a reserved teacher at the school; and instead subsection (5) below shall apply in relation to such a teacher as it applies in relation to a teacher at a voluntary aided school.

(4) In connection with the appointment of a person to be head teacher of the school (whether foundation or voluntary controlled) regard may be had to that person's ability and fitness to preserve and develop the religious character of the school.

(5) If the school is a voluntary aided school—

(a) preference may be given, in connection with the appointment, remuneration or promotion of teachers at the school, to persons—

(i) whose religious opinions are in accordance with the tenets of the religion or religious denomination specified in relation to the school under section 69(4), or

(ii) who attend religious worship in accordance with those tenets, or

(iii) who give, or are willing to give, religious education at the school in accordance with those tenets; and

(b) regard may be had, in connection with the termination of the employment of any teacher at the school, to any conduct on his part which is incompatible with the precepts, or with the upholding of the tenets, of the religion or religious denomination so specified.

(6) If the school is a voluntary aided school, no person shall be disqualified by reason of his religious opinions, or of his attending or omitting to attend religious worship, from being employed for the purposes of the school otherwise than as a teacher.

(7) Where immediately before the appointed day a teacher at a school which on that day becomes a school to which this section applies enjoyed, by virtue of section 304 or 305 of the Education Act 1996 (religious opinions of staff etc.), any rights not conferred on him by this section as a teacher at a school to which it applies, he shall continue to enjoy those rights (in addition to those conferred by this section) until he ceases to be employed as a teacher at the school.

(8) In this section 'reserved teacher', in relation to a foundation or voluntary controlled school, means a person employed at the school in pursuance of section 58(2).

PART 5A School Standards and Framework Act 1998

(added by The Independent Schools (Employment of Teachers in Schools with a Religious Character) Regulations 2003. No 2037)

124A. Employment of teachers at independent schools having a religious character

(1) This section applies to an independent school which has a religious character.

(2) Preference may be given, in connection with the appointment, promotion or remuneration of teachers at the school, to persons—

(a) whose religious opinions are in accordance with the tenets of the religion or the religious denomination specified in relation to the school under section 124B(2), or

(b) who attend religious worship in accordance with those tenets, or

(c) who give, or are willing to give, religious education at the school in accordance with those tenets.

(3) Regard may be had, in connection with the termination of the employment or engagement of any teacher at the school, to any conduct on his part which is incompatible with the precepts, or with the upholding of the tenets, of the religion or religious denomination so specified.

124B. Designation of independent schools as having a religious character

(1) Subsections (3) and (5) of section 69 (which relate to the designation of foundation or voluntary schools as having a religious character) apply in relation to an independent school as they apply in relation to a foundation or voluntary school, but as if—

(a) in subsection (3), the reference to Part 2 were a reference to this Part, and
(b) in subsection (5), the reference to subsection (4) of that section were a reference to subsection (2) of this section.

(2) An order made under section 69(3) by virtue of subsection (1) shall specify, in relation to each school designated by the order, the religion or religious denomination (or as the case may be each religion or religious denomination) in accordance with whose tenets education is provided at the school or the school is conducted.']

Harassment legislation

Regulation 5 The Employment Equality (Religion or Belief) Regulations 2003

Harassment on grounds of religion or belief

5.—(1) For the purposes of these Regulations, a person ('A') subjects another person ('B') to harassment where, on grounds of religion or belief, A engages in unwanted conduct which has the purpose or effect of—

(a) violating B's dignity; or

(b) creating an intimidating, hostile, degrading, humiliating or offensive environment for B.

(2) Conduct shall be regarded as having the effect specified in paragraph (1)(a) or (b) only if, having regard to all the circumstances, including in particular the perception of B, it should reasonably be considered as having that effect.

Protection from Harassment Act 1997

(Incorporating s 7(3A) added to the Act by s 44 Criminal Justice and Police Act 2001, ss 1(1A), 3A and 7(5) added by s 125 Serious and Organised Crime Act 2005. Also s 5A and amendments to s 5 made by a12 Domestic Violence, Crime and Victims Act 2004.)

An Act to make provision for protecting persons from harassment and similar conduct.

s 1 Prohibition of harassment

(1) A person must not pursue a course of conduct—

(a) which amounts to harassment of another, and

(b) which he knows or ought to know amounts to harassment of the other.

(1A) A person must not pursue a course of conduct—

(a) which involves harassment of two or more persons, and
(b) which he knows or ought to know involves harassment of those persons, and
(c) by which he intends to persuade any person (whether or not one of those mentioned above)—

    (i) not to do something that he is entitled or required to do, or
    (ii) to do something that he is not under any obligation to do.

(2) For the purposes of this section, the person whose course of conduct is in question ought to know that it amounts to or involves harassment of another if a reasonable person in possession of the same information would think the course of conduct amounted to or involved harassment of the other.

(3) Subsection (1) or (1A) does not apply to a course of conduct if the person who pursued it shows—

(a) that it was pursued for the purpose of preventing or detecting crime,
(b) that it was pursued under any enactment or rule of law or to comply with any condition or requirement imposed by any person under any enactment, or
(c) that in the particular circumstances the pursuit of the course of conduct was reasonable.

s 2 Offence of harassment

(1) A person who pursues a course of conduct in breach of section 1(1) or (1A) is guilty of an offence.

(2) A person guilty of an offence under this section is liable on summary conviction to imprisonment for a term not exceeding six months, or a fine not exceeding level 5 on the standard scale, or both.

(3) *(arrest powers now irrelevant)*.

s 3 Civil remedy

(1) An actual or apprehended breach of section 1(1) may be the subject of a claim in civil proceedings by the person who is or may be the victim of the course of conduct in question.

(2) On such a claim, damages may be awarded for (among other things) any anxiety caused by the harassment and any financial loss resulting from the harassment.

(3) Where—

(a) in such proceedings the High Court or a county court grants an injunction for the purpose of restraining the defendant from pursuing any conduct which amounts to harassment, and

(b) the plaintiff considers that the defendant has done anything which he is prohibited from doing by the injunction,

the plaintiff may apply for the issue of a warrant for the arrest of the defendant.

(4) An application under subsection (3) may be made—

(a) where the injunction was granted by the High Court, to a judge of that court, and

(b) where the injunction was granted by a county court, to a judge or district judge of that or any other county court.

(5) The judge or district judge to whom an application under subsection (3) is made may only issue a warrant if—

(a) the application is substantiated on oath, and

(b) the judge or district judge has reasonable grounds for believing that the defendant has done anything which he is prohibited from doing by the injunction.

(6) Where—

(a) the High Court or a county court grants an injunction for the purpose mentioned in subsection (3)(a), and

(b) without reasonable excuse the defendant does anything which he is prohibited from doing by the injunction,

he is guilty of an offence.

(7) Where a person is convicted of an offence under subsection (6) in respect of any conduct, that conduct is not punishable as a contempt of court.

(8) A person cannot be convicted of an offence under subsection (6) in respect of any conduct which has been punished as a contempt of court.

(9) A person guilty of an offence under subsection (6) is liable—

(a) on conviction on indictment, to imprisonment for a term not exceeding five years, or a fine, or both, or

(b) on summary conviction, to imprisonment for a term not exceeding six months, or a fine not exceeding the statutory maximum, or both.

s 3A Injunctions to protect persons from harassment within section 1(1A)

(1) This section applies where there is an actual or apprehended breach of section 1(1A) by any person ('the relevant person').

(2) In such a case—

(a) any person who is or may be a victim of the course of conduct in question, or

(b) any person who is or may be a person falling within section 1(1A)(c), may apply to the High Court or a county court for an injunction restraining the relevant person from pursuing any conduct which amounts to harassment in relation to any person or persons mentioned or described in the injunction.

(3) Section 3(3) to (9) apply in relation to an injunction granted under subsection (2) above as they apply in relation to an injunction granted as mentioned in section 3(3)(a)

s 4 Putting people in fear of violence

(1) A person whose course of conduct causes another to fear, on at least two occasions, that violence will be used against him is guilty of an offence if he knows or ought to know that his course of conduct will cause the other so to fear on each of those occasions.

(2) For the purposes of this section, the person whose course of conduct is in question ought to know that it will cause another to fear that violence will be used against him on any occasion if a reasonable person in possession of the same information would think the course of conduct would cause the other so to fear on that occasion.

(3) It is a defence for a person charged with an offence under this section to show that—

(a) his course of conduct was pursued for the purpose of preventing or detecting crime,
(b) his course of conduct was pursued under any enactment or rule of law or to comply with any condition or requirement imposed by any person under any enactment, or
(c) the pursuit of his course of conduct was reasonable for the protection of himself or another or for the protection of his or another's property.

(4) A person guilty of an offence under this section is liable—

(a) on conviction on indictment, to imprisonment for a term not exceeding five years, or a fine, or both, or
(b) on summary conviction, to imprisonment for a term not exceeding six months, or a fine not exceeding the statutory maximum, or both.

(5) If on the trial on indictment of a person charged with an offence under this section the jury find him not guilty of the offence charged, they may find him guilty of an offence under section 2.

(6) The Crown Court has the same powers and duties in relation to a person who is by virtue of subsection (5) convicted before it of an offence under section 2 as a magistrates' court would have on convicting him of the offence.

s 5 Restraining orders on conviction

(1) A court sentencing or otherwise dealing with a person ('the defendant') convicted of an offence may (as well as sentencing him or dealing with him in any other way) make an order under this section.

(2) The order may, for the purpose of protecting the victim of the offence, or any other person mentioned in the order, from conduct which—

(a) amounts to harassment, or
(b) will cause a fear of violence,
     prohibit the defendant from doing anything described in the order.

(3) The order may have effect for a specified period or until further order.

(3A) In proceedings under this section both the prosecution and the defence may lead, as further evidence, any evidence that would be admissible in proceedings for an injunction under section 3.

(4) The prosecutor, the defendant or any other person mentioned in the order may apply to the court which made the order for it to be varied or discharged by a further order.

(4A) Any person mentioned in the order is entitled to be heard on the hearing of an application under subsection (4).

(5) If without reasonable excuse the defendant does anything which he is prohibited from doing by an order under this section, he is guilty of an offence.

(6) A person guilty of an offence under this section is liable—

(a) on conviction on indictment, to imprisonment for a term not exceeding five years, or a fine, or both, or
(b) on summary conviction, to imprisonment for a term not exceeding six months, or a fine not exceeding the statutory maximum, or both.

(7) A court dealing with a person for an offence under this section may vary or discharge the order in question by a further order.

s 5A Restraining orders on acquittal

(1) A court before which a person ('the defendant') is acquitted of an offence may, if it considers it necessary to do so to protect a person from harassment by the defendant, make an order prohibiting the defendant from doing anything described in the order.

(2) Subsections (3) to (7) of section 5 apply to an order under this section as they apply to an order under that one.

(3) Where the Court of Appeal allow an appeal against conviction they may remit the case to the Crown Court to consider whether to proceed under this section.

(4) Where—

(a) the Crown Court allows an appeal against conviction, or

(b) a case is remitted to the Crown Court under subsection (3),

the reference in subsection (1) to a court before which a person is acquitted of an offence is to be read as referring to that court.

(5) A person made subject to an order under this section has the same right of appeal against the order as if—

(a) he had been convicted of the offence in question before the court which made the order, and

(b) the order had been made under section 5.

s 6 Limitation

In section 11 of the Limitation Act 1980 (special time limit for actions in respect of personal injuries), after subsection (1) there is inserted—

'(1A) This section does not apply to any action brought for damages under section 3 of the Protection from Harassment Act 1997.'

s 7 Interpretation of this group of sections

(1) This section applies for the interpretation of sections 1 to 5.

(2) References to harassing a person include alarming the person or causing the person distress.

(3) A 'course of conduct' must involve—

(a) in the case of conduct in relation to a single person (see section 1(1)), conduct on at least two occasions in relation to that person, or

(b) in the case of conduct in relation to two or more persons (see section 1(1A)), conduct on at least one occasion in relation to each of those persons.

(3A) A person's conduct on any occasion shall be taken, if aided, abetted, counselled or procured by another—

(a) to be conduct on that occasion of the other (as well as conduct of the person whose conduct it is); and

(b) to be conduct in relation to which the other's knowledge and purpose, and what he ought to have known, are the same as they were in relation to what was contemplated or reasonably foreseeable at the time of the aiding, abetting, counselling or procuring.

(4) 'Conduct' includes speech.

(5) References to a person, in the context of the harassment of a person, are references to a person who is an individual.

s 12 National security, etc

(1) If the Secretary of State certifies that in his opinion anything done by a specified person on a specified occasion related to—

(a) national security,

(b) the economic well-being of the United Kingdom, or

(c) the prevention or detection of serious crime,

and was done on behalf of the Crown, the certificate is conclusive evidence that this Act does not apply to any conduct of that person on that occasion.

(2) In subsection (1), 'specified' means specified in the certificate in question.

(3) A document purporting to be a certificate under subsection (1) is to be received in evidence and, unless the contrary is proved, be treated as being such a certificate.

Religious criminal offences

Religiously Aggravated Offences

(This is the wording of sections 28 to 32 of the Crime and Disorder Act 1998 as amended by section 39 of the Anti-terrorism, Crime and Security Act 2001. The racially aggravated offences provisions came into force on the 30th September 1998 and the religiously aggravated provisions came into force on the 14th December 2001. The provisions apply to offences after that date. Details are also provided of the actual offences which are aggravated by sections 28 to 32.)

Crime and Disorder Act 1998

s 28 Meaning of 'racially or religiously aggravated'

28.—(1) An offence is racially or religiously aggravated for the purposes of sections 29 to 32 below if—

(a) at the time of committing the offence, or immediately before or after doing so, the offender demonstrates towards the victim of the offence hostility based on the victim's membership (or presumed membership) of a racial or religious group; or

(b) the offence is motivated (wholly or partly) by hostility towards members of a racial or religious group based on their membership of that group.

(2) In subsection (1)(a) above—

'membership', in relation to a racial or religious group, includes association with members of that group;
'presumed' means presumed by the offender.

(3) It is immaterial for the purposes of paragraph (a) or (b) of subsection (1) above whether or not the offender's hostility is also based, to any extent, on any other factor not mentioned in that paragraph.

(4) In this section 'racial group' means a group of persons defined by reference to race, colour, nationality (including citizenship) or ethnic or national origins.

(5) In this section 'religious group' means a group of persons defined by reference to religious belief or lack of religious belief.'

s 29 Racially or religiously aggravated assaults

29.—(1) A person is guilty of an offence under this section if he commits—

(a) an offence under section 20 of the Offences Against the Person Act 1861 (malicious wounding or grievous bodily harm);
(b) an offence under section 47 of that Act (actual bodily harm); or
(c) common assault,
   which is racially or religiously aggravated for the purposes of this section.

(2) A person guilty of an offence falling within subsection (1)(a) or (b) above shall be liable—

(a) on summary conviction, to imprisonment for a term not exceeding six months or to a fine not exceeding the statutory maximum, or to both;
(b) on conviction on indictment, to imprisonment for a term not exceeding seven years or to a fine, or to both.

(3) A person guilty of an offence falling within subsection (1)(c) above shall be liable—

(a) on summary conviction, to imprisonment for a term not exceeding six months or to a fine not exceeding the statutory maximum, or to both;
(b) on conviction on indictment, to imprisonment for a term not exceeding two years or to a fine, or to both.

s 30 Racially or religiously aggravated criminal damage

30.—(1) A person is guilty of an offence under this section if he commits an offence under section 1(1) of the Criminal Damage Act 1971 (destroying or damaging property belonging to another) which is racially or religiously aggravated for the purposes of this section.

(2) A person guilty of an offence under this section shall be liable—

(a) on summary conviction, to imprisonment for a term not exceeding six months or to a fine not exceeding the statutory maximum, or to both;
(b) on conviction on indictment, to imprisonment for a term not exceeding fourteen years or to a fine, or to both.

(3) For the purposes of this section, section 28(1)(a) above shall have effect as if the person to whom the property belongs or is treated as belonging for the purposes of that Act were the victim of the offence.

Criminal Damage Act 1971

1(1) A person who without lawful excuse destroys or damages any property belonging to another intending to destroy or damage any such property or being reckless as to whether any such property would be destroyed or damaged shall be guilty of an offence.

s 31 Racially or religiously aggravated public order offences

31.—(1) A person is guilty of an offence under this section if he commits—

(a) an offence under section 4 of the Public Order Act 1986 (fear or provocation of violence);

(b) an offence under section 4A of that Act (intentional harassment, alarm or distress); or

(c) an offence under section 5 of that Act (harassment, alarm or distress),
which is racially or religiously aggravated for the purposes of this section.

(2) & (3) (now irrelevant).

(4) A person guilty of an offence falling within subsection (1)(a) or (b) above shall be liable—

(a) on summary conviction, to imprisonment for a term not exceeding six months or to a fine not exceeding the statutory maximum, or to both;

(b) on conviction on indictment, to imprisonment for a term not exceeding two years or to a fine, or to both.

(5) A person guilty of an offence falling within subsection (1)(c) above shall be liable on summary conviction to a fine not exceeding level 4 on the standard scale.

(6) If, on the trial on indictment of a person charged with an offence falling within subsection (1)(a) or (b) above, the jury find him not guilty of the offence charged, they may find him guilty of the basic offence mentioned in that provision.

(7) For the purposes of subsection (1)(c) above, section 28(1)(a) above shall have effect as if the person likely to be caused harassment, alarm or distress were the victim of the offence.

Public Order Act 1986, s 4 Fear or provocation of violence

(1) A person is guilty of an offence if he—

(a) uses towards another person threatening, abusive or insulting words or behaviour, or

(b) distributes or displays to another person any writing, sign or other visible representation which is threatening, abusive or insulting,

with intent to cause that person to believe that immediate unlawful violence will be used against him or another by any person, or to provoke the immediate use of unlawful violence by that person or another, or whereby that person is likely to believe that such violence will be used or it is likely that such violence will be provoked.

(2) An offence under this section may be committed in a public or a private place, except that no offence is committed where the words or behaviour are used, or the writing, sign or other visible representation is distributed or displayed, by a person inside a dwelling and the other person is also inside that or another dwelling.

(3) (arrest provisions now irrelevant).

(4) A person guilty of an offence under this section is liable on summary conviction to imprisonment for a term not exceeding six months or a fine not exceeding level 5 on the standard scale or both.

(s 6(3)) Mental element: miscellaneous

A person is guilty of an offence under section 4 only if he intends his words or behaviour, or the writing, sign or other visible representation, to be threatening, abusive or insulting, or is aware that it may be threatening, abusive or insulting.

Public Order Act 1986, s 4A Intentional harassment, alarm and distress

(1) A person is guilty of an offence if, with intent to cause a person harassment, alarm or distress, he—

(a) uses threatening, abusive or insulting words or behaviour, or disorderly behaviour, or

(b) displays any writing, sign or other visible representation which is threatening, abusive or insulting,

thereby causing that or another person harassment, alarm or distress.

(2) An offence under this section may be committed in a public or a private place, except that no offence is committed where the words or behaviour are used, or the writing, sign or other visible representation is displayed, by a person inside a dwelling and the person who is harassed, alarmed or distressed is also inside that or another dwelling.

(3) It is a defence for the accused to prove—

(a) that he was inside a dwelling and had no reason to believe that the words or behaviour used, or the writing, sign or other visible representation displayed, would be heard or seen by a person outside that or any other dwelling, or

(b) that his conduct was reasonable.

(4) (arrest provisions now irrelevant).

(5) A person guilty of an offence under this section is liable on summary conviction to imprisonment for a term not exceeding six months or a fine not exceeding level 5 on the standard scale or both.

Public Order Act 1986, s 5 Harassment, alarm and distress

(1) A person is guilty of an offence if he—

(a) uses threatening, abusive or insulting words or behaviour, or disorderly behaviour, or

(b) displays any writing, sign or other visible representation which is threatening, abusive or insulting,

within the hearing or sight of a person likely to be caused harassment, alarm or distress thereby.

(2) An offence under this section may be committed in a public or a private place, except that no offence is committed where the words or behaviour are used, or the writing, sign or other visible representation is displayed, by a person inside a dwelling and the other person is also inside that or another dwelling.

(3) It is a defence for the accused to prove—

(a) that he had no reason to believe that there was any person within hearing or sight who was likely to be caused harassment, alarm or distress, or

(b) that he was inside a dwelling and had no reason to believe that the words or behaviour used, or the writing, sign or other visible representation displayed, would be heard or seen by a person outside that or any other dwelling, or

(c) that his conduct was reasonable.

(4) (arrest provisions now irrelevant).

(5) (arrest provisions now irrelevant).

(6) A person guilty of an offence under this section is liable on summary conviction to a fine not exceeding level 3 on the standard scale.

s 6(4) Mental element: miscellaneous

A person is guilty of an offence under section 5 only if he intends his words or behaviour, or the writing, sign or other visible representation, to be threatening, abusive or insulting, or is aware that it may be threatening, abusive or insulting or (as the case may be) he intends his behaviour to be or is aware that it may be disorderly.

Public Order Act 1986, s 6 Mental element: miscellaneous

(5) For the purposes of this section a person whose awareness is impaired by intoxication shall be taken to be aware of that of which he would be aware if not intoxicated, unless he shows either that his intoxication was not self-induced or that it was caused solely by the taking or administration of a substance in the course of medical treatment.

(6) In subsection (5) 'intoxication' means any intoxication, whether caused by drink, drugs or other means, or by a combination of means.

Public Order Act 1986, s 8 Interpretation

In this Part—

> *'dwelling' means any structure or part of a structure occupied as a person's home or as other living accommodation (whether the occupation is separate or shared with others) but does not include any part not so occupied, and for this purpose 'structure' includes a tent, caravan, vehicle, vessel or other temporary or movable structure;*
> *'violence' means any violent conduct, so that—*
>> *(a) except in the context of affray, it includes violent conduct towards property as well as violent conduct towards persons, and*
>> *(b) it is not restricted to conduct causing or intended to cause injury or damage but includes any other violent conduct (for example, throwing at or towards a person a missile of a kind capable of causing injury which does not hit or falls short).*

s 32 Racially or religiously aggravated harassment etc

32.—(1) A person is guilty of an offence under this section if he commits—

(a) an offence under section 2 of the Protection from Harassment Act 1997 (offence of harassment); or

(b) an offence under section 4 of that Act (putting people in fear of violence),

which is racially or religiously aggravated for the purposes of this section.

(2) (arrest provisions now irrelevant).

(3) A person guilty of an offence falling within subsection (1)(a) above shall be liable—

(a) on summary conviction, to imprisonment for a term not exceeding six months or to a fine not exceeding the statutory maximum, or to both;

(b) on conviction on indictment, to imprisonment for a term not exceeding two years or to a fine, or to both.

(4) A person guilty of an offence falling within subsection (1)(b) above shall be liable—

(a) on summary conviction, to imprisonment for a term not exceeding six months or to a fine not exceeding the statutory maximum, or to both;

(b) on conviction on indictment, to imprisonment for a term not exceeding seven years or to a fine, or to both.

(5) If, on the trial on indictment of a person charged with an offence falling within subsection (1)(a) above, the jury find him not guilty of the offence

charged, they may find him guilty of the basic offence mentioned in that provision.

(6) If, on the trial on indictment of a person charged with an offence falling within subsection (1)(b) above, the jury find him not guilty of the offence charged, they may find him guilty of an offence falling within subsection (1)(a) above.

(7) Section 5 of the Protection from Harassment Act 1997 (restraining orders) shall have effect in relation to a person convicted of an offence under this section as if the reference in subsection (1) of that section to an offence under section 2 or 4 included a reference to an offence under this section.

(The wording of the Protection from Harassment Act 1997 can be found in Appendix D)

Offences involving disorder in Churches or Cemeteries

There remain on the statute book a small number of nineteenth century offences dealing with disorder in churches and cemeteries which are widely regarded as obsolete today. The type of behaviour they deal with can also prosecuted as either 'ordinary' or 'religiously aggravated' public order or violence offences.

Cemeteries Clauses Act 1847 s59

Disturbances and nuisances in cemetery

Every person who shall play at any game or sport, or discharge firearms, save at a military funeral, in the cemetery, or who shall wilfully and unlawfully disturb any persons assembled in the cemetery for the purpose of burying any body therein, or who shall commit any nuisance within the cemetery, shall forfeit for every such offence a sum not exceeding level 1 on the standard scale.

The Local Authorities' Cemeteries Order, 1977

Article 18 – Offences in Cemeteries

(1) No person shall—

(a) wilfully create any disturbance in a Cemetery;
(b) commit any nuisance in a Cemetery;
(c) wilfully interfere with any burial taking place in a Cemetery;
(d) wilfully interfere with any grave or vault, any tombstone or other memorial, or any flowers or plants on any such matter; or
(e) play at any game or sport in a Cemetery.

(2) No person not being an officer or servant of the burial authority or another person so authorised by or on behalf of the burial authority shall enter or remain in a Cemetery at any hour when it is closed to the public.

Article 19 – Penalties

Every person who contravenes—

(a) any prohibition under article 5(6);
(b) article 10(6);
(c) article 18;
(d) Part 1 of Schedule 2 shall be liable on summary conviction to a fine not exceeding level 3 on the standard scale (currently £1000) and in the case of a continuing offence to a fine not exceeding £10 for each day during which the offence continues after conviction therefore.

Ecclesiastical Courts Jurisdiction Act 1860, s 2

Penalty for making a disturbance in churches, chapels, churchyards, etc

Any person who shall be guilty of riotous, violent, or indecent behaviour in England in any cathedral church, parish or district church, or chapel of the Church of England, or in any chapel of any religious denomination, or in England in any place of religious worship duly certified under the Places of Worship Registration Act 1855, 18 & 19 Vict c 81, whether during the celebration of Divine service, or at any other time, or in any churchyard, or burial-ground, or who shall molest, let, disturb, vex, or trouble, or by any other unlawful means disquiet or misuse any preacher duly authorised to preach therein, or any clergyman in Holy Orders ministering or celebrating any sacrament or any Divine service, rite, or office in any cathedral church or chapel, churchyard, or burial ground shall on conviction thereof before two justices of the peace, be liable to a penalty of not more than level 1 on the standard scale, or may, if the justices before whom he shall be convicted think fit, instead of being subjected to any pecuniary penalty be committed to prison for any time not exceeding two months.

Offences Against the Person Act 1861, s 36

Assaulting clergymen etc

Whoever shall, by threats or force, obstruct or prevent or endeavour to obstruct or prevent, any clergyman or other minister in or from celebrating Divine service or otherwise officiating in any church, chapel, meeting house, or other place of Divine worship, or in or from the performance of his duty in the lawful burial of the dead in any churchyard or other burial place, or shall strike or offer any violence to, or shall, upon any civil process, or under pretence of executing any civil process, arrest any clergyman or other minister who is engaged in, or to the knowledge of the offender is about to engage in, any of the rites or duties in this section aforesaid, or who to the knowledge of the offender shall be going to perform the same or returning from the performance thereof, shall be guilty of a misdemeanour, and being convicted thereof shall be liable, at the discretion of the Court, to be imprisoned for any term not exceeding two years.

Burial Laws Amendment Act 1880, s 7

Burials to be conducted in a decent and orderly manner and without obstruction

All burials under this Act, whether with or without a religious service, shall be conducted in a decent and orderly manner; and every person guilty of any riotous, violent, or indecent behaviour at any burial under this Act, or wilfully obstructing such burial or any such service as aforesaid thereat, or who shall, in any such churchyard or graveyard as aforesaid, deliver any address, not being part of or incidental to a religious service permitted by this Act, and not otherwise permitted by any lawful authority, or who shall, under colour of any religious service or otherwise, in any such churchyard or graveyard, wilfully endeavour to bring into contempt or obloquy the Christian religion, or the belief or worship of any church or denomination of Christians, or the members or any minister of any such church or denomination, or any other person, shall be guilty of an offence.

(This offence is only triable on indictment)

Blasphemy

Blasphemy is a common law offence and so is not defined by statute. The last indictment for blasphemy in England was in the case of *Whitehouse v Gay News Ltd and Lemon* [1979] 2 WLR 281, and read as follows:

Statement of Offence

BLASPHEMOUS LIBEL

Particulars of Offence

Gay News Ltd and Denis Lemon on a day or days unknown between May 1 and June 30, 1976, unlawfully and wickedly published or caused to be published in a newspaper called 'Gay News No. 96' a blasphemous libel concerning the Christian religion namely an obscene poem and illustration vilifying Christ in life and in His crucifixion.

Racial and Religious Hatred Act 2006

An Act to make provision about offences involving stirring up hatred against persons on racial or religious grounds.

[16th February 2006]

BE IT ENACTED by the Queen's most Excellent Majesty, by and with the advice and consent of the Lords Spiritual and Temporal, and Commons, in this present Parliament assembled, and by the authority of the same, as follows:—

1 Hatred against persons on religious grounds

The Public Order Act 1986 (c. 64) is amended in accordance with the Schedule to this Act, which creates offences involving stirring up hatred against persons on religious grounds.

2 Racial and religious hatred offences: powers of arrest

In section 24A of the Police and Criminal Evidence Act 1984 (c. 60) (arrest without warrant by persons other than constables) after subsection (4) add—

'(5) This section does not apply in relation to an offence under Part 3 or 3A of the Public Order Act 1986.'

3 Short title, commencement and extent

(1) This Act may be cited as the Racial and Religious Hatred Act 2006.

(2) This Act comes into force on such day as the Secretary of State may appoint by order made by statutory instrument.

(3) An order under subsection (2) may make—

(a) such supplementary, incidental or consequential provision, or

(b) such transitory, transitional or saving provision,
     as the Secretary of State considers appropriate in connection with the coming into force of this Act.

(4) This Act extends to England and Wales only.

SCHEDULE Section 1
HATRED AGAINST PERSONS ON RELIGIOUS GROUNDS

In the Public Order Act 1986 (c. 64), after Part 3 insert—

Part 3A
Hatred against persons on religious grounds
Meaning of 'religious hatred'

29A Meaning of 'religious hatred'

In this Part 'religious hatred' means hatred against a group of persons defined by reference to religious belief or lack of religious belief.

Acts intended to stir up religious hatred

29B Use of words or behaviour or display of written material

(1) A person who uses threatening words or behaviour, or displays any written material which is threatening, is guilty of an offence if he intends thereby to stir up religious hatred.

(2) An offence under this section may be committed in a public or a private place, except that no offence is committed where the words or behaviour are used, or the written material is displayed, by a person inside a dwelling and are not heard or seen except by other persons in that or another dwelling.

(3) A constable may arrest without warrant anyone he reasonably suspects is committing an offence under this section.

(4) In proceedings for an offence under this section it is a defence for the accused to prove that he was inside a dwelling and had no reason to believe that the words or behaviour used, or the written material displayed, would be heard or seen by a person outside that or any other dwelling.

(5) This section does not apply to words or behaviour used, or written material displayed, solely for the purpose of being included in a programme service.

29C Publishing or distributing written material

(1) A person who publishes or distributes written material which is threatening is guilty of an offence if he intends thereby to stir up religious hatred.

(2) References in this Part to the publication or distribution of written material are to its publication or distribution to the public or a section of the public.

29D Public performance of play

(1) If a public performance of a play is given which involves the use of threatening words or behaviour, any person who presents or directs the performance is guilty of an offence if he intends thereby to stir up religious hatred.

(2) This section does not apply to a performance given solely or primarily for one or more of the following purposes—

(a) rehearsal,

(b) making a recording of the performance, or

(c) enabling the performance to be included in a programme service;

but if it is proved that the performance was attended by persons other than those directly connected with the giving of the performance or the doing in relation to it of the things mentioned in paragraph (b) or (c), the performance shall, unless the contrary is shown, be taken not to have been given solely or primarily for the purpose mentioned above.

(3) For the purposes of this section—

(a) a person shall not be treated as presenting a performance of a play by reason only of his taking part in it as a performer,

(b) a person taking part as a performer in a performance directed by another shall be treated as a person who directed the performance if without reasonable excuse he performs otherwise than in accordance with that person's direction, and

(c) a person shall be taken to have directed a performance of a play given under his direction notwithstanding that he was not present during the performance;

and a person shall not be treated as aiding or abetting the commission of an offence under this section by reason only of his taking part in a performance as a performer.

(4) In this section 'play' and 'public performance' have the same meaning as in the Theatres Act 1968.

(5) The following provisions of the Theatres Act 1968 apply in relation to an offence under this section as they apply to an offence under section 2 of that Act—

section 9 (script as evidence of what was performed),
section 10 (power to make copies of script),
section 15 (powers of entry and inspection).

29E Distributing, showing or playing a recording

(1) A person who distributes, or shows or plays, a recording of visual images or sounds which are threatening is guilty of an offence if he intends thereby to stir up religious hatred.

(2) In this Part 'recording' means any record from which visual images or sounds may, by any means, be reproduced; and references to the distribution, showing or playing of a recording are to its distribution, showing or playing to the public or a section of the public.

(3) This section does not apply to the showing or playing of a recording solely for the purpose of enabling the recording to be included in a programme service.

29F Broadcasting or including programme in cable programme service

(1) If a programme involving threatening visual images or sounds is included in a programme service, each of the persons mentioned in subsection (2) is guilty of an offence if he intends thereby to stir up religious hatred.

(2) The persons are—

(a) the person providing the programme service,
(b) any person by whom the programme is produced or directed, and
(c) any person by whom offending words or behaviour are used.

Inflammatory material

29G Possession of inflammatory material

(1) A person who has in his possession written material which is threatening, or a recording of visual images or sounds which are threatening, with a view to—

(a) in the case of written material, its being displayed, published, distributed, or included in a programme service whether by himself or another, or
(b) in the case of a recording, its being distributed, shown, played, or included in a programme service, whether by himself or another,

is guilty of an offence if he intends religious hatred to be stirred up thereby.

(2) For this purpose regard shall be had to such display, publication, distribution, showing, playing, or inclusion in a programme service as he has, or it may be reasonably be inferred that he has, in view.

29H Powers of entry and search

(1) If in England and Wales a justice of the peace is satisfied by information on oath laid by a constable that there are reasonable grounds for suspecting that a person has possession of written material or a recording in contravention of section 29G, the justice may issue a warrant under his hand

authorising any constable to enter and search the premises where it is suspected the material or recording is situated.

(2) If in Scotland a sheriff or justice of the peace is satisfied by evidence on oath that there are reasonable grounds for suspecting that a person has possession of written material or a recording in contravention of section 29G, the sheriff or justice may issue a warrant authorising any constable to enter and search the premises where it is suspected the material or recording is situated.

(3) A constable entering or searching premises in pursuance of a warrant issued under this section may use reasonable force if necessary.

(4) In this section 'premises' means any place and, in particular, includes—

(a) any vehicle, vessel, aircraft or hovercraft,

(b) any offshore installation as defined in section 12 of the Mineral Workings (Offshore Installations) Act 1971, and

(c) any tent or moveable structure.

29I Power to order forfeiture

(1) A court by or before which a person is convicted of—

(a) an offence under section 29B relating to the display of written material, or

(b) an offence under section 29C, 29E or 29G,

shall order to be forfeited any written material or recording produced to the court and shown to its satisfaction to be written material or a recording to which the offence relates.

(2) An order made under this section shall not take effect—

(a) in the case of an order made in proceedings in England and Wales, until the expiry of the ordinary time within which an appeal may be instituted or, where an appeal is duly instituted, until it is finally decided or abandoned;

(b) in the case of an order made in proceedings in Scotland, until the expiration of the time within which, by virtue of any statute, an appeal may be instituted or, where such an appeal is duly instituted, until the appeal is finally decided or abandoned.

(3) For the purposes of subsection (2)(a)—

(a) an application for a case stated or for leave to appeal shall be treated as the institution of an appeal, and

(b) where a decision on appeal is subject to a further appeal, the appeal is not finally determined until the expiry of the ordinary time within which a further appeal may be instituted or, where a further appeal is duly instituted, until the further appeal is finally decided or abandoned.

(4) For the purposes of subsection (2)(b) the lodging of an application for a stated case or note of appeal against sentence shall be treated as the institution of an appeal.

29J Protection of freedom of expression

Nothing in this Part shall be read or given effect in a way which prohibits or restricts discussion, criticism or expressions of antipathy, dislike, ridicule, insult or abuse of particular religions or the beliefs or practices of their adherents, or of any other belief system or the beliefs or practices of its adherents, or proselytising or urging adherents of a different religion or belief system to cease practising their religion or belief system.

Supplementary provisions

29K Savings for reports of parliamentary or judicial proceedings

(1) Nothing in this Part applies to a fair and accurate report of proceedings in Parliament or in the Scottish Parliament.

(2) Nothing in this Part applies to a fair and accurate report of proceedings publicly heard before a court or tribunal exercising judicial authority where the report is published contemporaneously with the proceedings or, if it is not reasonably practicable or would be unlawful to publish a report of them contemporaneously, as soon as publication is reasonably practicable and lawful.

29L Procedure and punishment

(1) No proceedings for an offence under this Part may be instituted in England and Wales except by or with the consent of the Attorney General.

(2) For the purposes of the rules in England and Wales against charging more than one offence in the same count or information, each of sections 29B to 29G creates one offence.

(3) A person guilty of an offence under this Part is liable—

(a) on conviction on indictment to imprisonment for a term not exceeding seven years or a fine or both;
(b) on summary conviction to imprisonment for a term not exceeding six months or a fine not exceeding the statutory maximum or both.

29M Offences by corporations

(1) Where a body corporate is guilty of an offence under this Part and it is shown that the offence was committed with the consent or connivance of a director, manager, secretary or other similar officer of the body, or a person purporting to act in any such capacity, he as well as the body corporate is guilty of the offence and liable to be proceeded against and punished accordingly.

(2) Where the affairs of a body corporate are managed by its members, subsection (1) applies in relation to the acts and defaults of a member in connection with his functions of management as it applies to a director.

29N Interpretation

In this Part—

> 'distribute', and related expressions, shall be construed in accordance with section 29C(2) (written material) and section 29E(2) (recordings);
>
> 'dwelling' means any structure or part of a structure occupied as a person's home or other living accommodation (whether the occupation is separate or shared with others) but does not include any part not so occupied, and for this purpose;
>
> 'structure' includes a tent, caravan, vehicle, vessel or other temporary or moveable structure;
>
> 'programme' means any item which is included in a programme service;
>
> 'programme service' has the same meaning as in the Broadcasting Act 1990;
>
> 'publish', and related expressions, in relation to written material, shall be construed in accordance with section 29C(2);
>
> 'religious hatred' has the meaning given by section 29A;
>
> 'recording' has the meaning given by section 29E(2), and
>
> 'play' and 'show', and related expressions, in relation to a recording, shall be construed in accordance with that provision;
>
> 'written material' includes any sign or other visible representation.

Index